Education for Survival

In Memoriam

For the most compassionate, articulate and spiritual man – our one and only 'Grandpa Fairy'. We know that you are smiling down on us. Your 74 years on this planet were filled with constantly campaigning for change to make the world a better place. This book, your parting gift to us all, will hopefully fuel the change you so eagerly sought.

We miss your cuddles, your stories, your wisdom and unconditional love.

Rest assured that you will NEVER be forgotten; the legend of Maurice Irfan Coles will live on.

From Nina, Lara and Rohesia (and your amazing 5 grandchildren/ bodhisattvas)

From Maurice and Bill

Education for Survival is dedicated to Maurice's five grandchildren and to Bill's two.
To the twins, Elias and Tobias (born 2015)
To the triplets, Elouisa, Annabella and Isla (born 2015)
To Charlotte (born 2008) and Lucy (born 2010)

At least we will have a response when they ask us 'Grandpa, what did you do in the great climate war?'

All proceeds from the sale of this book will go towards supporting the work of the Compassionate Education Foundation (CoED).

Education for Survival
The pedagogy of compassion

Edited by Maurice Irfan Coles
with Bill Gent

is an imprint of

First published in 2020 by UCL Institute of Education Press, University College London, 20 Bedford Way, London WC1H 0AL

www.ucl-ioe-press.com

British Library Cataloguing in Publication Data:
A catalogue record for this publication is available from the British Library

ISBNs
Paperback: 978-1-85856-919-2
PDF: 978-1-85856-921-5
EPUB: 978-1-85856-922-2
Kindle: 978-1-85856-923-9

Typeset by Quadrant Infotech (India) Pvt Ltd
Printed by CPI Group (UK) Ltd, Croydon, CR0 4YY
Cover designed by emc design ltd. The publisher was not able to discover the original source or rights holder of the cover image.

Contents

List of figures

About the contributors

Maurice Irfan Coles: CoED founder and trustee
The CEO and Founder of the Compassionate Education Foundation (CoED), Maurice published extensively on school improvement, race and faith equality, Islam and compassionate education. With over fifty years of practical classroom, lecturing, advisory and management experience, he was an inveterate traveller and had visited over a third of the world's countries. A TED speaker and Sufi sheikh, he was a proud father and grandfather. He died in 2020.

Bill Gent
Bill was a teacher, adviser and inspector. Writing extensively on religious education, he edited the journal of the National Association of Teachers of RE (NATRE). An associate fellow at Warwick University Centre for Education Studies, he researched and published on aspects of Islamic supplementary education. He was also a trustee of the CoED Foundation. He died in 2020.

Philip (Pip) Barlow
Pip is a freelance therapist expert in change and choices for a mindful life. He is a qualified NLP and mindfulness practitioner and has developed his own processes that make these practices more accessible to his clients. With his teacher partner Louise Darby he has developed the Compassionate Self/Compassionate Classroom project, a free monthly course for anyone working as an educator. Bringing together their unique talents, Pip and Louise utilize compassion, mindfulness and practical classroom techniques to provide a safe place for staff to develop higher skills for the classroom and life – and it works.

Gilroy Brown
Gilroy has been a headteacher of an inner-city school, a local authority adviser and an educational consultant. He has specialized in multicultural, antiracist education and leadership and management. He is also a writer and a successful artist who has been part of a number of innovative art projects. He is a practising pastor and a dynamic member of several community groups.

Rohesia Coles

Rohesia is a specialist occupational therapist in child and adolescent mental health in the West Midlands. Previously, she worked in Warwickshire and Sandwell within community mental health settings. Rohesia graduated from the University of Liverpool with a BSc in occupational therapy. She specializes in early intervention and prevention work for young people and is a trustee of the CoED Foundation.

Maureen Cooper

Maureen is the founding Director of Awareness in Action, which is dedicated to teaching how to combine wellbeing and excellence in the work environment by integrating meditation and compassion into everyday situations. She has over 25 years' experience in education and the private sector and is an accomplished practitioner of Buddhist meditation in which she leads workshops and training programmes. Her book, *The Compassionate Mind Approach to Reducing Stress*, brings together the best of modern science and the wisdom of the world's ancient contemplative traditions into a practical manual for thriving in today's world.

Louise Darby

Louise has worked for the past thirty years in education as a school teacher, school adviser and freelance consultant supporting schools in difficulty. Currently a supply teacher, she trains ITT students, and with her partner, Pip Barlow, delivers a teachers' course – Compassionate Self/Compassionate Classroom – which brings together compassion, mindfulness and practical teaching techniques.

Colin Diamond

Colin, currently CoED's chair of trustees and Professor of Educational Leadership, has long worked in the field of educational leadership. He has been a head of faculty, associate headteacher, local education authority adviser, assistant director and director of education/children's services. He led improvements in two local authorities, taking them from government intervention to strong performance.

Paul Gilbert

Paul is Professor of Clinical Psychology at the University of Derby and honorary visiting Professor at the University of Queensland. In 2006, he established the Compassionate Mind Foundation as an international charity to promote wellbeing through the scientific understanding and application of compassion, which has developed compassionate mind training for schools and businesses. He is the Director of the Centre for Compassion Research and Training at Derby University in the UK. Paul has written and/or edited 22 books and over 300 papers on evolutionary and contextual approaches to psychopathology and process-focused interventions.

James N. Kirby

James is a Senior Lecturer at the School of Psychology and Co-Founder of the Compassionate Mind Research Group at The University of Queensland. James also holds a Visiting Fellowship at the Center for Compassion and Altruism Research and Education at Stanford University. James has been developing compassion-based approaches to help parents engage positively with their children and thereby create nurturing family environments.

Frances Maratos

Frances is an Associate Professor and Reader in Emotion Science. For the past twenty years, her research has centred on understanding psychological, neurological, cognitive and physiological correlates of emotional wellbeing. She has published over thirty peer-reviewed papers as well as several book chapters and has become a key figure within the Compassion in Schools movement, leading on the UK arm of the international Compassion in Schools research programme. Currently, she serves as a consultant on UK 'Mindfulness Initiative Education Strategy' policy.

Marcela Matos

Marcela is a clinical psychologist and postdoctoral research fellow at the University of Coimbra, who has developed research in evolutionary clinical psychology and third-wave psychological approaches. Her PhD research centred on 'Shame memories that shape who we are'. Currently, her main research focus is investigating the impact of a self-compassion and mindfulness-based intervention on mental and physical wellbeing and on epigenetic mechanisms and physiological stress responses.

Catherine Knibbs

Catherine is a clinical researcher, trauma psychotherapist, functional coach, supervisor, speaker, trainer, vlogger and podcaster. She is currently completing a PhD in cyber-trauma. Cath has interests in the phenomena of cyber-related compassion as an antithesis to cyber-trauma, such as the phenomena related to cyber-bullying.

Manjit Shellis

Manjit, an educationalist with over thirty years' experience, helped transform the University of the First Age (UFA) into a national organization that has worked with over fifty local authorities, 50,000 young people and 7,000 adults in a variety of settings. The UFA has gained a national reputation for innovative practice in learning design and the development of young people's leadership in both schools and community settings. Currently, Manjit is the Wider Learning Lead for Birmingham Education Partnership and a member of the CoED Board.

Marilyn Turkovich

Marilyn started with the Charter for Compassion in 2013 as the Education Director and, since then, has moved into a number of different roles. Marilyn's background has been primarily in higher education, where she specialized in multicultural and global education and curriculum design and innovation.

Mick Waters

Mick, as well as being a headteacher, teacher trainer and founding trustee of the CoED Foundation, has held several senior leadership roles in Birmingham and Manchester local authorities. He was also Director of Curriculum for the national Qualifications and Curriculum Authority, which co-created one of the world's most progressive and dynamic national curriculums. He recently led an Independent Review of School Teachers' Pay and Conditions for the Welsh Government, with some exciting new proposals for teachers' careers and professional learning. This followed on from his work helping the Welsh Government to produce new Professional Standards for Teaching and Leadership.

Wendy Wood

Recently semi-retired from the University of Derby, Wendy was employed as a senior lecturer in counselling and psychotherapy for 19 years. More recently, she has concentrated on Compassion-Focused Therapy as a trainer and therapist. She also works in schools and other organizations as a Compassionate Mind Trainer to help facilitate compassion using the Compassionate Mind model.

Acknowledgements

The publishers would like to offer their condolences to the families of Maurice Irfan Coles and Dr Bill Gent, who died in April 2020 within a few weeks of each other, both of Covid-19.

We are grateful for the immaculately spelled manuscript we received from Bill.

Amarjot Butcher picked up the torch of compassion and worked tirelessly with us and the other contributors to make this book as near as we can to perfect. Thank you, Amarjot, for all you've done.

Those of us checking the book prior to print have done our best to verify all references and sources. Due to the tragic circumstances in which Maurice's manuscript is being resolved into this book, there may be a very small number of minor inaccuracies.

Gillian Klein, Publisher, Trentham Books

Foreword

Marilyn Turkovich
Director, Charter for Compassion

> We can only sound the alarm, again and again; we must never relax our efforts to rouse in the peoples of the world, and especially in their governments, an awareness of the unprecedented disaster which they are absolutely certain to bring on themselves unless there is a fundamental change in their attitude towards one another, as well as in their concept of the future.... The unleashed power of the atom has changed everything except our ways of thinking, and thus we drift to unparalleled catastrophe. (Albert Einstein, 1946)

Over seventy years ago, in this now well-known statement, Einstein foresaw the fundamental impact on the world of one major scientific breakthrough and warned of the need for corresponding fundamental changes in human thought and relationships. One could argue that we failed to follow his prescription for fundamental change in our ways of thinking and that the possibility of the terrible results of which Einstein warned has therefore mushroomed beyond a single catastrophe into multiple possibilities for disaster.

Yesterday, it was the split atom that should have made us reconsider our thinking and our relations with our neighbours on the Earth. Today, other conditions are challenging our ways of thinking – climate change and destruction of nature, global large-scale conflict, inequality, poverty, government accountability and lack of transparency, among other issues. The United Nations (UN) has provided us with a blueprint for peace and prosperity by 2030 in the adoption of the Sustainable Development Goals (SDGs). However, the goal outlining education does not instruct us on what a model for a new approach to education would look like, but rather, how we need to focus our efforts to 'improve learning outcomes for the full life cycle, especially for women, girls and marginalized people in vulnerable settings' (United Nations, 2019).

What, then, should we be doing? What are the necessary knowledge and skills for citizens to learn how to live effectively in an increasingly interconnected and interdependent world? What needs to be learned and why – not to mention *how*?

As the realms of citizenship expand from local and national to international in scope, schooling is increasingly being challenged to determine and transmit the skills needed for responsible citizenship. This means that education needs to help impart a sense of allegiance to the species of humankind, providing opportunities for citizens to interact more and become more consciously linked across national borders. We need to develop a meaningful conception of community and the multiple communities of which we can become a part. We need to use the mind in new ways, to think anew about time and space and other people. We need to develop not only cognitive skills but also emotional and intuitive skills – multiple intelligences – and, above all else, compassion. What the cognitive–analytical faculty cannot grasp, the emotional–affective faculty can reach through empathy and compassionate action.

As Thích Nhất Hạnh, the revered Vietnamese monk, puts forth, 'compassion is a verb'. *Education for Survival* therefore challenges the premise of schooling for success and material gain in favour of schooling for collaboration and service – to oneself, others and the planet. *Education for Survival* extends the process of moving from the pedagogy of the oppressed, so brilliantly addressed in the philosophy and practice of Paulo Freire, to acting on new processes for identifying and confronting the societal oppression that threatens our very existence. At the base of this re-thinking of education is hope. You will see it woven throughout the book. Without hope and resilience, how can we continue?

Education for Survival is a combination of science, reflection and action. The contents put before us the concept that loving kindness is a part of our nature that, in some ways, has become foreign to our understanding, and hence, to our practice. As Karen Armstrong, British writer and founder of the Charter for Compassion, has noted, returning to the premise of the Golden Rule – do unto others as you would have them do unto you – is a necessity if we are to survive as a human race. And, while we humans are undoubtedly capable of loving and caring for one another, *Education for Survival* extends the premise of the Golden Rule to caring for all sentient life forms and the planet.

There is both inspiration and challenge in the pages you are about to read. You will experience moments that will bring forth deep reflection and hopefully encouragement for further investigation into how compassion is grounded not only in science but is core to understanding how we can act with care and respect as we move responsibly and continuously to educate ourselves and guide future generations.

Preface

Maurice Irfan Coles

There is a world of light, of love and Oneness struggling to be born. 'Struggling' is probably too mild, for we live in an age of danger, disharmony and dishonesty. A continent burns. The Disunited Kingdom and The Disunited States of America are riven with ideological conflict; populism trumps reason, and abuse trumps debate. Since we started the Compassionate Education Foundation (CoED) from my house in Birmingham, England, in 2012, the world has become an even more perilous place. But, despite having no budget, we have managed to produce this work on the pedagogy of compassion whose central theme is the creation of an education system that encourages agency in the young so that they might co-create an interdependent and more compassionate world.

The struggles we have faced in completing *The Pedagogy of Compassion* are a microcosm of the planet's angst. In the two years since we conceived the idea for the book, several of the authors have lived through family tragedy, breakdown and trauma. Illness (including mine) has plagued production, and there were desperate times when I wondered if it would ever come to fruition. My empathy exceeded my capacity, and my compassion outstripped my industry and ability. And yet, against such odds, we have completed the task.

Compassion has been the glue that has bound the authors, and it has been my honour to be involved in the design, implementation and editing of this volume. I have known for many years that I am a most privileged man – privileged not by virtue of birth (growing up in social housing in London's Lambeth, there are not many silver spoons) but by virtue of a personality that allows me intuitively to see the world's interconnectivity. An acute sense of Oneness seems to be part of my ethical and spiritual DNA and it has enabled me to feel totally at home in my visits to over a third of the world's countries, and to feel at peace in all three major faith traditions – Christianity, Hinduism and Islam – with which I am intimately connected. But my greatest privilege and blessing is the ability to work with so many compassionate souls who have given of their time so freely.

Let me mention several people without whom this publication would never have happened. CoED's present and previous chairmen, Professors Colin Diamond and Mick Waters, both of whom have been unstinting in their support of this endeavour and their concern for my welfare. My co-worker, critical friend and design guru Amarjot Butcher, who has caught the compassion bug. My beautiful and long-suffering family who have borne my obsession with saintly stoicism. CoED trustee, Dr Bill Gent, whose brilliant copy-editing skills have been invaluable and without whom this book would never have been finished. Trentham's Dr Gillian Klein, who has supported the work from beginning to end. Most importantly, big respect to the writing team of Philip (Pip) Barlow, Louise Darby and Manjit Shellis (chapters 1.2 and 6.1). Throughout, they have helped conceive, shape, design and evaluate so much of the material. In this sense, the book really is co-created.

'What seems at first a cup of sorrow is found in the end immortal wine', says Krishna in the *Bhagavad Gita*. Let us hope that *Education for Survival* has a touch of that immortal wine. So let me end, as I always do, with my favourite Sufi paean, 'All praise is due to Him who has no name and comes by whatever name you call Him' – without whom this journey would never have happened, and to whom ultimately everything is owed.

Introduction

Maurice Irfan Coles

This work is born of love for our beautiful, interconnected and shared planet, in the certain knowledge that, unless we do all in our power to halt and reverse the ravages of ecocide, we will have failed in our duty as caretakers of the Earth and failed generations of young people, now and yet to come.

This work is born of love and amazing generosity of spirit, wherein the 23 authors have given of their time and effort without recompense. Indeed, some have sought funding to support their research and others have employed an editor to help reduce their word counts.

This work is born of research – field research conducted by several university departments, and book and electronic research that covered many disciplines. So vast are the academic references that these appear free of charge on the CoED website, as do the authors' biographies.

This work is born of practice. Many of the authors are practising teachers, lecturers, consultants and mental health practitioners working at the chalkface. Those who are not, still spend considerable time in direct contact with young people and have significant experience in project management, delivery and evaluation. Their collective expertise, often gained over a lifetime, is extraordinary.

This work is born of collaboration, creativity, innovation and vision. The authors are all experts in their respective fields and here they envision a compassionate future. The creativity, innovation and vision presented in this book are the result of entwining concepts together in a collective future-mapping exercise.

This work is born of hope. Perhaps amazingly, without reference to each other, so many authors use the word 'hope' throughout their work. There seems to be a genuine optimism that, despite all the many problems, education can make a significant impact on building a world fit for all our children.

This work is born of a threat to humans. So many of the authors make unwitting reference to the pandemic which was to rage across the planet and took two of them in the time between writing and publication. There are references to social distance, bubbles of support and the need for communities to exercise restraint of self for greater good. As we adjust to a 'new normal', let's do it with compassion.

The genesis of this book was a major conference on the subject of compassion financed by the City of Birmingham's Director of Children's Services, who, in 2018, brought together 200 headteachers, senior politicians and officers. Co-created and co-presented by the CoED Foundation, City of Birmingham and the University of the First Age, it presented *Towards the Compassionate School: From Golden Rule to Golden Thread* (Coles, 2015) as the baseline for building a compassionate world. Many headteachers commented that the conference 'reminded them of why they came into teaching'; some wanted such an event weekly! At the end of the conference, my elder daughter, Lara (herself a deputy head in a primary school) said, 'That's all very well, dad, but what do I do now?' This book outlines what to do now. It aims to:

- examine the nature of both compassion and pedagogy, locating these two overarching concepts within the wider social and geo-political contexts of our conflicted world
- justify the paradigm shift in the private sphere from consumerism and individualism to one of service and collaboration; and in the public sphere, from market ideology to public service
- offer a number of theoretical and practical models that support the development of a compassionate ideology and help schools and other institutions devise a curriculum with the learner at its heart, drawing insights from a range of scientific disciplines
- outline and justify the key skills, attitudes and knowledge required to co-create a compassionate world
- provide practical tips for teachers, schools and other institutions
- galvanize education so that it places compassion for planet as *the* key motivational force.

Each chapter has been devised as a stand-alone element but I suggest you begin with Chapters 1.1 and 1.2 of Section One. These provide the imperatives for change, the overview of compassion and the nature of pedagogy. Our first book, *Towards the Compassionate School* (2015), placed us at the foothills of compassionate education. Hopefully, the fact that we have completed this new work means we are now at base-camp. Others, God willing, will help take us to the summit.

Section One

Compassion and Pedagogy

1

Riding the crest of a compassionate wave: The horror and the hope

Maurice Irfan Coles

Abstract: This chapter examines the frightening imperatives that drive compassionate action: the climate catastrophe, poverty and inequality, the failed neoliberal and economic paradigm that buttresses the rich and disenfranchises the poor, and the crisis in mental health. It argues that there are, however, many reasons for hope. They are encapsulated in the acronym CREST: Compassion, Religion, Economics, Science and Technology. These can be galvanized by a compassionate education system designed to inspire young people's agency, through which they can help address these formidable imperatives.

The frightening imperatives that drive compassionate change

When I used to support schools in devising their institutional development plans, I often employed a future-mapping process whereby leaders envisaged their school five years hence, and then worked backward to outline how they might have got there. Similarly, we played the humorous 'yes but ... no but' game where participants list all the factors that would impede development. The game concludes with the organizer stating that 'You have expressed all the negatives today. We will address them, but that is the last time this year I want to hear the word BUT...'. In the same spirit, this chapter starts with all the 'buts' and then proceeds to the positives.

Towards the Compassionate School (Coles, 2015: 10–19) outlines 'ten self-evident truths: drivers for compassionate change'. With the exception of areas related to climate change, economics and equalities, they were framed to emphasize the positive rather than accentuate the negative. Five years on, the stark truth is that climate change and species extinction, inequalities and poverty, and physical and mental health have continued to deteriorate to reach crisis proportions. They are, of course, all interrelated but it's the impact of climate catastrophe that is fuelling the worsening crises. Alarmingly, the carbon industries have known about the damaging effects for over seventy years and yet have chosen to actively propagate an alternative vision in which they have invested billions (Alston, 2019).

We are cursed with political leaders who are, at best, disingenuous and, at worst, mendacious. The most powerful political leaders continue to see the world in terms of their narrow national interests. Yet, we have less than a decade to limit greenhouse gases to a rise of 1.5 degrees centigrade – or face devastating consequences.

Although the richer world will hardly be immune from the effects of climate change, the poor (who contribute the least to global warming) are on the front line.

Since 2008, poverty and wealth disparity in the UK have grown exponentially, and are further exacerbated by a broken welfare system that has forced an alarming rise in the poor seeking emergency help from food banks just to meet their basic needs (see Tyler, 2020, *House of Commons Briefing Paper*). The worsening position of the poor in one of the world's richest countries was highlighted by Alston in his searing report on extreme poverty and human rights in the UK, in which he argued that the Tory Government had pursued an austerity programme 'more as an ideological than an economic agenda' (Alston, 2019: 1).

The British Government responded to Alston by attacking him as 'too political', and rejected his conclusions. Similar denial tactics have been effectively used by the democratically elected leaders of some of the world's biggest polluters. In their election campaigns, heads of government Trump, Bolsonaro and Morrison all insisted that climate change was a myth, a hoax perpetuated to deny their citizens prosperity. But such figureheads don't exist in a vacuum. Toxic leaders require colluding followers; both peddle bad ideas that become the conduit for damaging behaviours. The bad ideas that prop them up are part of the neoliberal and economic worldview that elevates the individual above society and that idolizes growth–greed consumerism whose by-product has impoverished millions, and whose zeal for economic growth is rapidly destroying the planet. Its effects have the potential to undermine the very liberal democratic values for which our ancestors fought and died.

Neoliberals believe, despite all the evidence, that, as a matter of 'faith', big government is 'bad' – unless it involves spending on arms or subsidizing the fuel or farming industries – because the market will decide. They also believe that individual wealth-creation will trickle down to the rest of society. The authors of the Wikipedia entry on this ideology summarize neatly:

> Neoliberalism … is the 20th-century resurgence of 19th-century ideas associated with laissez-faire economic liberalism and free market capitalism. It is generally associated with policies of economic liberalization including privatization, deregulation, globalization, free trade, austerity, and reductions in government spending in order to increase the role of the private sector in the economy and society; … Neoliberalism constituted a paradigm shift away from the post-war Keynesian consensus which had lasted from 1945 to 1980. (Wikipedia, 2020b)

As a philosophy, neoliberalism is now at outright war with the compassion that drives the environmental movement, the proponents of the Green New Deal and mass global movements like Sunrise, Youth for Climate Justice and Extinction Rebellion. The impact of the neoliberal paradigm, with its belief in the efficacy of short-term austerity, has further exacerbated the growing global mental health crisis. *All* the evidence we have, in the UK, USA and internationally, provides a terrifying litany of decline in the world's mental health, especially among the young.

Figure 1.1: CREST on the hoopoe bird

Source: Courtesy of Johannes Obermeier, Vienna

So, these are the horrors, the many 'BUTS'. There is also hope. The TEDx talk 'Education for survival: Compassion for planet' (Coles, 2019) summarizes causes for hope in a simple acronym, CREST, which employs the powerful graphic metaphor of a hoopoe bird. Not only is the hoopoe the national bird of Israel but, in Sufi symbolism, it also represents the spiritual leader who, despite all the obstacles, leads others to salvation. The image (see Figure 1.1) is inspired by the beautiful twelfth-century Sufi poem *Conference of the Birds* by Farid al-din Attar, which Anne Baring has rendered for children in *The Birds Who Flew Beyond Time* (2009). CREST provides an acronym around which to cluster our positive compassionate arguments, many of which are developed in more detail in this book.

Compassion

Since we started the CoED Foundation in 2012, governments have displayed increasing indifference to the suffering they bring to their own and other populations. At the same time, there is a growing army of *compassionate souls* who individually and collectively perform innumerable acts of kindness and argue – increasingly vociferously – that we can no longer continue to allow our beautiful world (and hence ourselves) to be destroyed by the forces of power and greed. Compassion is the lightning rod and the lodestar to counter these forces, but what is it and why has it such an important part to play in education?

Remarkably, the concept of compassion, at least in Western cultures, has been somewhat of a contested space. In 1979, Matthew Fox, the prescient eco-warrior and Christian mystic, wrote:

> Compassion has been exiled in the west. Part of the flight from compassion has been ignorance of it that at times borders on forgetfulness, at times on repression, and at times on a conscious effort to distort it, control it and keep it down. This exile of compassion leads to the poison and pain that becomes incarnated wherever people are treated unjustly. (Fox, 1999: 1)

Many Christians would disagree with Fox's analysis, but, over time, compassion came to signify sympathy, often associated with patronizing attitudes related to pity. This is particularly true in the German, Italian and French languages. Schopenhauer (1839), for example, in his famous maxim 'universal compassion is the only guarantee of morality', uses the term *das Mitgefühl*, which implies sympathy and commiseration. But German speakers also employ *Mitleid*, which implies pity, and *Barmherzigkeit*, which is closer to mercy. Other languages, faiths and the contemplative traditions avoid this confusion. For Muslims, especially the Sufis, the root of faith is love (Rahman) and all Muslims are enjoined to do good works. For Jews, God is the Compassionate (Rahmana) and they, too, are exhorted to relieve distress in both human and other animals. Possibly the clearest exposition, however, is found in Buddhism and its *Metta* ideal of loving-kindness with the supreme manifestation of the bodhisattva, a person who has foregone nirvana to help the planet.

The English word 'compassion' derives from the Latin *compati*, which means 'to suffer with'. But it is not merely sympathy or empathy, for its original meaning implied action. Compassion as *love and action* has the same dual meaning in Arabic, Hebrew, Greek, Sanskrit, Pali and Punjabi. In 2009, as a result of the inspirational work of Karen Armstrong, representatives of all major faiths and humanist traditions came together to fashion, agree and disseminate the 'Charter for Compassion', which was based on the Golden Rule, *love others as yourself*. The charter has spawned a growing international movement that places compassion at the heart of everything we do. This, combined with major advances in neuro- and other sciences, has led to the restoration of the term to its original meaning. In addition, we have come to realize that, although individual and collective action can help to address suffering, and in some cases the causes of that suffering, our world will become an even more hostile and indifferent place unless we challenge the systems that underpin and maintain it. Thus, as shown in Figure 1.2, there are four key components of compassion:

- the **recognition** of a person's or group's suffering and a loving **response** to that misery
- an **understanding** of the causes of distress and the neoliberal and economic *systems* that perpetuate and increase suffering
- an **active determination** to alleviate the distress
- the **practical wisdom** (what the Greeks called *phronesis*), which is based not solely on the mind but also on the heart.

We are all genetically wired to recognize suffering, and the majority of us can empathize, can walk in another's shoes and feel both their joy and their suffering. It is difficult to act, however, if we allow ourselves to be overwhelmed by that suffering. Empathy, unlike compassion, does not demand action. Compassion does! It is predicated on 'feeling *for*, rather than a feeling *with* the other' (Singer and Klimecki, 2014). In addition, neuroscientific research indicates that the neural pathways for compassion and empathy are very different, which may help explain their different expressions (Bergland, 2013; Well, 2017).

Figure 1.2: The four components of compassion

Source: The CoED Foundation

Compassion, therefore, is love-in-action. CoED has devised a typology of compassion that works on four interlaced levels and that, like the Egyptian pyramids, represents the sense of harmony and unity within ourselves and with nature, and our connection to the soul and the sacred. Science was added because so many recent evidence-based insights validate the wisdom of Oneness and Love expressed in ancient contemplative knowledge and practice. Many of us, however, are happy with showing compassion for others but treat ourselves badly. Once again, however, the research demonstrates that non-judgemental kindness to ourselves is fundamentally important if we are to sustain our compassionate drive for others. Compassion for planet forms the gold-tipped apex (the benben) because it rests upon the three other levels (Figure 1.3).

To summarize, compassion is a perspective, a way of seeing the world, that places love-in-action at the heart of everything. Compassion renders love-in-action our zeitgeist, our worldview, the spirit of our age. Compassion is a radical way of living on this shared Earth wherein everything we do is permeated by love.

Presumptuously, we use the terms 'new' and 'radical'; but, in truth, this only relates to the immediate present. Love-in-action has always been at the heart of world religions and contemplative and spiritual traditions. The revival of this spirit is our second cause for hope.

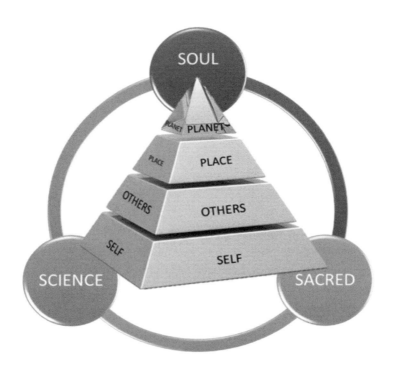

Figure 1.3: The typology of compassion

Source: The CoED Foundation

In our CREST, **Compassion** is followed by **Religion,** developed further in Chapter 5.1.

Religion

Good people of faith and spirit have always engaged in interfaith dialogue. Although the interfaith movement grew throughout the twentieth century, the rise of violent religious extremism and climate Armageddon provide the greatest present impetus for it to unite around the Golden Rule (as their common ethical base) and around the interconnection and Oneness of all creation and a common belief in humanity's role as 'caretaker' of the Earth.

SACRED ACTIVISM AND SPIRITUAL ECOLOGY

The concept of Mother Earth also exists in aspects of Taoist, Hindu and Buddhist thought. More recently, it became a central plank of 'engaged Buddhism', with its founder Thích Nhất Hạnh arguing that we must learn to fall in love with the Earth again. A manifestation of sacred activism is the 'new' discipline of spiritual ecology that combines the two great streams of secular science and ancient spiritual/religious/indigenous traditions. It aims to rescue our beautiful shared Earth by stressing the scientific and intuitive wisdom that we are all interconnected and that the health and wellbeing of the individual and the collective depend on the health and wellbeing of the planet and its entire species. The individual's spiritual journey becomes meaningful when it interacts and connects with the spiritual journey of others, when we move from the 'me' to the 'we', or, as Martin Buber (1923) put it, from the 'I' to the 'Thou'.

Humans, of course, can't live by spirit alone; they require bread – a metaphor for the economic system that should allow us to survive and prosper. The potential changes to our perceptions of economics and neoliberalism provide us with our third area of hope: economics.

Economics

Gandhi famously observed that the world has enough for everyone's needs, but not everyone's greed. For Gandhi, cooperation, not competition, was the natural state of humankind as 'he argued that all efforts to improve the human condition are bound to fail unless they put *dharma,* or a moral framework and a sense of higher purpose, above the pursuit of *arth* (wealth) and *kama* (pleasure)' (Bakshi, 2012: 10). Outside modern India, Gandhi's ideas have increasingly gained traction. The present dominant economic model presupposes that wealth will trickle down to the poor, ignores the fact that the world's resources are finite, offers harmful subsidies to fossil-fuel companies and acts as if all economies can develop to match the affluence of the most 'developed' nations. All of these actions are now vigorously challenged.

In her 2017 book, *Doughnut Economics,* for example, Kate Raworth cogently argues that the economic model that governments have religiously followed since the 1930s is demonstrably broken because it is predicated on perpetual growth. Governments worship at the altar of gross national product (GNP) because that has been so successfully marketed as a proxy indicator of progress. Many of its acolytes have grown richer (especially the 1 per cent super-rich) while the world's majority, poorer. Everybody is now paying a huge price because we have exceeded the 'ecological ceiling', the limit of what the planet can sustain. Raworth advocates a 'doughnut' model of economics with an outer ring of planetary constraints, an inner ring comprising the social foundation – the minimum basics for life – with a sweet spot in the middle that is both ecologically safe and socially just. This, she argues, requires a regenerative and distributive economy, which will change the mindset from one of endless growth to one that 'thrives in balance' (Raworth, 2017: 237).

Raworth is part of a wider movement redefining economics generally – seeking to end the GNP tyranny in particular – by widening the criteria through which we assess 'successful' nations. The UN Sustainable Development Solutions Network, for example, annually publishes its *World Happiness Report*, which grades countries according to a range of 14 measures. Interestingly, five Scandinavian countries consistently appear in the top ten, four of which also rate as those with the best education systems (and all of which have very different systems from the UK and the US).

Science

One of the main drivers of the compassion movement is the science that underpins it, particularly in the fields of psychology, neurobiology, physiology, evolutionary psychology and sociology. In addition, we have the science of creativity, and the 'unambiguous' climate science (Ban, 2014). All of these constitute our evidence-based drivers of change. Compassion has become a discipline in its own right. In 2017, Oxford University Press published its encyclopaedic *Oxford Handbook of Compassion Science*, which is the most detailed exposition to date. Similarly, in 2013, the Max Planck Institute for Human Cognitive and Brain Sciences released its comprehensive e-book *Compassion: Bridging Practice and Science* (Singer and Bolz, 2013), which summarizes the results of the science of compassion and outlines training programmes and practical experiences.

A most accessible, comprehensive, online and affordable training package has also been developed by the Charter for Compassion Education Institute. The Science of Compassion Course (2019) is divided into seven parts providing a wealth of resources and covering the latest science in the following areas:

- What is the science of compassion?
- What can the science of compassion teach us?
- How does mindfulness relate to the science of compassion?
- How does social and emotional learning fit into the science of compassion?
- Where does kindness fit into the equation of science and compassion?
- Do animals have compassion?

We know more about the science of the brain than we have ever done: we are all genetically and physiologically wired for compassion, but we are not hard-wired. Put simply, the mind sculpts the brain and is influenced by its experiences. Positive experiences reinforce the neural pathways so that, the more compassionate you are, the more compassionate you become; the more compassionate you become, the happier you are; the happier you are, the better you learn. It is a virtuous compassionate circle. The opposite is equally true.

The implications for education are profound. Christopher L. Kukk, in *The Compassionate Achiever* (2017), describes five areas in which research demonstrates the benefits of compassion, which:

- improve academic performance
- foster greater self-esteem and health
- strengthen resilience
- create a happier workplace, increase productivity and improve profitability
- strengthen the political, civic and economic health of communities.

Building on the work of Dacher Keltner and others, Kukk argues against social Darwinism, which maintained that the biological concepts of natural selection and survival of the fittest applied equally to human interaction. This ideology was used to justify the worst excesses of competitive, aggressive and evil behaviour. Kukk observes: 'Charles Darwin not only did *not* coin the phrase "survival of the fittest" ... but he argued against it' (ibid.: 10). As Darwin wrote in *The Descent of Man* (1871), 'I perhaps attributed too much to the action of natural selection or the survival of the fittest ...'. Darwin argued in favour of what he termed 'sympathy' when he wrote, 'those communities, which included the greatest number of the most sympathetic members, would flourish best and raise the greatest number of offspring' (cited in Kukk, 2017: 10–11). Since Darwin, other evolutionary biologists have developed the 'survival of the kindest' hypothesis. The point is simple: Darwinian science was used to justify competition but its twenty-first-century reappraisal endorses compassion.

The last cause for hope that I will mention here (the fifth in the CREST acronym) is technology.

Technology

The 'T' is for technology – or, more precisely, the compassionate use of technology in a range of areas. For example, there are now a host of mobile apps to support mindfulness and encourage emotional literacy. Goleman (2009) argues that new information technologies could create 'radical transparency', making us aware of the environmental, health and social consequences of what we buy. Such knowledge, intelligently applied, alters purchasing habits, which, in turn, change producer practice. Information technology facilitates wide and immediate knowledge in all facets of compassion and can encourage that Oneness of understanding required to build a compassionate world.

We already have the technologies to harness the power of the sun, wind and waves to build our carbon-neutral future. And we have the old technology of trees! George Monbiot, writing from a commercial food laboratory outside Helsinki, argues in the *Guardian*:

> We are on the cusp of the biggest economic transformation, of any kind, for 200 years. While arguments rage about plant-versus meat-based diets, new technologies will soon make them irrelevant. Before long, most of our food will come ... from unicellular life. After 12,000 years of feeding humankind, all farming except fruit and veg production is likely to be replaced by ferming: brewing microbes through precision fermentation. (Monbiot, 2020)

Compassionate technology can help us in our fight for planetary survival but, without a changed political mindset and culture, the shifts will be too gradual to avert climate – and, consequently, human – tragedy. A compassionate education system can help create a culture that builds on CREST because it is a way of seeing the world that places love-in-action at the heart of everything we do. The *golden thread* that must become part of the warp and weft of young people's lives.

From the pedagogy of the oppressed to the pedagogy of compassion

Philip Barlow, Louise Darby, Manjit Shellis and Maurice Irfan Coles

Abstract: Pedagogy *is* politics. One cannot divorce the values and ideologies of governments from what happens to the teaching and learning in the classroom and other settings. This is particularly true of England, where the educational worldview of one man has dominated practice and discourse concerning publicly funded education since 2010. This chapter unpicks this discourse and argues that there are five interrelated areas of enquiry and ten criteria that determine pedagogy. As long ago as 1968, the Brazilian educator and eco-warrior, Paulo Freire, highlighted the link between pedagogy, power and social justice in *The Pedagogy of the Oppressed*. Freire identified 'rage and love' as the basis of radical alternatives to neoliberalism. This chapter argues that there is a pedagogy of compassion that isolates the political drivers and the compassionate knowledge, skills, attitudes and modes of delivery that culminate in the practical wisdom required to build a compassionate world.

Introduction

When Hulagu Khan, leader of the conquering Mongol army, entered Baghdad in 1258, one of his first acts was to destroy all the libraries and, in particular, the House of Wisdom, which housed the greatest collection of books in the world. Eyewitnesses reported that the Tigris literally ran black with the ink of thousands of books. It ran red as the bodies of scholars and philosophers suffered a similar fate. When, in 2010, Michael Gove (the new English secretary of state for education) and the coalition forces entered the DfE's Sanctuary Buildings, his first act was to destroy the previous Labour Government's largely consensually crafted education and curriculum policies and the structures that underpinned them. These included multi-agency working, the *Every Child Matters* agenda and the detailed advice on tackling bullying, Metaphorically, the Thames ran black with the ink of

Labour's advice, strategies and resources, then red with the mass clear-out of most of the officials who had served a government with a different ideology. All semi-independent education bodies with responsibilities for leadership and teacher training were absorbed into the new all-conquering empire through the conformity to inspection and the threat of losing funding. The many educational professionals who opposed his approach were summarily dismissed and lampooned by Gove as 'The Blob'.

Prompted and assisted by his faithful satrap Nick Gibb, Gove set about centralizing government control, realizing the Thatcherite revolutionary dream of removing local authority influence over state-funded schools while returning the curriculum to the narrow 'traditional' subject-based model much loved by the Victorians. Strikingly, issues of climate change that had permeated Labour's curriculum were now restricted to geography and science. Claiming to give English schools greater 'autonomy', he encased them in a tight inspection, assessment and examination regime that, in effect, determined their agendas. As Professor Dorling puts it in his searing analysis of the unravelling of equality during six years of Tory rule:

> ... the National Curriculum was altered to suit one man's theory
> of the world ... more and more of what was taught in schools was
> what ... Michael Gove happened to believe in, and was taught in
> the rote-learn/exam-regurgitation way he believed worked best
> for his purposes. (Dorling, 2018: 11)

Dorling's words confirmed the worst fears of 'The Blob', who had launched a scathing attack in 2013 on Gove's proposed reforms. Professor Robin Alexander, editor of the encyclopaedic *Cambridge Primary Review* (2010), described the primary changes as 'neo Victorian', 'educationally inappropriate and pedagogically counter-productive' (Garner, 2013).

The pedagogy of the oppressed

An unabashed and unapologetic Gove had finally achieved what critics of the Education Act 1988 – which created the first English National Curriculum – had feared: a secretary of state who used his extensive powers to impose *his* political vision on the education system. Although the context was very different, the great Brazilian educator, Paulo Freire, in his seminal *Pedagogy of the Oppressed*, first published in English in 1970, unpicked the contextual link between pedagogy, power and social justice, arguing that the powerful used education as a means to maintain an unequal status quo and impose their own cultural perspectives. Freire believed that a relationship between teachers and students in which teachers have power and knowledge, but the students do not, failed to teach students to view the world critically. He described this as a 'banking model' of education, where a teacher 'deposits' facts into the minds of the students, who have to memorize and recall them (1970: 45–6) for regular testing that requires them to 'withdraw' the learning previously deposited.

Freire argued for a 'problem-posing model', in which teachers and students were more equal. Problem-posing education presents students with worldly difficulties that relate to their own lives and pushes them to analyse how and why those problems exist. Freire's model would directly combat oppression by empowering people to question their circumstances. It would encourage dialogue and the practice of 'co-intentional education' (ibid.: 43). Together, these measures would lead to praxis.

Partly because of Freire's influence, debates about pedagogy became part of popular educational discourse. For many practitioners, pedagogy is probably understood as nothing more than aspects of teaching and learning, content and delivery, and possibly the theories underpinning learning. The word 'pedagogy' itself has its roots in ancient Greek; it is a derivative of *paidagōgia*, which literally meant to lead a boy or a child. Rich Greeks would task slaves with looking after their children, often taking them to places of education, so a 'pedagogue' became, literally, a leader of children. Over time, as various education systems became institutionalized, the meaning evolved to incorporate people who taught and employed various methods of instruction. But, as with the word 'compassion', pedagogy took on nuanced variations in different contexts at different times. At its heart, however, were always issues of the key knowledge, skills and attitudes (KSAs) that educators (or politicians) wished to impart, as well as the means of transmission; but behind these KSAs sits a series of fundamental questions.

Five major areas determine pedagogy in its widest sense but all are underpinned by one overarching question: *Who decides?* The first area, the *context*, determines our vision of the *purpose* of public education and examines the implications of its funding streams. So what do the politicians want in return for public investment?

The second area, the *content*, relates to what we teach, the curriculum we offer and the KSAs we aim to develop in our learners. 'Curriculum' is not just subject-specific courses or cross-curricular themes; it is also the 'hidden curriculum', the attitudes, values and norms that children absorb from the institutional structures, relationships and systems around them. Since the late 1990s, schools have also become aware of the 'inner curriculum', which is to do with the inner life of students: their emotions, imagination, intuition, ideals, values, sense of spirituality and psychological wellbeing – all of which help to build their emotional resilience. Building on the pioneering work of Daniel Goleman (1995), the phrase appears to have been coined initially in the US by A.P. Johnson (2007) and popularized by Hawkes and Hawkes (2018).

The third area of enquiry, and possibly the most familiar, is the *methodology* we employ to transmit this content. How do we teach? What informs our choices? What are our theories of mind and of how children learn? Closely related to methodology are the initial training and continuing professional development teachers receive. Who decides its content, and who funds attempts to keep teachers up-to-date and using recent and relevant approaches?

Governments have been obsessed with the fourth area, *monitoring and evaluation,* both nationally via their own systems and internationally, driven by the PISA rankings. Who assesses students' work, and over what period? Who decides if teaching and schools are up to scratch? And how are the findings reported to the public? In England, all publicly funded schools are ranked in league tables and all are inspected by the Office for Standards in Education, Children's Services and Skills (Ofsted). Until 2019, Ofsted's judgements had been predominantly based on academic attainment, but the most recent Chief Inspector of Schools, Amanda Spielman, has altered the focus so that now schools are urged to concentrate more on the quality of education. Accordingly, Ofsted is emphasizing schools' processes for deciding what to teach and why, how well they are doing it and whether it is leading to strong outcomes for young people (Ofsted, 2019). Inspectors will now come to their judgements based on dialogue with schools and pupils – a much more compassionate system that encourages collaboration.

The fifth and final area of enquiry – and, in many ways, the most important – is *governance*. What structures are in place for schools to be managed and administered efficiently and effectively? But how do we define 'efficient' and 'effective'? Such questions go to the very heart of the values schools wish to impart and to the purpose of education, since, once we are clear about those, everything else follows.

The problem is that the word 'education' can mean many things. It has two different Latin roots: *educare* which means to 'train' or to 'mould', and *educere* which translates as to 'lead out', to 'elicit'. *Educare* presupposes a set body of knowledge and skills that young people are required to master and teachers pass down. *Educere*, on the other hand, assumes that we are born with skills and propensities and it is education's function to develop them. The scientific literature confirms that this is particularly true of compassion.

Educare and *educere* are not, however, polar opposites. Indeed Bass and Good (2004) argue for a better balance between knowledge-transmission and the eliciting of the key meta-skills such as questioning, thinking and creating. Citing Deming (1994), they also contend that:

> ... parameters and expectations for educators ... are established by the aims and structure of the organization itself. Thus, educators tend to assume roles shaped by the organizational design in place. To be effective, all educators must first understand the aims of the organization before they can organize their work. (Bass and Good, 2004: 165)

Our aims are closely related to our values, to the sort of society in which we want our young to grow and prosper and to our vision as to how this might be achieved. In their excellent *The Power of Pedagogy* (2008), Leach and Moon list ten criteria describing 'authentic' pedagogy: '[It] is invariably political', and 'is always about vision, values and educational purposes', which address 'big ideas' (Leach and Moon, 2008: 15). It is 'a collaborative iterative process between teachers, learners and other members of the community' and takes place in real changing settings. These authors acknowledge the relationships between learning and identity and laud the strengths of teachers as researchers and intellectuals (ibid.: 28–99). Furthermore, they maintain that the mind is complex and multifaceted, and believe that 'a broad understanding of the human mind and cognitive science is a crucial aspect of teacher knowledge' (ibid.: 168).

In another publication currently in development, Manjit Shellis and John Corrigan expand on this and explore how relationships between teacher and student have a biological basis that can provide us with greater insights into our own behaviour. Understanding the human brain even at a basic level can help us to learn to drive our own brain and build the sort of relationships that are deeply engaging, influential and compassionate. Drawing on Corrigan's *Red Brain, Blue Brain* (2019), they offer a range of activities and a rationale for enhancing our 'blue brain' where we are at our best – confident, collaborative and creative – while mitigating the negativity of the 'red brain', where we become self-focused, impulsive and overly emotional. In summary, then:

> ... pedagogy is the act of teaching together with its attendant discourse of educational theories, values, evidence and justifications. It is what one needs to know, and the skills one

needs to command, to make and justify the different kinds of decision of which teaching is constituted. (Alexander, 2010: 280)

Our 'attendant discourse' is, of course, compassion. But is there a distinct pedagogy of compassion that isolates the political values, key knowledge, skills and attitudes we wish to impart, all of which provide a compassionate learning environment? Categorically, yes!

We can best summarize our thinking in a simple diagram showing the pedagogy of compassion (Figure 1.4), which places 'compassion for planet' at the heart of all we do. The outer circles are common areas of enquiry for all pedagogies. The inner box contains our key values, purposes and processes. You get a very different outcome indeed if, in the central purpose box, you replace 'compassion for planet' with concepts like transmission of core skills, preparation for the life of work, individualism and competition. All the key questions remain the same, but replacing collaboration, co-construction and dialogue with a centralized, top-down model radically alters the dynamics as well as the outcomes.

The pedagogy of compassion

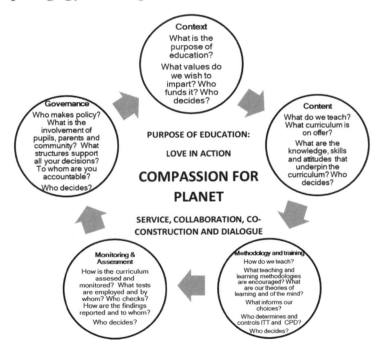

Figure 1.4: The pedagogy of compassion

Source: The CoED Foundation

Earlier, we offered love-in-action as our simple definition of compassion and justified 'compassion for planet' as the key overarching, interlacing driver because it contains within it compassion for self, for others and for place. Interestingly, some fifty years before compassion became a discrete discipline, Freire had arrived at a similar conclusion, when discussing the nature of dialogue:

> Dialogue cannot exist, however, in the absence of a profound love for the world and for people ... Because love is an act of courage ... love is commitment to others ... No matter where the oppressed are found, the act of love is a commitment to their cause. (Freire, 1970: 62)

The climate emergency means that we are now all oppressed. Ironically – and, for the majority, often unknowingly – we are all oppressors too, just by virtue of living in this society. Freire, one of the founders of eco-pedagogy, was well ahead of his time, perhaps unsurprising as he was much influenced by the pioneering work of Erich Fromm, whose *The Art of Loving* (1956) helped set the present compassionate trajectory.

We can translate love into educational activities by identifying the key compassionate knowledge, skills and attitudes (KSAs) required:

Knowledge: relating to facts and concepts, which can be divided into three areas – propositional (*knowing that*), procedural (*knowing how*) and intuitive (*knowing about*) – without necessarily having recourse to conscious reasoning.

Skills: the ability to perform a task that can be subdivided, for example, into soft or hard, interpersonal or social.

Attitudes: feelings, emotions, beliefs and values.

There are some important riders, however. First, this taxonomy is a useful method of organizing and assessing learning. The areas are not discrete but rather interrelate, as our knowledge of something often informs our skills – especially in relation to our attitudes, since we learn best when we value what we are learning. The second rider is this: knowledge is not wisdom!

When we refer to the four components of compassion (see Figure 1.2), we argue that compassion must lead to 'practical wisdom' – what the ancient Greeks called *phronesis* – which implied both good judgement and excellent character and habits. Wisdom is the synthesis of cognitive intelligence and sound judgement, based on knowledge, experience and intuition – the wisdom of the heart. Knowledge without wisdom can be, at best, fascinatingly sterile or, at worst, frighteningly dangerous. There are many examples throughout history of clever people acting without wisdom: for example, the letter that child psychologist Haim Ginott cites in his book *Teacher and Child* (1972). It is the letter a school principal sent every year to his teachers, which movingly encapsulates the dangers of knowledge without wisdom, of learning divorced from compassionate values:

> I am a survivor of a concentration camp. My eyes saw what no person should witness: gas chambers built by learned engineers. Children poisoned by educated physicians. Infants killed by trained nurses. Women and babies shot ... by high school and college graduates. So I am suspicious of education. My request is this: Help your children become human. Your efforts must never produce learned monsters, skilled psychopaths, educated Eichmanns. Reading, writing, and arithmetic are important only if they serve to make our children more human. (Ginott, 1972: 317)

More recently, Daisaku Ikeda, president of the Soka Gakkai International, in his inaugural address at the founding of the Soka University of America (2005), eloquently summed up the differences between knowledge and wisdom:

> Knowledge alone cannot give rise to value. It is only when knowledge is guided by wisdom that value is created. The font of wisdom is found in the following elements: an overarching sense of purpose, a powerful sense of responsibility and, finally, the compassionate desire to contribute to the welfare of humankind. (Ikeda, 2005)

Compassion can act as the alchemic formula that transmutes the lead of knowledge into the gold of wisdom. To create a compassionate school, we need to isolate the discrete elements of compassionate knowledge, skills and attitudes.

Compassionate knowledge

As a baseline, young people require knowledge about compassion – what it is, how it works and how it offers a sense of purpose and supports resilience. It helps also if they also know the importance of mindfulness and spirituality and of the benefits of self-knowledge (Coles, 2015: 54–5). It is imperative that they understand the science of the brain and the science surrounding ecocide, at an age-appropriate level. In addition, it aids learning if pupils and teachers know about the nature and variety of intelligences and their potential impact on learning styles.

In *Frames of Mind* (1983), Howard Gardner smashed the IQ paradigm that exalted linguistic and logical–mathematical intelligence, in favour of eight distinct intelligences that more fully account for the broad range of human potential in children and adults. In summary, the eight areas are:

1. Linguistic intelligence (word-smart)
2. Logical–mathematical intelligence (number/reasoning-smart)
3. Spatial intelligence (picture-smart)
4. Bodily–kinaesthetic intelligence (body-smart)
5. Musical intelligence (music-smart)
6. Interpersonal intelligence (people-smart)
7. Intrapersonal intelligence (self-smart)
8. Naturalist intelligence (nature-smart)

In 2001, Zohar and Marshall argued for a further and ultimate intelligence, spiritual intelligence (SQ). Cindy Wigglesworth, in *SQ21* (2012), develops the SQ concept into a set of 21 skills that we develop over time, with practice; her approach aims to create a 'helpful roadmap and diagnostic' (ibid.: xvi). Itzkow, in his innovative piece (in preparation), explores the relationship between SQ and leadership.

In this more sophisticated model, everybody has intelligence but in different ways. That knowledge can help raise learners' self-esteem and self-knowledge. As Manjit Shellis and John Corrigan put it:

> That knowledge is power. The power to drive our own brain rather than be taken on a hair-raising journey over which we have little control. Exposing learners to new ways of thinking about intelligence so that they grow confident in what they as individuals have to offer is fundamental to developing a mind-set characterized by resilience, drive, care and connectedness. This knowledge in the context of nurturing relationships gives us the tools with which to flourish compassionately. (Shellis and Corrigan, in preparation)

Schools can audit the compassionate knowledge components of their curriculum to determine if they are teaching the science, the spirituality and mindfulness, and the compassionate characteristics outlined. That knowledge translates into the second element of a compassionate school: compassionate skills.

Compassionate skills

Each school can review its own skill-set against the best compassionate practice. The award-winning work of Theo Gilbert from Hertfordshire University provides an excellent baseline. As part of his PhD, *Using the Psychological Concept of Compassion to Inform Pedagogic Strategies for Higher Education Seminars*, he developed 'a theoretical basis for designing a pedagogy that attends explicitly to compassion in HE teaching, learning and assessment' (Gilbert, 2015: 3). For Gilbert, compassion relates to cooperative behaviours and is 'recognised across disciplines and it is valued across cultures' (ibid.). In the five years since then, he has developed and sharpened his thinking and the practical and theoretical aspects of his work. His excellent website, Compassion in Education (https://compassioninhe.wordpress.com) offers helpful strategies via a range of short films and PowerPoints. He is an advocate of teaching the micro-skills of compassion that support positive group-work skills while countering disruptive group behaviours such as monopolizing debate or avoiding participation. Although focused on higher education, his work applies also to other age ranges.

Unsurprisingly, there is considerable overlap between Theo Gilbert's work and that of Louise Darby, CoED Foundation Associate. Darby has rendered the thinking of this book's organizing group on the skills of compassion into a simple mnemonic – NEAR – as it dwells on the higher-order skills of **N**oticing, **E**mpathizing, **A**cting and **R**eflecting. Each is broken down into a series of sub-skills and accompanied by a range of activities that can be used in any educational setting and for all abilities. Figure 1.5 sets out the essence of her thinking:

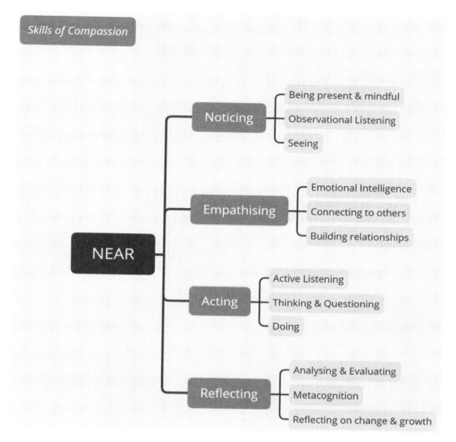

Figure 1.5: NEAR: Skills of compassion

Source: Louise Darby

Gilbert's and Darby's work complement Bronwyn Hayward's wonderful book, *Children, Citizenship and Environment* (2012), which directs us 'conceptually and practically towards ways of building capacity and desire in children for collaborative work, involving critical debate and collective democratic action' (Hayward, 2012: x). Hayward's conclusions were based partly on her field research in New Zealand into the citizenship and environmental concerns of young people aged 8–12 years. She considers the ecology of a neoliberal childhood and issues of importance to the young in English-speaking countries. The book details the development of what she terms the 'SEEDS' approach to citizenship and environmental education: 'Social Agency', 'Environmental Education', 'Embedded Justice', 'Decentred Deliberation' and 'Self-Transcendence'. She strongly endorses the approach of Andrew Dobson (2003, 2016) who argues that we must teach citizenship, not from a narrow civics-based perspective, but from an ecological perspective. Dobson developed the concept of 'ecological citizens' who accept and act on their global obligations to tackle the climate emergency. To achieve this, Hayward argues, young citizens will require: 'critical thinking skills, the ability to reason, reflect and communicate clearly… and the virtues of empathy and tolerance, co-operation, moral reasoning, determination and courage' (Hayward, 2012: 16).

We now turn to the third of the three elements necessary for creating a compassionate school: compassionate attitudes.

Compassionate attitudes

As a prelude to the final version of *Towards the Compassionate School*, Coles and Brown brainstormed the characteristics of a compassionate person. The result was a list of some thirty attributes or attitudes for schools to actively promote. After much reflection, they rendered these as an acronym – 'Acts for Love' (Figure 1.6).

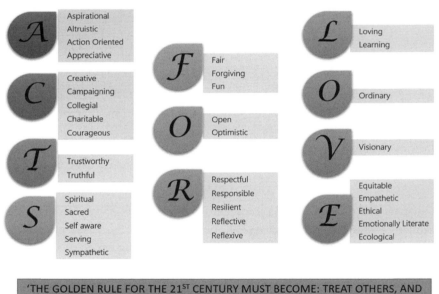

Figure 1.6: Acts for love: A compassionate person is …

Source: The CoED Foundation

Most of these attributes are self-explanatory but several require clarification because they might, at first glance, appear contradictory. For example, how can one be both 'visionary' and 'ordinary'? Some thinkers and activists (like our authors) might envision and dynamically endeavour to create a compassionate world. Others, more prosaically, might perform countless random acts of kindness, equally valid but not, in themselves, earthshattering. As Saint Teresa of Calcutta eloquently put it, 'Not all of us can do great things, but we can do small things with great love'.

Implicit in much of the discussion surrounding compassionate KSAs are a range of styles conducive to compassionate pedagogic approaches that aim to empower the young to challenge the existing paradigm that has brought our world to this perilous state and equip them with love and resilience to help them fashion a better future. UNESCO'S three working papers, *The Futures of Learning* (2015), confirm the broad thrust of compassionate pedagogy, arguing that 'the transmission model' is not at all effective for teaching twenty-first-century skills (Scott, 2015c: 2). Instead, UNESCO emphasizes a humanistic vision, collaborative learning and the power of dialogue. In paper 14 of the series, it stresses:

> ... the importance to the twenty-first century workplace of personal skills such as initiative, resilience, responsibility, risk-taking and creativity; social skills such as teamwork, networking, empathy and compassion; and learning skills such as managing, organizing, meta-cognitive skills and 'failing forward'. (Scott, 2015b: 1)

Children learn about compassion by acting compassionately. But schools have found that classifying delivery styles into 'taught', 'caught' and 'cultivated' not only helps organize compassionate learning but also provides a useful audit tool with which to judge the quality of existing practice:

- **TAUGHT characteristics** refer to the *explicit* teaching of the KSAs through lessons on compassion, on neuro- and climate science, on prominent compassionate people and on the compassionate moral compass.
- **CAUGHT characteristics** refer to the actions that young people *implicitly* absorb through example, such as observing random acts of kindness, which are often inspired by your behaviours and the respect and love you show. Your modelling of the Golden Rule can speak volumes.

- **CULTIVATED characteristics** refer to the conscious fostering of compassionate values, which can be achieved through *what* we teach and *how* we teach. Furthermore, compassion can be fostered through our approach to the subjects we teach and how we transmit and promote culture and identity. Compassion can be particularly encouraged through, for example, the teaching of the creative arts, citizenship, ecology (personal, social and health education), mindfulness and meditation and also religious education.

Conclusion

As we have seen, the pedagogy of compassion has 'compassion for planet' as its overarching moral and political driver. Contained therein is compassion for self, for others and for place/community. It is based on sound science of the mind, of compassion and of climate. It stresses the importance of multiple intelligences and SQ. It encourages models that co-create and utilize dialogue and collaboration. Compassion for planet is a perspective that should permeate everything we do in education because it encompasses both the pedagogy of compassion and the pedagogy of the oppressed, having rage, love and justice as its bedrock.

Towards a compassionate school system

Mick Waters

Abstract: This chapter outlines some principles by which school systems work and describes some attempts to make them more productive. It questions whether this emphasis on productivity is well placed in light of its impact on the people who work within such systems. As long as measurable outcomes and results take precedence over compassion, headteachers are treated as branch managers, with teachers as operatives and learners as units of production. However, there is hope.

The chapter highlights examples from across the world where nations are realizing that there are other ways to structure society and address the future – better ways. The recent pandemic has seen a rethink of what matters in society and human relationships, with consideration of the roles of schools and systems. The chapter concludes with some thoughts about how those within the system can influence and support change towards an outlook that is compassionate in every respect.

School systems: Why they exist

School systems are established to meet the needs of every learner. Underneath lurk other reasons, however: profit, economic benefit and the manipulation of people, for example. Whatever the driving force, the strapline is usually the ultimate benefit for the learners. Nations and local jurisdictions 'invest' in schooling with the espoused intent of offering fulfilment. Private schools invite parents to pay for the sort of learning experience that will release their children's human potential. The parallel purposes of schooling are the economic benefits to a nation of a better-educated workforce, profit to the schools' owners, the social cohesion of community and the exercise of influence by those in power. Some of these purposes are foregrounded to validate performance against investment, emphasize success relative to competitors and reassure the users of the service.

It is the relationship between the ambitions for the learner and the driving purpose of the system as a whole that determines the degree of tension to which an individual school system is subject: whether its behaviour is ethical, measured, unscrupulous or compassionate towards its students, workers and community.

How systems have tried to manage school quality – and their investment

Schools are run by professionals. Investors, be they government or private, need to see their investment being maximized, and therefore they are interested in ensuring that schools are delivering cost-effective practice. Schools are influenced by the system that 'owns' them and within which they work. Increasingly, the system seeks to improve its schools. Where previously it was the job of the system to provide schools and leave the running of them to the professionals, there is now a tendency to control the work of the schools to render them better than before and better than their competitors. National governments constitute by far the largest group of systems, although the extent to which they devolve control at federal level or to localities and jurisdiction varies.

Over the last fifty years, as school systems have gradually extended control over their schools, they have limited the professional autonomy of teachers and manipulated operating conditions and structures to increase the effectiveness of their system. Why have they done this? The schools could be left alone, autonomous and independent. After all, most professions recognize the need to look at other approaches and learn from the best. Schools are no different; sharing of practice is natural.

Those who lead systems exert influence for several reasons. The wish to ensure that every school is optimally effective is one reason, but there are others too because ensuring that their system is 'performing' acceptably means exerting influence of a different kind. Recognizing performance can be a means to provide support or it can be a test of effectiveness – which becomes complicated when the performance of different schools is compared and turns support into competition, both between individual schools and between school systems. There is a fine balance between the notion of professional self-improvement and being driven to 'deliver' top performance. When the stakes are high, compassionate outlooks may well diminish.

Nearly all school systems exert control via five primary features:

- a centralized curriculum
- the provision of well-trained and highly skilled teachers
- highly effective school leadership

- accountability
- testing and examinations.

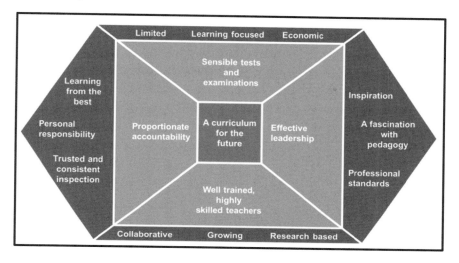

Figure 1.7: Practices for system influence on schooling

Source: The CoED Foundation

The premise and intentions of the system's control are set out in Figure 1.7. The starting point is the agreed or expected curriculum, while the other measures are designed to ensure that the curriculum is supported and able to do its job. It is keeping these in balance that has proved difficult for most school systems and, in the last few decades, testing and accountability through a managerial approach have been seen as the way to improve outcomes.

Too often, such good intention is so focused on the system's effectiveness in gradually narrowing its parameters that the future of the young people it seeks to educate is no longer the main concern. We are fiddling with the education systems of the world while the planet burns.

A curriculum for the future?

Any school or school system is essentially built around its curriculum. There is an underlying belief that certain things we can teach our young will be most effectively learned in a school. Most school manifestos begin with a statement about the curriculum. The decision of the Department for Education (DfE) in England in the late 1980s to establish a National Curriculum prompted other nations to consider what the entitlement for learners in their schools should be. This essentially simple concept has become the catalyst for the evolving nature of system influence on schooling.

Most national curriculums are built backward. They begin by establishing what students will need so they can pass examinations at the end of their school careers, and work back from there to establish the route that those able to complete the course will follow to reach 'A' standard. In many countries, only about half the students reach the desired goal. For a significant proportion of the other half, the process of being threaded through the eye of the educational needle leaves them so discouraged that life feels too difficult and they can become a cost to their nation in terms of needing health, social care and judicial resources. Although fine words are written about the need to address the future by attending to the learning of the young, we find a retreat to the trusted content of previous generations and to curriculums that can be tested.

Efforts are made to present the curriculum in a different way. New Zealand, for example, talks of 'natural connections' between subjects. Few take the step into organizing learning in a truly integrated way, although Finland details seven cross-curricular themes including 'cultural identity and internationalism', 'responsibility for the environment', 'wellbeing' and 'a sustainable future'. The nations of the UK have pursued different courses. Scotland and Northern Ireland produced their own curriculums and 2010 saw the DfE in England establish what many commentators regarded as a regressive national curriculum consisting of knowledge and facts. Subsequent amendments included additions around the social and emotional wellbeing of pupils and concern for the planet. Wales regards the curriculum as being at the heart of its transformation of the school system and builds on four purposes for learning, which they defined in 'Areas of Learning Experience'.

While a national curriculum can look exciting on paper, it rarely serves the learner well. The focus on exam success or inspection criteria often distorts the curriculum experienced by the students. Across the globe, nations develop forward-looking versions of curriculum intentions, but the leverage of tradition is powerful and inertia prevails.

Later in this volume, we consider the climate emergency. Young people across the globe are moved to protest about the inadequacy of action taken, enthused by media interest around Swedish environmental activist Greta Thunberg. A dilemma arises when schoolchildren put into practice the knowledge of democracy they learned in school, thereby finding themselves challenging the authority of society. As teenagers 'March for Our Lives' in response to gun crime in the USA, or others build support for Malala Yousafzai's efforts to provide education for all girls worldwide, we see tensions arising as young protesters use their knowledge to confront issues that affect them. As these youngsters seek to influence their world, they condemn the efforts and actions of authority that insist they remain children until they leave school having learned compliance. Faced with this, the system is inevitably wary.

The ambitions of curriculums can easily end up as compliance. Campaigns such as 'No Child Left Behind' or 'Every Child a Reader' are set up with good intentions and there is no doubt that young people have better prospects if they are literate. But their prospects will also be better if the world becomes a more loving place and the climate is less at risk. In England, the New Labour policy of 'Every Child Matters' was swept away following a change in government. What then took centre-stage was a new approach to literacy-acquisition by teaching phonics.

However, the notion of young people as souls that must be controlled persists. We continue urging young people to strive to achieve curriculum requirements lest they otherwise lose out in later life. Do we see campaigns for 'Every Child a Conservationist' or for 'No Child Unloved'? As Ben Newmark puts it, in his blog: 'Our curriculum should whisper to our children, "you belong. You did not come from nowhere. You are one of us. All this came before you, and one day you too might add to it"' (Newmark, 2019).

The recent pandemic has drawn all of this into sharp focus. It has made people consider what matters in society and, for a short while, there has been a recognition that we need to be kinder to each other and the planet, and we need to value parts of society we have taken for granted and maybe not chase some of the goals we had previously sought. Whether this is sustained as the emergency passes and we work towards a 'new normal' remains to be seen. We humans crave the familiar; we even rebuild cities in the same places after earthquakes. Can we use what we have learnt in a few months of panic to take advantage of the opportunity to change? It depends on what we seek and how we hold each other to account.

Proportionate accountability

As determining a curriculum's content is fraught with difficulty, its existence sets in train many levers, drivers and checks to enable the system to support its schools. Once it is decided *what* all students should be entitled to learn, it is possible to check *whether* they are doing so and, it follows, to check whether they are being taught effectively. Through that process, it becomes apparent that some schools perform better than others and that, by implication, their students are better taught. Many reject this implication, believing that children's performance is the result of many factors besides the school. The more nagging doubt for many is whether 'better taught' is the same as 'better educated'.

The concept of variability leads the system to exert its influence on its schools. If there is variability, then there must be ways for the system to secure consistency for its learners. This logic is defeated when the focus on performance sharpens to such a narrow furrow that people are driven by the ends rather than the means. That's when pressure outpaces support – and when the system becomes dehumanized.

Overstating the evidence?

In schools, learning and testing have always held hands. Tests can motivate, help the teacher to determine need or provide comparisons of performance over time or against a norm. With the introduction of a national curriculum comes the potential for national testing of every school student. In the UK, it was called 'assessment', a softer-sounding term that suggests analysis *and* support.

In itself, testing is no bad thing, offering information and insight. However, the introduction of testing in the UK came at a time when computers were starting to offer possibilities in terms of data management. In just a few years, the analysis of results at national level had become an end in itself, pitting school against school, local area against area, local against national and school against national. The 'assessment' was no longer about just testing but became a process whereby each child was being treated as a unit of production.

The school results analysis conducted by the Organisation for Economic Co-operation and Development (OECD) and its Programme for International Student Assessment (PISA) has hugely influenced the system. Established to seize the growing measurement of outcomes in individual school systems, PISA tests now dominate the accountability agenda for national governments. While the OECD's work has strength in depth, few know its work other than in reference to the triennial publication of comparative test scores for schoolchildren across the globe. Governments, wary of public opinion fuelled by the media, vow that they will strive to maintain – or improve – their position in PISA's international league tables. This, in turn, puts pressure on systems to improve their unit output. The OECD has developed excellent papers and resources to enable systems to learn from its programme analysis. These go comparatively unnoticed by evolving 'self-improving school systems'. In terms of compassionate approaches in particular, OECD's four transversal themes – Trust, Time,

Technology and Thinking Together – encapsulate much of the valuable work that was going on.

Yet, for individual school systems, the collated analysis of their units of production indicates their own success or otherwise, suggesting that they seek to enhance their productivity. To do this, the science of 'drilling down' to identify the performance of sub-groups against different criteria has developed, leading to improvement-driven ways of thinking and acting.

Again, this is no bad thing in itself. Who would not want every child to succeed? Used judiciously, insight can enhance effectiveness. However, the apparent difference in performance between individual schools and their comparative *productivity* created an expansion of the impulse to look closely at the work of individual schools. Consequently, Ofsted was established in the UK in 1992 to carry out inspection of all schools. For the first time, they were routinely and publicly identified as succeeding or failing, and the repercussions for local area control were significant. Computer-generated analysis of inspection outcomes indicated that some local areas were performing better than others, and so Ofsted moved into inspecting school *systems*.

Beginning with London in 2000, inspection has highlighted, over twenty years, a range of failing local authorities and has proffered a hypothesis for failure that should be addressed. From the shortcomings of the urban metropoles to those of provincial cities, coastal towns, rural areas and satellite towns, there is virtually nowhere in the UK that has been immune from a 'rapid improvement strategy' initiated by concerns drawn from Ofsted's analysis. Like the Victorian doctors who neglected to wash their hands between examinations, so passing infections between patients, Ofsted inspections spread dubious managerial practice based on questionable evidence on a national scale. Schools were answerable for their own performance as measured by government criteria, which created a climate of hostile 'managerialism'. But a system in fear finds little space for compassion.

How inspection affects behaviour

Inspection has long been part of the infrastructure of most education systems. In the Victorian era, schools were inspected where there were concerns about propriety or standards of provision. Across the globe, systems – state or private – mirrored one another in establishing inspectorates that could be called upon for reassurance and to investigate concerns. In the UK, this changed as part of the education reform agendas of the late twentieth century. In his political memoir, Conservative politician Ken Clarke recalls his creation of a wholly new inspection regime when he was secretary of state for education: 'The creation of Ofsted resulted in another enormous leap forward in the general public's knowledge and understanding of what was happening in local schools' (Clarke, 2016: 273). But he notes that, among schools: 'A sense of near paranoia and victimhood reared its head' (ibid.).

This notion of needing to address perceived shortcomings in schools by scrutinizing them so as to improve outcomes has resisted professional opposition for a quarter of a century and has spread across the globe. In Australia or Scotland, for instance, the inspection regime is seen as more supportive towards the teaching profession, but the central premise remains that 'stakeholders' can be reassured that their school system is effective because of the existence of an inspectorate deemed to be objective.

While that may be the case, the adverse impact on the professionals themselves can, over time, be significant as they experience what they believe to be excessive scrutiny and limited trust – the opposite of compassion.

The side-effects of inspection: Panopticon theory

In the late eighteenth century, social reformer Jeremy Bentham developed the basic idea of the 'panopticon' prison – with an internal design configured in such a way that it led inmates to believe they were under continuous surveillance. Consequently, they *acted* as though they were being watched by their jailers at all times. Their perception of being constantly scrutinized had a controlling effect on their behaviour (Bentham, 1791). Eminent philosopher Michel Foucault noted that 'the Panopticon is a marvellous machine which, whatever use one may wish to put it to, produces homogeneous effects of power' (Foucault, 1978: 202). Within the panopticon, 'one is totally seen, without ever seeing', while those observing 'see everything without ever being seen' (ibid.).

The panopticon concept, which generates the sensation of being continually watched and thus influences the behaviour of those who believe they are under surveillance, has gradually been applied to schools, hospitals and other institutions in different forms by their respective managing systems. The omnipresent feeling of being monitored is designed to secure the practices the system believes would produce the accountability and outcomes it is seeking. In turn, by achieving its desired outcomes, the system can justify its own behaviours.

In his doctoral thesis, Doug Lowes outlines how inspection in England has seeped into every pore of the education body. As schools have been encouraged by Ofsted and government to self-evaluate their work, the process enables inspectors to observe schools 'at arms' length and out of sight … and being under constant but unseen observation, schools will be forced into moving the inspection criteria to a daily focus, as they comply with and eventually internalise inspection norms and procedures' (Plowright, 2008, cited in Lowes, 2016: 38).

Inspection has promoted the use of common criteria and language between schools and inspectors as a good thing. In reality, through the process of self-evaluation, schools have adopted the criteria of inspection rather than developing their own. In this way, the strength of discourse within the process of school self-evaluation has been defined by inspection and not by the schools themselves. In his work on school self-evaluation, Plowright suggests that one consequence of schools being in a constant state of readiness for inspection is that 'they have been in their own version of the Panopticon and that, in their eyes, escape now appears impossible' (Plowright, 2008: 121).

In a similar vein, Jane Perryman uses the expression 'panoptic performativity' to describe 'a regime in which the frequency of inspection and the sense of being perpetually under surveillance lead to teachers performing in ways dictated by the discourse of inspection in order to escape the regime' (Perryman, 2006: 148). The feeling of trying to escape a regime could hardly be described as compassion in action. At some point, those responsible for school systems have to take control of the agencies that they set up to inspect their schools. To many across the globe, the equivalent of a sheepdog that is eating its own flock has been created.

Effective leadership?

As leaders have been held accountable for success or otherwise, so leadership has become a science in itself, and the study of effective leadership of schools has spawned approaches to improving the level of production. Two significant things have resulted. First, those aspects of any defined curriculum that can be measured have come to the fore and others have receded in importance. How far can global sustainability be tested annually in each pupil? What chance kindness, generosity or love? Second, an accountability-driven mentality leads to a separation of functions in people's work. To ensure that the impact of their work can be measured, their remit is closely defined in terms of 'outcomes'. Part of the difficulty here is that education systems have tended to work discretely within their own siloed organizations.

In nations or jurisdictions, the requirement to provide the 'best' schooling is accepted and pursued by those responsible and separated from 'other agendas' or the corporate body. The same system that is providing education is also providing other services, ranging from health to law and order, defence or social care. These services usually run in parallel, held together by some overarching mission, and responsibility is gradually devolved to those deemed specialists in their field.

Where a school system is just that, a private entity offering schooling for sale, the effectiveness of the provision is judged on its profitability or economy, its effectiveness at marketing the provision and the provision itself; and the latter is usually in parallel with the other functions. Management effectiveness, then, became the key function, and the move to enable education to learn from the private sector's methodology – generally based on a principle of value-for-money – has been very influential. And so grew 'managerialism', as opposed to true leadership. Managerialism is that sense of being busy and decisive, highly organized and structured, clear about objectives and outputs while simultaneously losing sight of the underlying values of the community being led.

The McKinsey report (2010) asserted that the system can only be as good as the best of its teachers. This gave impetus to the notion that teachers were 'operatives' to be improved by 'leaders', motivated by rewards associated with results, and fear of the consequences of negative accountability. The business model, with its emphasis on line-management and the use of military language – such as 'front line', 'targets' and 'parachuting-in' expertise – gained strength but narrowed the arena of learning. As Diane Ravitch, a former education adviser to the US government argues:

> The new corporate reformers betray their weak comprehension of education by drawing false analogies between education and business. They think they can fix education by applying the principles of business, organization, management, law, and marketing. They purposefully develop elaborate good data-collection systems to incentivize the workforce ... with appropriate rewards and sanctions. (Ravitch, 2010: 12)

To Ravitch's list of influences, we could add 'sport'. The competitive nature of sport was exploited by all manner of well-meaning contributors attempting to help the education system perform better and deliver the best of itself. The availability of data enables the analysis of sports psychologists, who revel in concepts such as 'marginal gains' and 'previous best' to pursue higher scores. These models were adopted by the school system and embraced by system leaders.

The problem is that children are not mere units of production. However hard a teacher works, however refined their skill, however determined their effort, the student is still the crucial element. For a surgeon, the patient lies still as the technical operation is performed. The teacher works with minds that fly anywhere: teaching is one of the few jobs where the work is measured in the performance of others. In addition, the teacher who is trying to affect the hearts of learners as well as their minds is bound to feel aggrieved when the accountability settles exclusively on the measurable.

Too many such managerially efficient systems and processes fail to support learning. Worse still, many of them detract from precisely the work we seek to manage better. Computer technology has brought benefits but it has also made it easier to create mission statements, visions, strategies, plans, risk assessments, records, reports, flow charts, spreadsheets, data sets and the like – all of which tend to only increase in complexity and volume. Our managerial deadlines drive us, we seek evidence to prove the value of our analysis, we fret over presentations, we record or report at unnecessary length for fear of falling short on detail. Our plans cover every eventuality and risk. Our managerial efficiency is scrutinized almost as much as our teaching work, so we endeavour to cover any anomalies and sometimes game the system to avoid discomfort. The model of scrutiny used by those above us offers a model for our scrutiny of juniors; and they, in turn, replicate these demands to impose on others. This is the case at every level in the school system; so much of it builds up in tiers. It is no surprise, then, that people talk of 'chasing their tails', of 'tails wagging dogs', or of 'losing sight of the big picture'.

In the quest for effectiveness and efficiency, the culture of schooling may have shifted too close towards relying on the computer screen and paperwork and too far from the central purpose of our work. Schools should focus on the benefit to learners and those who work to support them. Our shorthand lets us talk in terms of agencies 'supporting schools' when we should see agencies as supporting learners in everything they do. Why are we meeting to follow up meetings, often under such pressure that paperwork is incomplete or late – which then necessitates a further meeting?!

The time taken to produce papers, reports, records, documents and the like should be measured against the amount of attention they receive and their usefulness to learners, rather than the managerial effectiveness of their production. This is one of the features of the managerialism culture that urgently needs to change, lest the young people have to carry the burden of managerialism on their own shoulders. Otherwise, they too will be groomed into performing and demonstrating the outcomes needed, channelled into production, and used as evidence. All of this is a far cry from the principles of learning and teaching.

A new era: Is system leadership changing?

In the 2019 Priestley Lecture at Birmingham University, Professor Sir Tim Brighouse talked of the four ages of schooling. He described the period from 1988 to the present as one of 'centralisation, marketisation and managerialism', and suggested that the next era, the one now emerging, would be characterized by 'ambition, purpose and hope' (Brighouse, 2019). As school systems across the globe seek to redefine themselves, the gap is growing between those who flog the horse of the previous age and those who unleash the spirit of hope. The systems that recognize that leadership needs to drive ambition, purpose and hope will emphasize professionalism and leave the era of managerialism behind.

At its best, such an approach will secure the education we want for children in the future. It will help support our commitment and passion and release the energy in the system for good. At the same time, we need to analyse the benefit of many aspects of work that we have come to take for granted, and question whether the effort spent on them benefits the students.

Examples of hope

Some nations and jurisdictions have recently started to see their schooling provision as part of a holistic approach to not only childhood but their society at large. Schooling is part of the society's outlook on its own future. Determining what is needed in the future is not the same as striving for wealth or economic prosperity. Thus a reassessment is taking place. Is the purpose of schooling what we have always been led to believe, or is there another vision for our children's future?

For about 150 years, we have separated our young from society at large and left it to the schools to 'prepare them for life' without necessarily considering the life we are preparing them for, or whether schools alone should be charged with that function. We are frustrated with the futility of attempts by school systems to improve provision, and with our misguided urgency to create an image of success about which we have become embarrassed. That we now have a more highly educated population that is capable of doing greater damage to our environment and to itself is an uncomfortable truth.

Typically, change is starting in smaller countries. New Zealand has embraced a new approach that puts consideration for one another at the centre of school learning. The United Arab Emirates is building new outlooks on personal education. Tunisia is working on sustainable development. Costa Rica is engaged in a national agenda for environmental sustainability – with schoolchildren involved in planting trees across the nation, for instance. The UN Rights of the Child are being respected in more countries across the world. In Wales, the 2015 Well-being of Future Generations Act outlined seven wellbeing goals (Figure 1.8) (Commissioner for Wales, 2015).

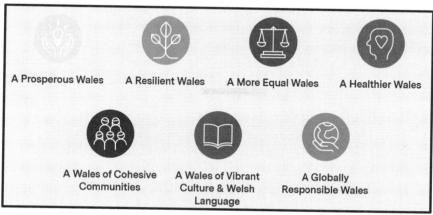

Figure 1.8: Seven wellbeing goals: Well-being of Future Generations (Wales) Act 2015
Source: The Welsh Assembly

These goals for the nation are to be embraced by schools as part of a system positioned within a national 'futures outlook'. Recycling levels in Wales are among the best in the world and plans for new road systems have been amended to take account of the environment.

The notion of a 'wellbeing economy' is central. Most education systems are traditionally built on mega-economic trends, watching how the world is changing, trying to anticipate the future and adapting their education provision accordingly. The issues have been noted: the ageing population, the transport that creates a shrinking planet, the movement of people across the world, the widening gap between rich and poor, the growth of new economic giants, concerns about global sustainability – much of this fuelled by the growth in technological capability.

Previously, schooling in Wales has responded by redoubling its efforts to achieve greater 'output' that would maintain and improve the country's status in the world. The belief was that, if a greater proportion of the Welsh population were to attain certain designated goals of learning and knowledge, Wales would somehow survive the next threat to its prosperity. The problem is that other countries, too, were applying these principles to their own systems and entering the competitive stakes of educational output. The differences between test scores in different countries' performance across the globe are recorded by rank order, but the highest-performing students and schools are actually similar everywhere. That is to say, for Wales and many other nations, chasing a rise in test scores in the pursuit of improved ranking is largely futile in terms of improving the future of young people.

What Wales is doing is changing the paradigm. It is making statements about the future for young people as part of its ambitions for the whole population, now and in the future. Sophie Howe, Future Generations Commissioner for Wales, argues that 'Our obsession with exams is failing to equip young people with the right skills for the future' (Howe, 2019).

System leadership for a new era

Developments in approaches to schooling such as co-construction of the curriculum, professional learning and revision of accountability need to be informed by purpose, ambition and professionalism and supported by agencies intent on upholding the philosophy of the agenda. We have to guard against using managerial devices such as paperwork to provide evidence of commitment and engagement. People in schools need confidence to take the steps they want to take on this new journey rather than relying on a map with its distant finishing line and checkpoints along the way.

If we want school leaders to be part of a self-improving school system, we shouldn't treat them as branch managers, teachers as operatives, nor treat children as units of production – faceless letters and numbers. Our community of parents must become partners, not customers, and our middle-tier agencies should give practical support, instead of just recording their own impact to show to their scrutinizers.

Certainly, strategic planning and *analysis* are important in ensuring thoroughness, but what matters above all is helping our young to grow and flourish, and our documentation and procedures must enable that to happen. Trust has to build at every level – trust to try, trust to ask for support, trust to adapt and improve.

As CEO of England's National College for School Leadership, Steve Munby was responsible for the professional development of all the school leaders in England's 22,000 state schools. In *Imperfect Leadership* (2019), he argues that one of the greatest flaws of leadership is to believe you have to be the perfect leader: never weak, always right, free from self-doubt and impervious to failure. Ethical leadership, according to Munby, means being clear about your values and hanging on to them rather than doing the expedient thing just to keep the government off your back, get performance numbers up or avoid pushback (Munby, 2019: 14).

Many would agree with this sentiment but school systems, too, need to respond. Ethical leadership should not rest completely on individual conscience. We also need to make policy environments more principled so that educational leaders can address impossible dilemmas such as having to implement policies they believe will harm children or feeling pressured to raise results quickly by concentrating disproportionate attention on those students closest to minimal proficiency targets.

The Atlantic Rim Collaboratory (ARC) has taken an exemplary step forward in this regard. This group of ten systems – each comprising a minister, deputy minister and head of a professional association – convene in an annual summit to progress their shared interests in advancing excellence, equity, inclusion, democracy and human rights in education, within professionally run systems. ARC's work rests on three core principles:

- School visits should get close to policy and practice in action, followed by a debriefing.
- Feedback and analysis should be structured.
- Peer feedback should be facilitated in triads, in an environment of confidentiality and trust, based on strategic and ethical codes of practice.

The system leaders report having remarkably productive discussions with their own teams that may lead them to occasionally adapt their policies on accountability, creativity or practice. Ethical leadership, according to an analysis by Andy Hargreaves is about:

> … being courageous and staying true to your values. It's about letting right be done, even when it's uncomfortable or poses personal risk. It's about confronting complex dilemmas like competing human rights with others rather than trying to resolve everything alone. And it's about creating and fighting for a positive educational and ethical environment together that removes ethical dilemmas between serving the child and complying with the system that are neither necessary nor desirable. (Hargreaves, 2019: 4)

So what needs to be done?

So long as managerialism drove the system, people in schools learned to do as the system required. The result is that those within the system feel controlled by a power over which they have little influence. However, there are signs that the system is changing and that politicians recognize the growing concern about our young people and the role of our schools and services. Accordingly, at every level in the system, people will have to exert their individual influence, commitment, belief and will. These are the tasks ahead:

For headteachers and principals:

- Hold on to what matters – the things you said at interview about changing lives, equipping young people for their futures, shaping society and changing the world.
- Resist the pressure to become too managerial and 'feed the machine' of accountability that others drive.
- Require of 'system leaders' the support they profess to offer, and remind them when they deviate from the agreed support.
- Stand by teachers and others who work with children, literally. This means being close to wherever the learning is taking place: in classrooms, workshops, laboratories and gymnasiums. The closer we are to the action, the more influence is possible. And stand by them metaphorically too – by recognizing how systems have become managerial constructs and working for change.

For teachers and others who work with children and young people:

- Recognize that you are a professional and that you have been entrusted with the hopes, ambitions and dreams of young people for the future.
- Ask questions, make suggestions and propose approaches based on what the mission statement for your school promotes.
- Balance effort between the big picture and the small details that foster learning.
- Help your students to see the wide world: its opportunities, threats and beauty.
- Seek professional contributions, get involved, read, don't wait to be told or invited to join in decision-making.

For system leaders at every level:

- Make sure that the processes and practices put in place serve the ambitions of the curriculum.
- Co-construct processes for support with, and alongside, those in schools and the community to provide what is needed.

- Base your work physically within schools for as much of the time as you can. If you need an office, base it in a school, where you'll be able to see schooling in the raw.

Conclusion

This chapter has examined how school systems treat their people, and questions whether an intensively managerial approach can achieve the ambition the systems have for themselves and for the learners they seek to serve.

The reality is dawning that the world has to be kinder to itself, that we have to take care of our planet and each other. Compassion is spreading around the world. The world no longer revolves around nation states. We have communication systems that circle the world. We have pandemics that respect no boundaries. People are asking fundamental questions about the world in which they live.

While there are forces that seek to create a new world order in their own interests, there are also growing numbers of people questioning their own community, state, country and government and seeking a more collaborative, sensitive and gentle way of life. School systems are a part of the ecosystem of society. They are gradually changing from the chasers of economic capital to the builders of human capital. If they are to succeed, the way systems treat the schools in their care will need to balance demand with sensitivity, temper the pressure to secure improved data with wider concepts of success, and entwine notions of wellbeing with traditional measures of learning.

It can be done. It is being done. But everyone everywhere needs to do it. People must encourage their systems to re-think, and those who work within them need to ask the awkward questions of those who run them. Optimism has to prevail.

The compassionate mind and the conflicts between competing and caring: Implications for educating young minds

Paul Gilbert, Marcela Matos, Wendy Wood and Frances Maratos

Abstract: The evolution of mammalian caring behaviour brought with it a range of physiological systems that play a crucial role in emotion-regulation and prosocial behaviour. This chapter explores the evolutionary origins of caring behaviour and how human cognitive competencies facilitate the emergence of compassion as a specifically human process. We explore how the motive for compassion has to compete with other motivational systems that have also evolved, such as status-seeking, belonging and social competition. Compassion, like all motives, has inhibitors and facilitators, and it is important that educational settings can identify both of these if they are to promote compassion among growing minds and within the organizations in which they are growing and maturing.

Introduction

Among the many reasons that compassion should become a core focus for education are: equipping children with emotional coping skills; addressing bullying; creating safe, collaborative, encouraging and supportive learning environments; developing ethical behaviour; and promoting prosociality (among others, Coles, 2015; Goleman and Davidson, 2017; Lavelle, 2017; Maratos *et al.*, 2019a; McAdam and Lang, 2009; Roeser *et al.*, 2018; Peterson, 2017; Welford and Langmead, 2015). These efforts dovetail with international initiatives for social and emotional learning programmes, such as those being developed by the Collaborative for Academic, Social, and Emotional Learning (CASEL). Some innovations towards compassion training in schools stem from the contemplative traditions, others from

Western-based social and emotional education training (Coles, 2015; Welford and Langmead, 2015).

This chapter discusses an evolution- and biopsychosocial-based approach to compassion for informing, educating and nurturing teachers and young minds. This approach essentially aims to contextualize compassion within an evolutionary and physiological context that recognizes that motives for being caring can conflict with, or be inhibited by, motives including self-focused competitiveness and threat-defensiveness. Working in these contexts is part of compassionate mind-training or CMT (Gilbert, 1989, 2009, 2017a, 2019a, b).

The problems faced by modern societies, including the contexts of how and what we teach children, are different from those faced by the small, hunter-gatherer groups that supported human strategies of caring and sharing and learning basic life skills (Dunbar, 2014; Narvaez, 2017; Spikins, 2017). This 'mismatch hypothesis' – that the modern cultures that create comforts, medicines and technologies are also associated with many challenges for humanity, such as criminality, poor mental health and problems such as obesity, drugs and alcohol dependency (Gilbert, 2018; Li *et al.*, 2017; Sapolsky, 2017) – places various demands on child learning. We are educating our children in, and to cope with, quite different environments from those of our ancestors.

Some of these differences usefully point to the challenges of modern education. The origins of modern societies and their divergences from hunter-gatherer societies were facilitated by agriculture. Agriculture created opportunities for resource growth and larger groups. Caring and sharing seem to be major strategies for survival in low-resource environments, whereas holding and controlling resources tend to be common in high-resource environments. Piff and Moskowitz (2017) review considerable evidence that poor, lower-class individuals tend to be more sharing and caring than the rich upper-classes.

As the availability of resources increases, so does competitiveness for control and access to them, thereby creating social hierarchies of 'haves', 'have-nots' and 'have-lots'. Wang *et al.* (2018) found cross-national evidence that a greater desire for wealth and status was associated with higher social classes (captured in the title of their paper 'The more you have the more you want?'). Today, the economic success that schools and parents encourage their children to pursue may not stimulate the sharing and caring that were crucial for hunter-gatherers. Rather, the neoliberal idea of competing for, holding and controlling resources for oneself – and wanting ever more – prevails. The question is the degree to which education can offset the potentially harmful tendencies that promote competitiveness and self-interest, particularly in the context of education.

Modern cultures: The dark side and the bright

The *how* and *what* of education are socially contextualized. Western cultures are high-resource and competitive, characterized by major discrepancies in social class, wealth and opportunity. These discrepancies have been linked to social difficulties including crime and mental health problems (Durante and Fiske, 2017; Wilkinson, 2001). The drive to gain control over resources partly explains why humans are a species of extremes (Marsh, 2019). We are capable of being extremely compassionate, self-sacrificing and moral, and we can demonstrate immensely prosocial behaviour that benefits others (Ricard, 2015). However, tragically, the last 4,000–5,000 years have also shown humans to be among the most callous, vicious and sadistic species on this planet. We have inflicted intense suffering with our wars and holocausts, torture, Roman games, slavery, Chinese foot-binding and female genital circumcision, while our treatment of factory-farmed animals remains shocking (Gilbert, 2018).

Commentators have observed that it was the educated who developed the poison gas chambers that killed millions of innocent people in the Holocaust. It is the educated who invent increasingly terrifying weapons (including artificial intelligence), who develop and refine nuclear weapons, who created the businesses of slavery and who negotiate unfair trade deals. It was the educated who presided over the financial crash of 2008, despite being aware of the potential consequences of their sharp practices in moneymaking (Sachs, 2011). It is often the educated who are involved in corruption, harmful computer hacking and the callous behaviour of companies that pollute the world, exploit their workers and avoid paying taxes (Bakan, 2011). Human history warns us of two key things. First, let us not be naïve about the human potential to be brutally callous and harmful; and, second, let us acknowledge that education without a moral focus is dangerous because it ignores the reality of that potential in us. When education is solely focused on self-advancement, problems arise (Coles, 2015).

Yet, we are also a species that can be strongly motivated to be helpful to others, even at a cost to ourselves (Preston, 2013). Humans show extraordinary compassion in many contexts (Seppälä *et al.*, 2017). Consider how medicines and treatments have eased much suffering. Think about those who risk their lives to combat the Ebola crisis or fire-fighters who threaten their own safety to save the lives of others. And we have seen massive cultural change in our preparedness for moral and prosocial behaviour, abolishing the slave trade (albeit sadly not all slavery) and improving human rights – although, as modern protest movements around the world show, there is still much to do. So, compassion can – and must – stand firm against the dark side. It is no soft option. Much depends on how families, communities, schools and cultures stimulate different potentials within us and our children – what our relationships inspire us to become and to stand for.

Socially embedded and embodied minds

Cultural contexts shape our physiologies and our motives for compassion (Chiao, 2017; Koopman-Holm and Tsai, 2017). Siegel (2016, 2019) makes the point that minds are essentially intra- and inter-neuronal networks of information flow. It is not only within the mind but also what goes on *between minds* that creates dynamic, reciprocal sources of information flow. The flow of information generated in verbal and non-verbal communication stimulates physiologically based algorithms driving motivational systems (*if* A *then* do B; *if* X *then* do Y). These algorithms choreograph physiological responses to specific stimuli throughout the brain and body (think of the different physiological response we have to a food stimulus, a threat stimulus/signal, a sexual stimulus/signal, or winning the lottery!). Although learning plays a role, the basic pathways of each type of stimulus–response (algorithm) activation were laid down through evolution. For example, when we are threatened, this stimulus–response reaction will activate various areas of the brain, including the amygdala (Maratos and Pessoa, 2019). In contrast, signals of friendship will result in the activation of the reward areas of the brain found in the insular and frontal cortex regions.

This idea is captured by the concept of 'social mentalities' (Gilbert, 1989, 2017b, 2019b). A social mentality facilitates the sending and decoding of social signals that enable the formation of specific role relationships, algorithms and 'interpersonal dances'. The roles they serve include building friendships and alliances; competing for resources and status; engaging in reproductive (sexual) behaviour; and caring for offspring.

Different social roles require different social signals and different emotional reactions to those signals. For example, a signal of distress from a friend may be upsetting or worrying because we don't want to see our friend in distress, whereas the same signal from a competitor or someone we don't like might be more gratifying or simply ignored. A social signal of sexual interest will activate very different physiological patterns if it is from someone liked or disliked, and, again, it will be different from a signal of aggression or one of emotional distress. Hence, compassion is a social mentality attuned to signals of distress that trigger behavioural outputs (responses) designed to react to, and impact helpfully on, the recipient. Social mentalities are crucial to the nature of information flow because they are role-specific – that is, they vary in relation to status or roles of mentoring, cooperation, caring or sexuality.

With our socially embedded, embodied and contextualized minds, the nature and forms of the relationships we have with each other create a social field of information flow (Siegel, 2019) that can influence many aspects of our physiology including genetic expression (Cowan *et al.*, 2016). For example, two people who are supporting each other will have a very different information flow (and physiological attunement and 'dance') within and between them compared to a couple in conflict and hostile towards one another.

Groups also create contexts for these relational patterns. For example, in some classrooms, emotional textures between teachers and learners, and between the learners, can be playful, supportive, open and curious, whereas in others they can be stressed, threatening and competitive (Chance, 1998). When we consider compassion, therefore, it is not just about what's happening inside individual minds, but also how expressions of compassion can impact on the minds and physiologies of recipients. Ideally, expressions of compassion can create reciprocal flows and ripples of compassion between people. In other words, when people experience the caring of others, they are more likely to feel safe and be supportive and caring towards others, in turn (Gilbert, 2018; Maratos *et al.*, 2019b).

The physiological responses that compassionate behaviours and signals trigger in a recipient depend on the state of the receiving mind. For example, people might be open to compassion or resistant to it; our minds and bodies will respond quite differently to receiving compassion from somebody we like, in contrast to somebody we dislike or depending on whether or not we feel deserving of it.

Being motivated to be caring and sharing, as opposed to being self-focused, competitive and non-sharing, creates very different patterns in the mind and body. When individuals are caring and sharing, for example, this stimulates the vagus nerve, oxytocin and various brain areas associated with supporting wellbeing (Keltner *et al.*, 2014; Petrocchi and Cheli, 2019). In contrast, conflict and competition are stressful and stimulate various areas in the brain associated with the threat-processing system, which in turn can raise blood pressure and cortisol levels (Heinrichs *et al.*, 2003).

Moreover, relationships impact on the physiologies of the actors, even at the epigenetic level, especially in the child–parent relationship (Conway and Slavich, 2017; Cowan *et al.*, 2016). How specific role relationships are played out is related to social context. Social contexts, be they within families, schools or other organizations, can facilitate cooperative, friendly relationships or intense competitive and threat-saturated ones. Hence, schools can provide important contexts to support reciprocal relationships between students, teachers and one another along the paths of caring–supporting versus self-focused competitiveness.

Basic motivational systems

The human brain consists of a number of conflicting motivational systems and social mentalities that guide us in the species-specific life tasks of survival and reproduction (Huang and Bargh, 2014). These life tasks include: detecting and avoiding threats and harm, seeking food and shelter, competing with others over resources and status, cooperating and developing friendships, sexuality and raising offspring (Buss, 2016; Gilbert, 1989, 2019b; Neel *et al.*, 2016). Supporting these life tasks and their social mentalities are a range of physiological systems.

In schools, the population's multiple and varied motivational systems and their biological patterns become choreographed and are played out. Their students learn history, language, geography and mathematical skills, but they also develop relational networks with their peers and with authority figures (Coles, 2015; Peterson, 2017). Schools are contexts for children's maturation, where they learn how to compete or cooperate, to support or bully, and to respect authority or contemptuously defy it. Schools are a primary source for children to learn to communicate, develop the motivation to share and care, acquire empathy skills and develop ethical values and respect, without being overly deferential or submissive to authority (see also Yeager *et al.*, 2018). In addition, schools should enable young people to make valued contributions to their communities and the wider world (Coles, 2015).

The question is, how effectively are schools able to do this when all kinds of other demands are made on them? Current trends suggest that this endeavour is difficult, partly because both the students and their educators are under intense competitive pressures.

The motivation to compete

Self-focused competitive behaviour, which operates through the evolved competitive motivational system and the social ranks and hierarchies created, is an obvious feature of human behaviour (Anderson *et al.*, 2015). Whether or not it is helpful depends on its context, intensity and focus (Gilbert 1989/2016). Recent evidence suggests that competitive motives and social mentalities have become unhelpfully intensified in Western societies, at the expense of other prosocial motives. In 2014, Harvard School of Education reported on a study of 10,000 middle-class high school students from 33 schools (https://mcc.gse.harvard.edu/reports/children-mean-raise). They found that the majority of children prioritized personal success and achievement over caring for others. Concepts of fairness were not given priority, and many of the students surveyed were prepared to cheat to achieve something of value to them. Indeed, the students suggested that their parents and teachers valued personal achievement over caring and sharing.

The Harvard authors believe there has been a change over the last twenty years or so, stimulating intensely individualistic and personal competitive motives and values rather than community values. Such a change is apparent in many countries: they now prioritize academic performance as the overriding indicator of a school's worth. In the UK, for example, the introduction of open access league tables (Gov.UK, 2019) means that judgements are made according to competitive social ranking and hierarchy, thus pushing both parents and teachers to rate students' academic success above their other skills and qualities. Consistent with this are the findings of studies measuring the rise of narcissism over the last twenty years. They come to similar conclusions – exemplified by the findings of Twenge in *Generation Me against Generation We* (2013). She reports that the shifting priorities have major consequences; empathy, concern for others, civic engagement and general community prosocial interest are now of little consequence.

Western schools, then, are contextualized in increasingly self-focused and self-concerned environments. Curran and Hill (2019) conducted a major meta-analysis of 41,641 participants across 164 samples on the effects of the pressures of perfectionism, which increased markedly between 1989 and 2016. They found that the levels of self-orientated perfection, socially prescribed perfection (thinking others want perfection from the self) and other-orientated perfection (wanting others to be perfect) have increased. They argue that what sits behind this is: 1. the emergence of neoliberalism and competitive individualism; 2. belief in meritocracy – that success is all down to effort and competitive striving; and 3. anxious and controlling parenting. Added to this, competitive stress is one of the major causes of mental health problems (Wetherall *et al.*, 2019).

Curran and Hill also note that the role schools play in supporting neoliberal and striving ideals linking status and wealth-seeking to one's perceived social value, and how one comes to judge oneself, can both have adverse ramifications. They observe: 'Because individuals cannot avoid being sorted, sifted, and ranked by schools, universities, and the workplace, neoliberal meritocracy places a strong need to strive, perform, and achieve at the center of modern life' (ibid.: 413).

Part of the problem of meritocracy, they say, is that it gives children unrealistic expectations of what is possible, and this can fuel the narcissistic sense of entitlement, unrealistic expectations and the fall into self-criticism when things don't work out (Curran and Hill, 2019; Holt, 1964). Central to understanding the impact of excessive focus on competitiveness, not just in schools but in social media and other domains, is the fact that mental health problems are increasing among young people (Rodway *et al.*, 2016).

Teacher stress is multifactorial, linked to time pressures, bureaucracy, disruptive classroom behaviours and underfunding, the resulting resource shortages pushing educators to continually strive to do more for less (Maratos *et al.*, 2019a). These pressures are having negative impacts on mental health and retention in the profession (ESP, 2018). The psychology and physiology of competitiveness and striving, while feeling that one is falling behind and failing, underpin the potential for a range of mental health problems (Sapolsky, 2005, 2017; Wetherall *et al.*, 2019). The psychology of competitiveness tunes attention to social comparison. Teachers become overly concerned about keeping up and keeping going, about how others view them, and about possible marginalization, and they become self-critical in the face of perceived failure and setbacks (Conroy *et al.*, 2002; Gilbert *et al.*, 2004). Evidence is accumulating that suggests that one reason why mental health problems are increasing among children and younger people (Rodway *et al.*, 2016) could be because of competitive pressures within educational settings and beyond (Curran and Hill, 2019). Mental health problems are associated with feeling inferior, rejected, lonely, self-critical and even self-disliking (Gilbert *et al.*, 2004).

With regard to social rank, there is increasing evidence that, as people become more successful, they become less sensitive to subordinate concerns (Keltner *et al.*, 2003) and, as they become wealthier, they become less compassionate (Van Kleef *et al.*, 2008). Thus, in high-resource (economically wealthy) environments, status and resource competition along with 'control and hold' strategies can become accentuated at the expense of 'share and care' behaviours (Gilbert, 2018; Basran *et al.*, 2019). These themes help us to recognize the degree to which schools are over-stimulating competitive behaviour in children along with the fear of not being good enough – or doing well enough, but at the expense of more prosocial orientation towards themselves and others.

Competing for what?

Schools are places where children can implicitly and explicitly pick up the notion that life is a competition and life satisfaction depends on winning and excelling. Individuals, however, compete for a number of reasons. Some forms of competition called 'scramble competition' have little impact on the behaviour of others. Birds feeding on an open field can eat as much as they want without affecting others, whereas if they are competing for bread on a lawn they will fight. Although competing by physical fighting and establishing fear-based hierarchies are generally prohibited in schools, they still occur, and bullying and intimidation can be a serious problem (Smith and Brain, 2000; Williams *et al.*, 2013).

However, the way humans compete for social position is mostly by trying to be attractive and desired. Succeeding in this way presents opportunities for developing helpful relationships, choosing a mate and claiming such resources as well-paid careers and salaries (Barkow, 1989; Etcoff, 1999; Gilbert *et al.*, 1995). To be deemed unattractive or undesired is to court shame and rejection (Gilbert, 1997, 2006; Sznycer *et al.*, 2016). The process of competing for social attention-holding potential (SAHP) entails trying to monitor how we exist in the minds of others and orientate our plans and behaviours to ensure high SAHP (Gilbert, 1989, 1997). Schools inevitably offer one place where children learn about their relative SAHP through the kinds of attention, help and esteem they can stimulate from others around them to avoid rejection (Williams *et al.*, 2013).

Gilbert *et al.* (2007) explored the type of competitive stress linked to depression and anxiety. Competition may be about being superior to others but also about avoiding being inferior and rejected; the two concerns are motivationally quite different. These authors labelled the two types of competitive styles as 'secure' and 'insecure'. Insecure competition involved 'striving to avoid inferiority' and was associated with fear of failing, falling behind, loss of status, being rejected, marginalization and losing out. It was associated with hyper-competitiveness and seeking to achieve and perform well to win validation from others rather than wanting to achieve for personal growth. Moreover, striving to avoid inferiority was strongly correlated with unfavourable social comparison and with experiencing stress, anxiety and depression. In contrast, secure competition was typified by individuals who felt that others accepted them, regardless of their successes or failures, and they did not associate failure with rejection or missing out. Their striving was associated with valuing achievement for its own sake (such as intrinsic rather than extrinsic reward), including prosociality rather than others as competitors. These people scored lower on measures of stress, anxiety and depression. In a further study, Gilbert *et al.* (2009) found that depressed clients presented the same relationships: striving to avoid inferiority was associated with external shame (beliefs that people look down on the self), anxious attachment and higher stress and anxiety.

These studies are not dissimilar to 'fears of failure' studies. Conroy *et al.* (2002) developed a self-report scale for fear of failure, identified by five basic factors and themes: a sense of shame and embarrassment; having to lower one's self-evaluation; concerns about the future; losing interest in the self; and worry over upsetting important others. Added to this, throughout the world of social media there are many anecdotal stories of how young people are worried about these possibilities, fearing that if they don't keep up, succeed or achieve, they will be rejected, marginalized or not be chosen. Bergold and Steinmayr (2016) found that fear of failure is detrimental to children's intellectual development. Although narcissism is sometimes seen as a form of entitlement and self-centredness and an up-rank motivation (Twenge, 2013), Basran *et al.* (2019) found measures of hyper-competitiveness and narcissism were also highly correlated with 'competing to avoid inferiority'. Hyper-competitiveness and narcissism were also correlated with fears of compassion.

Fear of rejection

Evidence is growing that the underlying drivers of current competitiveness may be fears of not being good enough. Such fears underpin both depressive and narcissistic-type problems (Conroy *et al.*, 2002; Curran and Hill, 2019). Depressed individuals adopt low-rank strategies, while those with narcissistic, grandiose orientations pursue up-rank strategies. Anecdotal evidence suggests that Western societies are increasingly witnessing fear of rejection, both over-stimulating competitiveness and heightening attention to rejection (Tweng, 2013). For example, the Olympic ideal of competition was to celebrate winners, and little attention was given to those who dropped out or fell behind. Recent forms of competition from popular culture, however – such as reality TV shows like Big Brother and Love Island, as well as various talent shows, from cookery to gardening – have increasingly focused on those who are to be rejected, dwelling on their responses to that rejection. During these weekly competitions or when pronouncing their final decisions, judges can be highly critical and even shaming. The participants are made to wait in a state of obvious anxiety so as to increase the tension for audiences until the judges finally announce their verdict. Interestingly, the audience may also be invited to vote on whom to accept and whom to reject – not unlike in the ancient Roman games! This focus on whom to reject may stimulate core archetypal fears that may have physiological consequences for observers and participants alike (Williams *et al.*, 2013).

These fears are also revealed in a different type of research. In a number of studies, Crocker and Canevello (2008, 2011) explored two types of interpersonal behaviour that they called 'compassionate' and 'self-image' goals. All the items on their assessment scale began with the phrase, 'In the past week, in the area of friendships, how much did you want to or try to …?' Items were rated on a scale ranging from 1 (*not at all*) to 5 (*always*).

Seven items assessed compassionate goals, namely: 'be supportive of others', 'have compassion for others' mistakes and weaknesses', 'avoid doing anything that would be harmful to others', 'make a positive difference in someone else's life', 'be constructive in your comments to others', 'avoid being selfish or self-centred' and 'avoid doing things that aren't helpful to me or others'. Six items assessed self-image goals, namely: 'get others to recognize or acknowledge your positive qualities', 'convince others that you are right', 'avoid showing your weaknesses', 'avoid the possibility of being wrong', 'avoid being rejected by others' and 'avoid taking risks or making mistakes'. Their research revealed that compassionate goals tend to be associated with creating supportive environments and wellbeing, whereas self-image goals tended to be associated with conflictual relationships and increased vulnerability to depression and anxiety.

Kirby *et al.* (2019) explored the compassionate versus the self-image goals of parents. In their online survey of 151 mothers, they found that self-image goals were associated with more psychologically controlling parenting styles, whereas compassionate goals were associated with more facilitative parenting styles. Maratos *et al.* (in preparation) investigated compassionate versus self-image goals in teachers and found that teachers with higher levels of compassionate goals showed increased compassion to others and openness to receiving compassion from others, greater interpersonal mindfulness, heightened feelings of vitality and enthusiasm at work and greater satisfaction with a teacher's life. In contrast, those with heightened self-image goals demonstrated higher levels of self-criticism, experiential avoidance related to teaching, threat-based emotions at work and stress, and lower levels of intrapersonal mindfulness. To the best of our knowledge, there have been no studies looking at teaching styles in relation to controlling versus facilitating interpersonal styles and their impact on children's learning.

Competing to secure social acceptance and self-esteem

One obvious way of coping with the feared consequences of failing is to compete harder – to focus on how to do better, how to succeed, how to prove oneself and how to raise one's social and self-esteem. Many training programmes seek to do just that, but they risk being outcome- rather than process-focused. If children still fail, no matter how hard they try not to, what are they left with? And if you are trying to prove yourself and better yourself when everybody else is doing the same, the bar (such as passing grade boundaries) is simply raised for all. In some contexts, we might raise achievements for everybody, but someone may still be bottom of the class. Half a century ago, in his book *How Children Fail,* John Holt (1964) raised this issue about how we energize and stimulate children to not just achieve particular goals but to competitively achieve goals that have been deemed 'worthy of achieving' by one's culture. There is evidence that successes that support self-esteem are related to what we think other people will value and what we will be praised or admired for (Santor and Walker, 1999).

In a major review paper entitled 'The costly pursuit of self-esteem', Crocker and Park criticize a number of such educational efforts to raise self-esteem, highlighting that:

> When people have self-validation goals, they react to threats in these domains in ways that undermine learning; relatedness; autonomy and self-regulation; and over time, mental and physical health. The short-term emotional benefits of pursuing self-esteem are often outweighed by long-term costs. (Crocker and Park, 2004: 392)

Hence, attempts to inspire and mobilize children or raise their self-esteem by achieving and competing can unwittingly stimulate social comparisons and exacerbate fears of failing. And, as Bergold and Steinmayr (2016) found, fear of failure is detrimental to children's intellectual development.

Group-based competition

Tribalism and intergroup competition are also important issues. Study after study has shown how easy it is for individuals to create in-groups and out-groups, becoming highly tribal and aggressive to those deemed outside their particular group (Hobfoll, 2018). Simple manipulations that persuade people they belong to one group rather than another (such as having different preferences in art) can produce conflict (ibid.; Bargh, 2017). Tribalism is rife in primates, and aggressive and violent interactions are common between groups. While studying chimpanzees in the Gombe Valley in East Africa, primatologist Jane Goodall witnessed a large group split into two, with the smaller group moving into the south of the territory (Goodall, 1990). Within a short time, the chimpanzees from the north group systematically ambushed and killed individuals in the south group, with whom they had been happily co-existing inside the bigger group until the split triggered the 'chimpanzee wars'. The problem of people identifying with their in-group, coming to see it as superior to others, is now well recognized and is labelled 'social dominance orientation' (Ho *et al.*, 2012).

Regarding one's own group as superior can significantly undermine empathy for other, less well-off groups (Sidanius *et al.*, 2013). One manifestation of this form of bullying is that of ostracizing others. There is much evidence that ostracism and rejection are very harmful to children, especially if they do not have a primary group of their own to relate to (Williams *et al.*, 2013). Schools can educate children about the dangers of the ease with which we form in- and out-group psychology, of group identification, of acting out ostracism and prejudice, and of the 'isms' such as racism, sexism and ageism. Children can, however, be alerted to how certain political and media-generated messages try to feed tribal conflict that serve their own self-interests, deliberately seeking to create divisions, accentuate tribal differences and privilege the elite few over the many. In addition, there is growing concern over digital tribalism and the tagging of 'fake news' on anything that challenges our in-group status.

Another area where this can be problematic for schools is in sport. Children can learn to compete with respect for their opponents and understand the importance of 'fair play'. It is well known that serious problems arise in sport through cheating, drug-taking, racism, showing contempt for opponents and other forms of problematic group-competitive behaviours. Domestic violence has also been found to increase after a favourite football team loses.

Schools can foster the process of competing without developing a 'win at any cost' attitude by exploring issues with their students such as: how to deal with losing, how to treat competitors with respect, respect the rules and the referee, and how to behave in a friendly manner after a competitive event. Many anecdotal stories are told about how the excessive money in professional sport has dissuaded professionals from being socially engaged with their competitors, as they were in amateur days, especially in cricket. At the end of the 2019 Ashes series, England cricketers David Gower and Sir Ian Botham spoke of how, when they played cricket with the Australians in the 1980s, they would frequently go into the changing room and socialize after a game. That is now apparently discouraged, lest it blunt the edge of competition.

Motivating compassion and balancing the mind

We know that there are health and social costs to overly intensive competitiveness; it can be stressful and socially divisive. So we need to cooperate, care and share – to opt for getting along versus getting ahead (Wolfe *et al.*, 1986). Refocusing on life tasks and life goals that are closer to those of our hunter-gatherer forebears can help people to shift the intensity of self-focused competitiveness. Followers of spiritual and contemplative traditions have, for centuries, argued that heightened competitive self-interest is not conducive to our wellbeing and that ethical or prosocial behaviour and caring, compassionate goals are the route to happiness and wellbeing (Ricard, 2015). Researchers have highlighted the fact that humans flourish best – physiologically, psychologically and socially – in caring, sharing and compassionate environments, not self-focused competitive ones (Baumsteiger, 2019; Bloom, 2017; Cassidy and Shaver, 2016; Colonnello *et al.*, 2017; Crocker and Canevello, 2011; Narvaez, 2017; Ricard, 2015; Penner *et al.*, 2005; Seppälä *et al.*, 2017). In short, promoting caring and sharing (in oneself and others) has a range of physiological and social benefits on wellbeing and prosocial behaviour (Goleman and Davidson, 2017). Such knowledge needs to be prioritized and incorporated into teacher education and in schools.

Although intragroup hierarchical competitiveness and intergroup tribalism are potentially core motives in humans, so too is our ability to take an empathic interest in, and care for, each other. Caring is clearly part of our evolutionary history (Brown and Brown, 2015; Dunbar, 2014; Marsh, 2019; Mayseless, 2016; Navarz, 2017; Spikins, 2017). Research has shown that we have a set of physiological systems that evolved in the brain and body specifically designed for giving and receiving care (Mayseless, 2016; Porges, 2017). As mammals have evolved over millions of years, the autonomic nervous system has adapted, such that one part of the parasympathetic system – the ventral, myelinated vagus nerve – is now highly regulated through social (especially friendly and supportive) relationships (Petrocchi and Cheli, 2019; Porges, 2017). Specific hormones, such as oxytocin and vasopressin, are linked to the evolution of caring and they play fundamental roles in the development of prosocial and affiliative behaviour (Carter *et al.*, 2017). Recent evidence even suggests that there are genetic variations in the oxytocin gene that underpins prosocial behaviour (Tost *et al.*, 2010). Such findings have direct implications for the cultivation of compassion.

The evolution of caring

Motives and algorithms for human caring evolved in first relationships between mammalian parents and their offspring. Usually, it is the mother who provides a range of resources to the infant, although, in species such as penguins, fathers share the care (Bowlby, 1969; Gilbert, 1989, 2017b; Mayseless, 2016; Cassidy and Shaver, 2016). Parents protect the infant from danger, give them food and thermal regulation, act to regulate emotion, support growth and encourage and facilitate the learning of survival skills. For the infants' part, they need to have physiological systems that respond to the inputs of the parent, and they are physiologically affected by those signals. Early life experiences are important in that experiences of being cared-for and supported (in contrast to lacking care and support) have major effects on epigenetic profiles – that is, on how certain genes get turned on and off in us and how that can influence the development of emotion-regulation systems and other processes.

Although parenting involves many functions, a particularly important one is for the parent to be sensitive to any stressful needs in the infant and then be motivated to do something about it. So, for example, parents will be sensitive to a distress call requiring rescue, or a hunger cry requiring feeding, or the shivering of an infant requiring thermal regulation. The basic algorithm of caring that underwrites compassion is therefore 'a sensitivity to suffering in self and others with a commitment to try to alleviate and prevent it' (Gilbert, 2014: 19). Most definitions of compassion have that kind of focus to them, although there are also differences and controversies (Coles, 2015; Gilbert, 2017a, 2019a). In 2013, Gilbert and Choden added the concept of prevention (of suffering) to the earlier definitions.

Compassion and the new brain

Human compassion necessarily differs from mammalian caring, or else other animals who care for their young (rats, for instance) could be described as compassionate, thereby rendering the notion of compassion meaningless. The evolutionary model, however, highlights processes that are unique to humans and underpin compassion. In the last two million years, our ancestors went through radical evolutionary changes to their – hence, our – cognitive competencies (Raghanti *et al.*, 2018; Suddendorf, 2018). Competencies are different from motives and emotions. A competency enables us to perform certain functions. Birds need wings to fly, but also a brain that will equip them to fly and become competent at flying. The competency to fly is neither an emotion nor a motive. Similarly, the cognitive competencies facilitate increasingly complex means for engaging in life tasks.

Humans have an impressive array of recently evolved cognitive competencies – far too many to explore here. But, among the most salient are our capacities for self-awareness, knowing awareness, knowing intentionality, systematic thinking and reasoning, thinking in time (that is, we can reflect on the past and imagine a future), various forms of metacognition, theory of mind and empathy, and capacities for self-observation that underpin processes such as mindfulness (see Gilbert, 2019a). These competencies can alter many forms of motivation, not just caring. For example, we would not regard the suffering a lion causes its prey as cruel or sadistic. This is because the lion has no insight into, or intention to, cause suffering. Humans do have such insight, and it is that intentional knowing behind our harming behaviour that defines aspects of human behaviour as cruel and sadistic. The same applies to compassion. It is when we knowingly and intentionally engage in suffering by trying to be helpful and not harmful that we call our behaviour 'compassion' (Gilbert, 2017b, 2018) (see Figure 1.9).

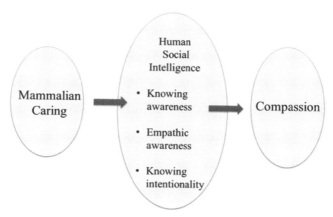

Figure 1.9: From caring to compassion

Source: Gilbert (2009), reproduced with permission
from Constable and Robinson Ltd

Our newly developed brain allows us to time-travel (Suddendorf, 2018). Not only can we intentionally and wisely pay attention to suffering 'now', but we can also think about preventing suffering in the future. We can reflect on how we might have caused it in the past. We can generate very complex models of the causes and cures of suffering. We can create a sense of compassion that is fundamental to our ethical values. We can gain insight into the effects of training our minds to be compassionate and intentionally choose to do so. As far as we know, no other animal can make a choice like this.

Our new brain competencies enable us to knowingly and wisely cultivate the different attributes of compassion. A number of therapies place the cultivation of compassion as central to the therapeutic process (Germer and Siegel, 2012; Kirby and Gilbert, 2017), such as compassion-focused therapy (CFT) (Gilbert, 2000, 2010) based on the evolutionary model of compassion. To facilitate this training, the *process* of compassion is broken down into constituents, trainable attributes and competencies. Keeping in mind the definition of compassion that is rooted in the caring stimulus–response algorithm of 'sensitivity to signals of distress (the stimulus) triggering appropriate behaviour for alleviation or prevention (the response)', CFT has articulated 12 basic dimensions for compassion training. These are outlined in Figure 1.10.

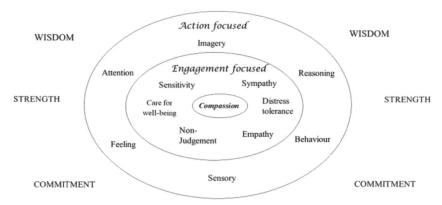

Figure 1.10: The 12 competencies of compassion

Source: copyright P. Gilbert, reproduced by permission

The two circles in Figure 1.10 have been called slightly different things over the years. In earlier versions, they were described as attributes and skills (Gilbert, 2009) and later as first and second psychology (Gilbert, 2017a). Today, they are referred to as engagement- and action-focused, which is the more logical label.

There are six basic processes for engagement with suffering and distress, and six for responding to, and cultivating, compassionate action. Stimulus-sensitive engagement competencies include:

1. being motivated to attend to suffering
2. being attentive to suffering (rather than dissociative)
3. being open to be emotionally moved by suffering (sympathy)
4. being tolerant of the distress aroused
5. having empathic insight into the causes and relief of suffering
6. being non-judgemental.

Each competency supports the others. For example, the more tolerant we are of distress, the more likely we are to be able to engage with it and empathically understand it. Each can be a focus for therapeutic intervention and training. The response or action function involves:

1. switching attention to what could be helpful
2. running imaginary scenarios of potentially helpful actions through one's mind
3. utilizing problem-solving and reasoning skills to address suffering
4. behaving courageously and wisely to address and prevent suffering
5. being able to regulate bodily aspects of compassion (for instance, the vagus nerve)
6. experience emotions and feelings appropriate to the context.

Again, each of these can be a source for therapeutic intervention and for the cultivation of compassion in general (Matos *et al.*, 2017, 2018).

Training is also linked to context because context determines the specific additional emotions and skills needed for a specific act of compassion. So a firefighter saving a family from a burning house might, for instance, need to tolerate anxiety and have appropriate skills to move into life-threatening environments. A person fighting injustice may feel anger at its causes and will need a way of turning that anger into effective, assertive action. Somebody sitting with a dying person may feel sad and need to tolerate deep sadness in others as well as themselves.

CFT will help individuals develop some or all of the following: mindful awareness; sensitivity to, and tolerance of, distress; empathy; problem-solving skills; and awareness of how to use the body to settle the mind (Gilbert, 2010; Gilbert and Choden, 2013). On the outside of the circles in Figure 1.10 are three core qualities for compassion:

1. wisdom, which is derived from many sources of knowledge and insight
2. a sense of inner strength that enables us to find the courage to engage and to act
3. the commitment and motivation to address suffering – to live to be helpful, not harmful.

Although derived from the 12 competencies, they form the core domains for personal practice and living.

Empathy

This competency has seen significant development during human evolution (Decety and Ickes, 2011). Empathy is an interpersonal competency of social intelligence that supports a range of social mentalities (Gilbert, 2017b). It has a number of prehuman precursors but evolved most of all in humans. Empathy has two aspects. One is emotional attunement where we can experience similar emotions to the other person. Emotional empathy is sometimes called emotional 'contagion' where we literally 'catch and feel' the emotion of others. The other aspect is cognitive empathy or perspective-taking. This allows us to stand back, think, reflect and work out what somebody else might be thinking or feeling or recognize the motives behind their behaviours. Emotional contagion is automatic whereas perspective-taking is more considered, effortful and reflective. Empathy allows us insight into the causes of interpersonal behaviours. As a competency, however, it can be used in many ways. Machiavellian individuals can be very empathic, and this powers their manipulative abilities. Empathy can be useful in cooperating, competing and sexual courting. Empathy training and guidance can be very important for children, not as a competency but just in itself, not driven by prosocial motivation.

We can behave compassionately for many different reasons (Böckler *et al.*, 2016). Sometimes we behave helpfully to others so that we will be liked, or because it's expected of us in our group, because we can see the logic of it or see it as a moral value, rather than because we are closely attuned empathically or have 'compassionate feelings' (Loewenstein and

Small, 2007). Similarly, we don't need empathy to be moral (Decety and Cowell, 2014). People can think they're being empathic when they're not, because certain aspects of other people's experiences are not in their domain of experience. This has been argued in terms of ethnic diversity when people from one ethnic group think they can naturally empathize with people from another, or that one gender can easily empathize with what it means to be a different gender when, in reality, they can't – they're guessing (Edge and Lemetyinen, 2019). How empathic are men to the processes of giving birth to another life? Part of compassion, therefore, is recognizing the limits of our empathy and distinguishing it from projection or guessing (Gilbert, 2019a; Loewenstein and Small, 2007).

The flows of compassion

If we think of compassion as a socially embedded information flow, we can identify three orientations: the compassion we have for others; our ability to be open and receptive to compassion from others; and the compassion we demonstrate towards ourselves. All competencies flow in these three directions. When we are compassionate towards others, we may be empathic with them and tolerate their distress and any distress we may feel about it. When we are open to compassion from others, we are sensitive to the empathy they have for us and their ability and desire to help us. We may be moved by their concern and more able to manage our distress. And when we are compassionate towards ourselves, we are trying to be helpful, empathic and courageously engaged with our own suffering. These are called 'the three flows of compassion' and they have been operationalized in a set of self-report measures (Gilbert *et al.*, 2017).

Crucially, we can gain insight into the fact that the human mind is full of competing motivational systems, and that if we focus only on the competitive ones – those that feature heavily in modern society – we risk having less ethical and more mentally unwell individuals populating our communities.

Contrasting compassion with competition

We can compare caring with competitive motivations according to how they orientate attention, focus our thinking, trigger emotions, choreograph our interpersonal behaviour with people around us, and physiologically pattern our bodies (see Figure 1.11).

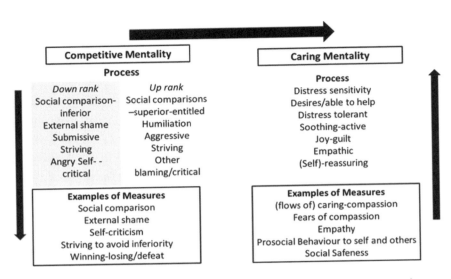

Figure 1.11: Moving from a competitive to a caring social motive and mentality
Source: Gilbert (2009), reproduced with permission
from Constable and Robinson Ltd

Figure 1.11 shows that competitive psychology is focused on social ranks and one's position within them: whom to compare with, who can threaten or support us, whom to associate with and so on. Individuals who focus down-rank tend to be concerned with being inferior to others and are submissive and self-critical. In contrast, individuals who focus up-rank tend to be narcissistic and have a sense of superior competencies and a sense of entitlement, and blame others for any difficulties that arise. They can also become aggressive if confronted – as do many of today's leaders (Basran *et al.*, 2019).

Given that the competitive motivational system, with its focus on social rank, may underpin certain psychological difficulties, what compassion training and compassion-focused therapies seek to do is help people engage in motivational shifting. In other words, they aim to shift the individual's attention, thinking and actions from competitiveness towards caring. Developing insight into caring and compassion-focused mental states creates more meaningful experiences in life, fosters physiological wellbeing and creates prosocial and supportive social contexts (Goleman and Davidson, 2017). Neither compassion training nor compassion-cultivation can simply focus on itself, however; both must also recognize the other motivational systems that compete for attention. Compassion will, at times, mean helping people with less benign motivations.

A focus for compassion training and compassion-cultivation

There are a number of innovative interventions for schools and children that focus on moral prosocial development (Coles, 2015). For example, the social and educational programmes of CASEL (2019) focus on five core domains:

1. helping children develop self-awareness and build their confidence
2. teaching children emotion awareness and self-regulation skills
3. developing social awareness and understanding the views and needs of others and issues of diversity
4. forming relationships and maintaining skills
5. moral reasoning and decision-making.

Running in parallel to these general programmes, specific interventions have evolved over the last twenty years to bring both mindfulness (Kuyken *et al.*, 2013; Weare, 2013; Jennings, 2019) and compassion into schools (Coles, 2015; Roeser *et al.*, 2018; Peterson, 2017) and are aimed at both teachers and students. Given the variations in the underlying theoretical frameworks and practices this chapter has touched on, we must guard against naïveté in compassion training. It is vital that compassion address our human dark side as well as promoting wellbeing (Gilbert, 2009, 2018; Marsh, 2019). Compassion training can be tough, requiring us to face painful realities and build competencies for empathy, distress-tolerance and courage.

Tricky brain

So far, this chapter has offered an evolutionary framework for guiding the understanding of compassion and the interventions derived from it, such as CMT (Gilbert, 2010; Gilbert and Choden, 2013). This approach identifies the core issues for compassion training and cultivation. We start by considering why we are a species of extremes and why we have a 'tricky brain' (Gilbert, 2018; Marsh, 2019). One reason is that the human brain evolved in a piecemeal way with a suite of complex cognitive competencies that can accentuate or attenuate our basic motives and emotions for good or ill. The human brain easily creates problematic loops between our emotions, motives and ways of thinking. This is why we are capable of such horrors as war, torture, the Holocaust and other genocides, slavery, sexual exploitation and an epidemic of mental health problems. Today's schools can be a major source of help for children to understand how tricky the human brain is and how dangerous it can be. Certainly, when the authors of this chapter were growing up, none of us was given any insight into the inherently problematic nature of our minds or any guidance on how to be careful of our minds' dark side (Gilbert, 2018).

Competing motivations

Psychoeducation should also teach mind/brain awareness to raise children's awareness of their inner competing motivations (Huang and Bargh, 2014). Gaining insight into motivational conflicts was once central to psychodynamic therapies but rather fell away with the advent of cognitive behavioural therapies. It is useful to help children understand that their minds come with built-in algorithms for motives and emotions that are inherently conflictual and can create helpful or hurtful behaviour to self and others. The mind also creates dilemmas that are sometimes self-focused or sometimes other-focused, and so compassion training can help children to make decisions that follow a moral and ethical path. Once compassion motives become central to our self-identity, we seek to be helpful, not harmful, in our lives (Gilbert, 2009). Providing clarity on 'living to be helpful' as opposed to 'competitive self-interest regardless of the potential damage to others' is a significant dimension of education.

Insight into the nature of one's motives and emotions

Children need to be helped to understand and become mindfully aware of fluctuating patterns and sometimes intense conflicts between their motives and emotions (CASEL, 2019). While many mindfulness interventions help children to become more attentive to the flow of desires, thoughts and emotions that emerge in their minds, they don't necessarily provide clear mind awareness or knowledge of how and why. Therefore, evolution-informed compassionate mind-training for schools must help children understand the evolved basis, and tricky nature, of their emotions. For example, an evolutionary functional analysis approach to emotions reveals that we can identify three major functions of emotions – namely, that they:

1. may help us detect and respond to threats such as anger and anxiety
2. may activate and encourage us to go out and secure resources
3. are associated with neither defending against nor seeking resources, but enable us to 'rest and digest'. Rest and digest states bring peacefulness and contentment.

Children can also think about how they experience and work with the three emotional systems. What is it that, for example, triggers their 'threat emotions' (anger or anxiety), and how might they deal with these? What triggers pleasurable emotions of joy, excitement, fun, or a sense of purpose or achievement? What helps them to rest, feeling safe and content – and thus cultivate good vagus nerve tone? Helping children understand the importance and use of 'rest and digest' states rather than stress is important for their long-term welfare. The ability to balance the autonomic nervous system with good vagal tone is linked to feelings of safeness and being supported, of 'cheerful calmness' (Geisler *et al.*, 2010) and prosocial behaviour (Gilbert, 1989; Petrocchi and Cheli, 2019; Porges, 2017).

Unfortunately, children are not taught how to access and cultivate the physiological states that calm the body and mind and facilitate the sense of safeness so conducive to wellbeing and prosocial behaviour (Porges, 2017). Instead, modern environments overstimulate mental states that activate drive and threat at the expense of dopaminergic and sympathetic pathways (Pani, 2000). We live in environments that lead patients to seek help from their GPs today because they feel perpetually tired and exhausted, sleep badly and are close to burnout.

Cultivating one's inner ideal compassionate self

While we can develop values and ideals about how we would like to be – for example, to be fit, a good athlete or piano player – we have to train for it. Simply living day-to-day won't cultivate these talents and skills. The more we practise our competency or talent, the better we get. Yet, children are rarely taught that we can also cultivate the patterns within our brains and bodies. Left unchecked, our sense of self will simply unfold according to the contexts in which it grows. The mind is like a garden, in that it will grow even without a gardener – but we may not like the way it turns out. Cultivation nurtures what we most want in our gardens – and in our minds.

A number of researchers have turned to the contemplative traditions to explore the impact of deliberately training ourselves in particular motivations and values (Goleman and Davidson, 2017) – in Gilbert's terms, CMT (Gilbert, 2010; Kirby and Gilbert, 2017). Evidence shows that we can train our minds so that we live in a particular way and our physiological states evolve accordingly (Goleman and Davidson, 2017; Weng *et al.*, 2018).

Using the body to support the mind

Many physiological systems can be targeted to help promote wellbeing and prosocial behaviour (Goleman and Davidson, 2017). We have noted that the ventral vagus nerve supports 'rest and digest' and is strongly associated with wellbeing and prosocial behaviour (Petrocchi and Cheli, 2019; Porges, 2017). Practising deepening and slowing the breath to around five breaths per minute can improve vagal tone. As well as the benefit of such breathing practices (Lin *et al.*, 2014), research is revealing how diet impacts on the brain and vagus nerve, be it for good or ill (Breit *et al.*, 2018). This raises the crucial question of how we can use diet and exercise in schools to engender compassionate mental states.

A compassionate mind-training programme for schools

CMT was developed as a psychosocially informed set of practices within CFT (Gilbert, 2000, 2010) for use in non-clinical populations such as schools (Gilbert and Choden, 2013; Matos *et al.*, 2017, 2018; Maratos *et al.*, 2018; McEwan and Gilbert, 2016; Sommers-Spijkerman *et al.*, 2018). The authors of this chapter developed a set of six two-hour modules, based on established CMT programmes (Matos *et al.*, 2017), which have been applied in schools in Derby (England) (Maratos *et al.*, 2019b) and in Coimbra and Viseu (Portugal). The first endeavours of the Compassionate Schools Project have been directed at teachers and educators. There are four reasons for this:

1. It helps to address teachers' own stress by affording them compassion-focused ways of coping. Not only is this good for them personally but it will also inform their interactions with their students.
2. It provides teachers with a science-informed model of compassion that gives them insight into how their minds and those of their students work.
3. As they become aware of the processes of CMT and the contexts that nourish it, they can build contexts that support compassion in the classroom.
4. They will ultimately be able to teach the children those compassion skills, forms of mind-awareness and compassion-based self-regulation.

In the next phase, our research programme will be looking more directly at the impacts of a) a pupil version of the compassionate mind-training programme, implemented alongside a brief parents' compassion mind-training intervention and b) the scaleability of the programme, including training teachers to guide pupils into the flows of compassion.

The programme modules

Our CMT programme for schools was developed and organized around six basic modules. These psychoeducation exercises and practices were adapted from CFT (Gilbert, 2000, 2010; Gilbert and Choden, 2013). They were first developed by Paul Gilbert and tested in a general population in Portugal, yielding promising results (Matos *et al.*, 2017, 2018). The main themes in the CMT programme for teachers are as follows:

MODULE 1

This module focuses on the definition of compassion, as a basic stimulus–response (S–R) algorithm using an evolutionary model: there is a stimulus (sensitivity to distress and need) followed by a response (an endeavour to alleviate and prevent suffering). This approach highlights the courage and dedication aspects of compassion. The module also indicates that compassion has to address the way that evolution has created problematic 'designs', particularly in relation to humans' complex cognitive competencies – our aforementioned 'tricky brain'. Participants explore how using compassion as a motivation can organize our minds, develop mind awareness and regulate emotion. This will involve mindfulness and attention to the 'contents and products' as one goes through the course.

The evolution and process of caring are interpersonal. Therefore, participants explore the concept of 'the flows of compassion' and discover how the course helps to develop compassion for self, be open to compassion from others and be compassionate to others. The participants also focus on competencies for compassionate relating, such as empathy skills. There are processes for studying both the flows and the fears of compassion (Gilbert *et al.*, 2017).

Practices introduced in this module

The idea of how to use the body to support the mind is taught using posture and breathing patterns, beginning with slow, deep breathing at around 4–5 breaths per minute that supports the vagus nerve (Soothing Rhythm Breathing). Participants are guided on how to adopt a friendly facial expression that influences the parasympathetic system and the vagus nerve, and are guided on how to generate friendly emotional tones and textures in thinking about the self and life's difficulties. They also learn the process of compassionate and empathic listening and behavioural practices such as performing one compassionate act for themselves and one for another person each day.

MODULE 2

This module provides an evolutionary functional analysis of emotions, focusing on three main functions:

1. emotions that evolved to help detect and respond to threats
2. emotions that energize and orientate individuals to seek out and acquire resources

3. emotions that support 'rest and digest' regulation of the sympathetic system and offer feelings of contentment, openness and safety.

Participants are invited to tune into how these emotional systems work, what triggers them and how we can move from one to another.

Practices introduced in this module

Participants are supported in distinguishing safety (threat prevention) from safeness (facilitating open attention and exploration). They are guided to explore their mindful awareness of their own motivations, emotional states and emotion-triggers. They are shown how to do this in ways that generate felt-body states that tap into the ventral vagus and create experiences of safeness, using imagery such as imagining a safe place. Because our sense of safeness and compassion and our ventral vagal activation can also be derived from experiencing the helpfulness and friendliness of others, participants are guided to imagine relating to another compassionate mind, by imagining an ideal friend, wise mentor or support figure relating to them compassionately.

MODULE 3

Here, the focus is on building the compassionate mind. Participants are guided to use the insights from Modules 1 and 2 to practise generating a compassionate mind state. Participants reflect on the attributes they would have if they were at their compassionate best. Then they are invited to engage with these attributes and step into becoming compassionate. They are also guided into the three core compassionate aspects (see Figure 1.10): wisdom, particularly about the nature of the mind; strength and courage; and commitment to live to be helpful, not harmful, to self and others. They are invited to use acting techniques to practise acting as a compassionate individual. The compassionate mind is also linked to creating an internal sense of a secure basis and safe haven, a concept taken from attachment models of relating.

Practices introduced in this module

Participants are introduced to the process of developing mindful awareness, imagining and then engaging with qualities of their own ideal compassionate self. These might be being helpful, friendly, patient, warm, considerate or thoughtful, for instance. Three core qualities also relate to wisdom about the nature of mind, courage and commitment to be helpful. Here, the wisdom aspects are about keeping in mind that one did not design or choose one's mind (with its potential to be stressed and angry, as well as helpful and joyful – a mind that has been built for each of us but not *by* us) but has to learn how to cope with its content and dispositions. This understanding is practised along with body-based activities. Individuals practise remembering to switch into a compassionate mind when stressed. They also explore how to show compassion to others and to self and to be sensitive to compassion from others.

MODULE 4

This module invites participants to explore the nature of complex and multiple emotions that can be part of our on-going experiences. Exercises are designed to facilitate in-depth exploration of emotions such as noting the motive behind emotion, the thoughts associated with a desire or motive and an emotion, and with the tendencies to act, and the body-feelings of them. For example, having an argument with somebody we care about arouses feelings of anger, anxiety and sadness. The experience is multi-textured. Participants learn to identify the different types of thinking, body-state and actions associated with each emotion and how they can all be activated at the same time. This facilitates emotion-differentiation learning. Participants then explore how switching into a compassionate mind state can offer new insights into the nature of the argument, how to handle (accept and work with) their emotions and what would be helpful versus unhelpful.

Practices introduced in this module

Here we explore how a combination of emotions can arise in response to a single event. Exercises include: how to note the motives behind emotions; how to become more mindful of our multiplicity of emotional experiences; and how to practise switching into and engaging one's compassionate motive and state of body and mind, to work with both the situation itself and the emotions it aroused. Switching into our compassionate mind can help with empathic listening, mentalizing, communicating and being assertive rather than aggressive.

MODULE 5

The focus here is on exploring the triggers, nature, frequency and intensity of self-criticism. Despite the notion that it can be helpful, functional analysis of self-criticism reveals it to be more hostile and undermining of confidence than people recognize. Rather than trying to argue with their inner criticism, participants explore how to generate compassionate self-correction when things go wrong. They note the difference between hostile forms of self-criticism and empathic, compassionate self-correction. Thus, compassion is not about avoiding responsibility when things don't go well or we have failed in some way, but taking responsibility in a way that encourages honesty, insight, development and new learning. Notice that hostile or shame-based self-criticism tends to undermine confidence and increases stress, anxiety and depression.

Practices introduced in this module
Functional analysis of self-criticism enables participants to notice and explore the (common) hostility of self-criticism and its detrimental effects on the self. Participants then learn how to switch into compassionate self-correction and compassionate encouragement. They are guided in the process of generating compassion for the inner critic by seeing that behind self-criticisms are often fears and previous unresolved difficulties. These are typically fears of rejection or social exclusion. Participants learn how not to suppress or fight with self-criticism or other aspects of the mind but, rather, to shift into compassionate ways of engaging with these difficulties.

MODULE 6
This module focuses on how to build compassionate ways of living into everyday life: how to turn compassionate values and behaviours into habits and thereby generate compassionate ways of living, interacting with others and relating with oneself. Collaboration with the school on how to take compassion forward as part of the school ethos is explored. The aim here is to identify the areas of their lives to which they would like to bring more compassionate courage, wisdom or engagement.

Practices introduced in this module
The emphasis here is on helping participants to make conscious efforts to notice things or people that are helpful to them, such as with appreciation and gratitude. Participants explore how to maintain self-compassion space and to mindfully remember to shift into compassionate mind states including regular breathing exercises and attention-focusing. They practise compassionate behaviour towards self and others, write compassionate letters and reflect on how to take CMT further into dealing with life as it unfolds.

Evidence of the effectiveness of the Compassionate Schools Project

The first version of the programme was evaluated with a sample of over seventy UK educators. The intervention had reduced self-criticism, increased self-compassion and revealed benefits of CMT for dealing with emotional difficulties (Maratos *et al.*, 2019b). In a second, randomized control trial study, Maratos and colleagues (in preparation) demonstrate that the intervention resulted in reductions in systolic and diastolic blood pressure and total peripheral resistance. As the latter is linked to parasympathetic nervous system activity and vagal tone, these findings accord with hypotheses and research that compassion-based practices directly benefit neurobiological emotion-based systems. At the time of writing, further data is being analysed. In our Portuguese research wing, a pilot study conducted with 41 teachers demonstrated that this programme was feasible and well-received cross-culturally, increasing teachers' professional satisfaction and compassionate motivations, attributes and actions towards others and themselves. It also reduced self-criticism burnout, depression, anxiety and stress symptoms (Maratos *et al.*, in preparation).

Furthermore, in a randomized controlled trial of the final version of the programme, one study (conducted with 153 teachers) has revealed that the aforementioned effects hold, unlike in the control group. Here, Maratos *et al.* (ibid.) found that teachers who completed the intervention showed improvements in a host of compassion-related motivations, behaviours and positive affect, and also diminished their self-criticism, fears of compassion, and threat-related emotions at work, reducing symptoms of burnout, depression, anxiety and stress. Again, the control group remained unchanged.

These studies demonstrate that the Compassionate Mind Schools Programme is a feasible, useful and effective intervention in educational settings. The programme not only promotes a compassion-based school ethos but also benefits the psychological and physiological wellbeing of those working in education. Our results hold across different cultures and languages, at least in Europe (Maratos *et al.*, in preparation). These interventions will continue to be developed over time with feedback from participants, basic compassion research, and learning from other innovations – a vital part of the cycle.

Compassion in communities

In addition to programmes that support compassionate development for individuals, a major challenge is to cultivate compassionate families, communities and cultures (Gilbert, 2018; Chiao, 2017; Jennings, 2019; Koopman-Holm and Tsai, 2017; Sachs, 2011). This has been one fundamental driving force of the Charter for Compassion (2019). Brown and Coles (2015) identify a number of processes that can further aid the building of compassionate schools. These include: building collaborations with parents; providing compassionate training for parents; identifying compassion advocates – teachers and children – within each classroom;

supporting compassion role models; rewarding compassionate behaviours; implementing a 'compassion heroes' programme; or profiling compassion as a school process with classroom projects for compassion (such as projects to consider global compassion).

As noted, to bring compassion into schools also requires combating some of the problematic aspects of self-focus competition. Competitive motives are easily stimulated through the media, political rhetoric and how a school prepares children to be economic competitors and live in unjust societies (Sachs, 2011). So compassion trainers should not be fearful about engaging children and teachers in reflections on how the culture in which they are immersed can shape their values for good or ill, consciously and unconsciously. Currently, few compassion training programmes are engaging with this issue, but it will be important for the future (Charter for Compassion, 2019). Given that increasing wealth tends to be accompanied by a reduction in compassion (Piff and Moskowitz, 2017; Van Kleef *et al.*, 2008), a further important consideration is how to educate rich and wealthy children whose privileges shuttle them into the higher ranks of power in society. Some forms of schooling are known to be damaging, engendering difficulties with empathy and compassion. When these privileged young individuals filter into the higher ranks of industry and politics, they can cause problems (Duffell, 2014).

Compassion and the rule of law

The rule of law and respect for the rule of law is part of compassion in the world of social competition. However, the linkage between the rule of law and compassion has also been seen as controversial (Bandes, 2017). Given what we know about the nature of the human mind, compassion recognizes that, without a referee and a clear set of rules and guidelines, many forms of competition would provoke cheating. In sport, for example, even with strict rules and legal sanctions, competitors will still find illicit ways, including drug-taking, to enhance performance or undermine competitors.

Those teaching a compassionate approach to self and others and a just society recognize that, without the rule of law, we can end up with tribal conflicts like drug gang warfare and criminality, which can terrorize entire nations. We realize that, in business, where the rule of law or surveillance may be weak, we may end up with companies avoiding paying taxes, damaging the ecology and exploiting their employees. Poorly regulated companies can become psychopathic and harmful (Bakan, 2011).

As we write, tropical rainforests are disappearing at the rate of an area the size of the UK every year. The seas are being fished-out. Both are the result of inadequate regulation and dismal law enforcement. One reason for this is the ecological disinterest shown by the political Right, who are highly competitive and threat-self-focused, including being fearful of status attacks and being shamed or rejected (Janoff-Bulman, 2009). Part of compassion ethics, therefore, is educating children in the importance of how we relate to, respect and regulate our relationships with each other and the planet. It follows that compassion training in schools is, and should be, more than self- and emotion-regulation. Compassion is a way of living and relating to all other sentient beings.

Conclusion

This chapter has highlighted the motives underpinning human compassion that evolved from mammalian caring behaviour. This evolution affords humans brain competencies for knowing, awareness, insight, reasoning and complex empathy, and a helpful, aware intentionality that turns caring into compassion. Compassion training tunes up these competencies. Caring and compassion, however, are among a number of motivational systems. Two others that need to be considered in relation to compassion are: 1. self-focused competitiveness for social place and resources; and 2. group identification, belonging and tribalism. When poorly regulated, these motive systems can lead to high levels of stress, depression and anxiety, on the one hand, and narcissistic self-focus and social conflict, on the other.

The means of resource-creation and distribution in the modern world are very different from the sharing and caring origins of hunter-gatherer societies (Narvaez, 2017). Understanding how and why the brain evolved the way it has, what it is set up to do and the contexts that bring out the best and worst in us needs to be central to compassion training (Gilbert, 2017b, 2018; Sapolsky, 2017). Given the theme of this chapter, it is important to explore the steps by which we can inform and help societal and educational leaders to reorientate the focus and context of education – from a Westernized self-interest and competition-driven philosophy, to a compassionate, caring, nurturing philosophy. This will not only provide a secure basis for learning, but also holds the prospect of improved wellbeing across individual and societal relationships. Competitiveness will always be part of human nature but it can be held in check with compassion.

Acknowledgements
We are greatly indebted to the support of Sarah and John Rockliff at the Reed Foundation, which funded our work, including the writing of this chapter.

Section Two

Compassion for Self

Self-compassion

Maureen Cooper

Abstract: Compassion is the recognition of a person's suffering combined with an active determination to alleviate that suffering and its causes. Self-compassion means adopting the same attitude towards one's own suffering. It could be said that compassion begins with oneself, and then our practical wisdom of heart and mind permeates our environment to touch people and our planet. To work with our own suffering compassionately, we need to know when we suffer, rather than try to avoid or distract ourselves from it. Research shows that practising self-compassion increases happiness, lowers our stress levels and promotes wellbeing. We may worry lest self-compassion be seen as selfish or weaken how we manage difficulties. We may fear being seen as self-indulgent or self-pitying. But these are fear-based responses to self-compassion, which can be overcome by gaining a deeper understanding of how self-compassion works.

Why we need self-compassion: The brain

To begin with, let's take a look at the basic building blocks of self-compassion and how it is important for us, starting with our brain and our emotional systems.

A simple way to understand the brain is to look at it in terms of an old and a new brain. The old or 'reptilian' brain dates back over 200 million years. Reptiles are not interested in community-building and they make poor parents, abandoning their offspring at birth. The old brain is all about individual survival and passing on our genes by enabling us to recognize and respond to threats as they arise. By contrast, the new or 'mammalian brain' has uniquely human qualities, such as interest in caring for offspring and establishing the bonding and social communication needed to provide a safe and nourishing environment to raise them.

Human beings today live with these two aspects of our brain. We have our deep-rooted 'fight, flight or freeze' responses to potential threat operating alongside our newer skills of reasoning, imagination, planning for the future, reflecting on the past and even thinking about how our minds work. Most of the time, we work with these newer skills but, when confronted by severe stress or a challenging situation, we can experience what is known as an amygdala hijack. The reasoning powers of our neocortex or new brain are overwhelmed by emotions and reactions triggered by the threat – to fight, flee or freeze. Have you ever found yourself suddenly furiously angry and hardly able to contain yourself? That's an example of an amygdala hijack. At such times, our need for self-compassion is most acute but the very fact that we are not engaging with our rational minds can make this difficult.

There are less dramatic but equally damaging ways in which the old brain might undermine the new. Eastern traditions have long described the way we can fixate on our thoughts, making them into stories that go way beyond the original event and causing us difficulty and unhappiness. The research conducted by Paul Gilbert, founder of CFT, presents a psychological perspective on how this happens (see Figure 2.1).

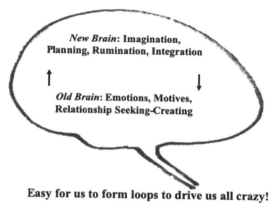

Easy for us to form loops to drive us all crazy!

Figure 2.1: Old brain, new brain

Source: Gilbert (2009), reproduced with permission
from Constable and Robinson Ltd

Think about a zebra fleeing a lion who wants to eat it. If the zebra escapes, it quickly settles and resumes grazing. For humans, it's different. The monologue in our mind could go something like this: *Will the lion come back? It knows where I hang out now and it got a good look at me. It will probably be back to have another go. Maybe I should move to another part of the savannah? But what about the rest of the herd? Would they come too? ...* This wonderful imagination that can achieve so much can also keep us awake at night worrying about taxes, losing our job or a family reunion coming up. Professor Gilbert calls these 'loops in the mind', when the mind turns in on itself and gets caught up in an on-going process of rumination that stresses and undermines us. The loops are hard to escape and tend to spawn more loops as we attempt to negotiate our way out.

Our emotional systems

We can see that underlying these mental loops are emotions that trigger them. Gilbert categorizes these into three systems (Figure 2.2).

Figure 2.2: Our emotional systems: The interaction between the three major emotion-regulation systems

Source: Gilbert (2009), reproduced with permission from Constable and Robinson Ltd

Our threat system

This is the system that alerts us to danger and helps us protect ourselves from it. It works by enabling us to stand and fight, or run and hide, or simply freeze and submit. It comes into play when we are personally threatened but also when our friends and family are threatened.

Our drive system

This is the system that motivates us to seek out the resources we need for survival for ourselves and those we care about. It guides us towards our life goals and enables us to experience pleasure in accomplishing them. If it is over-stimulated, this can result in frustration and disappointment, which can, in turn, topple over into a threat.

Our soothing system

When we are under no threat or if we don't need to accomplish anything in particular, we can be in a state of quietness or equanimity. This state is linked to affection and kindness: parents generally calm and soothe a child, or a friend will reach out to support us if we're distressed. The soothing system is essential to our wellbeing and fundamental to our understanding of self-compassion. It is linked to the production of endorphins and oxytocin.

These are some of the raw materials that we need to navigate as we learn to practise self-compassion. Now, let's look more closely at how self-compassion works.

How our thinking mind responds to threat

We have seen that, when we face a threat from an external source, our reaction can be to fight it, to run away from it, or to freeze and hope it passes us by. The clinical psychologist and author Christopher Germer is one of the pioneers in the field of self-compassion. He identifies the process we might go through when we face threat from within our own minds:

- The 'fight' response can become self-criticism.
- The 'flight' response becomes self-isolation.
- The 'freeze' response leads us to become caught up in our own thoughts to the extent that we are unable to act and tend to become self-absorbed.

Think about this for a moment. How often do you find yourself being very critical of yourself? When you're anxious and worried, do you feel like hiding away? Or does the worry turn into such a knot in your mind that you can think of nothing else?

The three elements of self-compassion

Let's look further. Kristin Neff is an Associate Professor in human development at the University of Texas and another pioneer in the field of self-compassion. One of her outstanding contributions has been to identify the three elements that make up self-compassion (see Figure 2.3):

- self-kindness: being gentle and understanding with ourselves
- recognizing our common humanity: feeling connected to others rather than isolated by our suffering and pain
- mindfulness: holding our experience with a balanced perspective, neither exaggerating nor avoiding it.

Figure 2.3: The three elements of self-compassion

Source: Kristin Neff

How self-compassion works as an antidote to threat

Germer and Neff, who have been collaborating since 2007, have come up with a way to consider how the three elements of self-compassion can act as antidotes to the original threat response:

- *Self-kindness* acts as an antidote to the *fight* response of self-criticism.
- *Recognizing our common humanity* is an antidote to the *flight* response that causes self-isolation.
- *Mindfulness* is an antidote to *freezing*, becoming trapped in our fears and self-absorbed.

So, what does this mean for the practice of self-compassion?

Making self-compassion work in your life

We have seen that we humans are capable of looking at how our own minds work. To practise self-compassion in a meaningful way, it is essential to develop awareness of our habits, learn what triggers distress for us and what antidotes are available. Increasing our self-awareness will help us to see how self-compassion can help us. We can learn to soothe our own distress and to be good friends to ourselves.

So many of us have a voice in our heads that is forever berating us and telling us that we aren't good enough. Sometimes echoing a disappointed parent or a disapproving teacher, this voice can crush our confidence and our ability to deal with difficulties. This voice deepens our sense of shame and makes us feel unlovable. As we learn to apply self-kindness, we can begin to change our relationship to this inner critic. Somewhere in its commentary may be some helpful advice. We just need to be able to reorganize how we hear what is being said.

Along with struggling with our inner critic, we try to maintain an ideal of perfection. We are afraid that, if we do not manage to project a perfect image of who we are, people won't like us or want to be with us. We fear rejection and being left alone. Becoming a good friend to ourselves, whatever happens, is the most sustainable and reliable way of practising self-kindness. We see that we are loveable and capable of loving.

Changing your relationship to your inner critic: Loving-kindness

As we look more deeply into self-compassion, we gradually begin to realize that, just as we get things wrong sometimes, struggle to manage, and feel unlovable, so does everyone else. We are all in this together. Just as each of us wants to be happy and live a good life, so does everyone else. Just as we don't want suffering, none of the people around us wants suffering either.

Once we recognize this on a deep level, we also realize that everyone struggles and sometimes makes mistakes. As human beings, we are flawed, but we're also full of courage and the possibility of growth and understanding. There is no shame in needing to work with challenges. Making mistakes and working out how to grow and develop are part of the human story, the story of common humanity. The meditations 'Changing your relationship to your inner critic' and 'Loving-kindness for yourself' are a great place to start.

Meditation 1: Changing your relationship to your inner critic

- Sit quietly and comfortably.
- Take time to listen to your self-critic and the tone it takes in your mind.
- Does it speak to you like a good friend who is interested in your wellbeing?
- Or does it use a harsh and judgemental tone?
- If a friend or colleague spoke to you in a harsh manner, would you find it helpful?
- Would you talk to someone else using this kind of language and tone?

- Perhaps your own self-criticism is not as reliable as you first thought?
- Take a piece of paper and make a list of all the ways your self-criticism is unhelpful and even harmful.
- Note the threat that you experience when you engage with it.
- See that the self-critic is always focused on the past and what has gone wrong.
- Imagine how it would be if the approach were kinder, more understanding and less judgemental, and consider trying to use kinder language when you review your behaviour.

   (Adapted from Paul Gilbert: *The Compassionate Mind*, 2009: 340)

Meditation 2: Loving-kindness for yourself

- Sit quietly and rest your attention on your breath.
- When you feel settled, bring to mind a person who you feel embodies kindness (it could be your grandmother, the Dalai Lama, Desmond Tutu ... anyone who truly means 'kindness' to you).
- Imagine this person is sitting in front of you, smiling, warm and accessible.
- Now feel their kindness emanating from their heart like rays of light.
- Let this light enter *your* heart, filling you with a feeling of being loved.
- As the light pours into you, allow yourself to feel deeply well and happy.
- Quietly repeat to yourself: *May I be happy, may I be well. May I be happy, may I be well.*
- As you repeat the phrases, let the feeling settle deeply in your being.
- When you're ready, return to being aware of your breath for a few moments.

You might also like this exercise: 'Connecting with other people'.

Connecting with other people

- Turn your attention to the people around you – walking in the street, sitting in a café, travelling on public transport.
- Notice the people near to you.
- Take a moment to scan the area you are in and to see as many people as you can.
- Take note of the thoughts and emotions that pass through your mind as you do this.
- Notice if you make a comment in your mind about someone. Notice the people you're drawn to and those you don't like the look of.

- Try to imagine how they might see you as you sit, stand or walk alongside them.
- Take a moment to be aware that everyone around you wants their day to go well and to avoid any unpleasantness – just like you.
- Then realize that, inevitably, for some people, some things will go wrong during their day.
- Let that feeling touch you and help you to feel a common humanity with the people you see.
- Allow yourself to feel the interconnection between you and others.

Understanding the importance of meditation

Meditation is the most effective and reliable way of working with our minds and learning to work with the loops we get into with our thinking. When we're caught in a process of rumination, we can become completely caught up in our own worries and isolated from what's going on around us. Meditation enables us to become more self-aware and more aware of other people and what's going on in our environment. It is the basis of self-compassion and the best way of being kind to ourselves.

Perhaps you already have a meditation practice but, if you would like a very simple technique, try this exercise.

Simple meditation

- Sit up straight but relaxed.
- Close your eyes for a moment to settle, then open them again.
- Become aware of your breathing.
- Stay with where the sensation is vivid for you – moment by moment, by moment, breath by breath, by breath.
- Notice any changes in the breath.
- Notice when the mind is not on the breathing. Where has it gone?
- Dissolve the distraction.
- Bring your attention back to the breath.
- Begin again as if for the first time.

Conclusion

As a former school teacher, I am only too aware of the opportunities that the profession provides for being hard on yourself and demanding perfection in everything you try to do. If you find yourself struggling with these kinds of feelings, you can create a moment of self-compassion at any time in your working day (see Figure 2.4)

Taking a self-compassion moment

Where I find myself now is stressful and challenging

Feeling like this some of the time is part of life

Many people in the world will be going through something similar

I want to be able to give myself th compassion that I need right now, so I can learn from this situation for the future.

Figure 2.4: A self-compassion exercise

I suggest that holding your hands over your heart provides a strong feeling of comfort and peace. You can play with the words to make them fit your own needs and personality.

Then, of course, there are your pupils, who are going through challenges of their own that create opportunities for giving themselves a hard time. I am sure that, as teachers, you deal with the power of the internet in a child's life every day. Perhaps it is helpful to draw attention to two phenomena:

- fear of missing out: pervasive apprehension that others might be having rewarding experiences from which we are absent
- social comparison: our tendency to look at what people are doing on social media and thereby feeling dissatisfied with our own situation.

Both of these tendencies, although a potential source of suffering, can be very responsive to self-compassion and finding self-worth, rather than always looking outwardly for justification. All the exercises used in this chapter can be adapted to the needs of your pupils. The next exercise, 'Reflection on facing challenges', affords a simple way of examining how we react when facing difficulties and incorporates the three elements of self-compassion. It could also provide a good basis for discussion and exploration with teenagers.

Reflection on facing challenges

This reflection is based on the three elements of self-compassion:

1. Do you try to ignore the fact that you are suffering and focus on fixing the problem? Or do you take some time to give yourself comfort?

2. Do you feel cut off from others when things go wrong and feel as if it is happening only to you? Or do you take some time to think of others in a similar situation?
3. Do you get carried away by the drama and tend to make a big deal of what is happening? Or do you keep a balanced view of what is going on?

A good way to end this chapter is to draw attention to the Japanese art of *kintsugi*. This is the art form of mending broken china by going over the cracks with gold or other precious metals. It is a way of showing that imperfection can be an enrichment of a piece of art, rather than a reason to reject it. The parallel with self-compassion is clear.

Compassion in cyberspace

Catherine Knibbs

Abstract: It can be difficult for us to acknowledge, feel or engage in compassion when interactions on the internet seem empty of a human being to share these feelings with, especially if we can't see them. Some years ago, a proposition was put forward that we tend to change our behaviour when we use digital media. This chapter extends the idea and explains why we do what we do in digital space and why compassion for others through electronic devices is so greatly needed in this world of superfast communications.

Since much of the information about the sixth mass extinction and climate change is shared via the medium of cyberspace – through forums, social media or news and marketing – it is interesting to see how these messages are often met with compassion and a desire, by some, to act to help the planet. They contrast starkly with responses that are utterly devoid of compassion and it is these that I explore here. My chapter offers a window onto the behaviours that occur online, so that we adults can help the younger generations become more compassionate towards one another via social media. We need to create a gentler environment in which to communicate and share, particularly at this time of crisis. In the spirit of hope, the drive to create an active movement to save the planet can succeed. Although I am aware that we're looking at 4 billion active users of the internet, we can begin the narrative of change today, right here, one transaction, conversation and post at a time.

To do this requires consideration of the behaviours of ourselves and others. We can assume that, in most cases, the intent is to hurt another person through unkind words or images and that such behaviour lacks compassion. Now, cyberbullying is a complex issue and it is difficult to define what it is exactly without considering many overlapping areas such as harassment, stalking and so on. I could tell you my academic definition of what I call cybertrauma, of which cyberbullying is one aspect. But I'm afraid this might turn readers away from this chapter.

So I've chosen to talk here like I do to my psychotherapy clients, as I suspect you would appreciate the no-nonsense approach. I am proposing, therefore, that cyberbullying generally describes any behaviour that a person engages in, using online technology, that leaves another person feeling hurt and distressed. This doesn't match the definitions by some of the anti-bullying organizations, and I'm not seeking to provide a definitive guide to what it is and how to spot it. Any parent or professional working with children and young people will grasp the general gist of the idea.

In cyberspace, users of the technology face a screen and keyboard that allow them to communicate in the digital space of social media. What's often missing is the perception (the seeing) and recognition of the person on the other side of the computer screen, unless they're communicating through video. This disconnect may partly explain why cyberbullying happens. Although there are also more complex reasons, this is a fairly common response when people are asked why they cyberbullied. They often say they 'forgot' about the other person being there or, as Suler (2004) suggests, they were influenced by aspects of the 'online disinhibition effect' whereby our behaviours online change because we become disinhibited about the consequences of our messages. This is a fairly substantial area of theory but, to put it simply: if we cannot see our victim we are less likely to care about our behaviour towards them.

However, I posit that this is not the only reason we behave less compassionately towards each other in cyberspace. I would like to introduce a more nuanced theory to help us understand why we can be so quick to respond, so vitriolic, and display cyberbullying behaviours, particularly concerning issues we feel passionate about. It is largely to do with early life experiences – feelings as well as thinking styles – and the human need for connection through relationships.

To give you a little background into the theory of why we behave as we do in cyberspace, I am going to introduce to you a biological theory about who we are as human beings, as this underpins our actions and reactions to our environment – including, I suggest, the digital space. (The references will guide you to reading on the subject if you wish to probe deeper.)

We human beings have a biological safety system that is hard-wired into our bodies and brains. We have evolution to thank for passing on this mechanism, as it has allowed us to maintain our species by avoiding anything that could harm, hurt or kill us. Porges (2001) calls this the polyvagal system because it relates to several branches of the autonomic or automatic nervous system in our bodies. Through the process of neuroception, the nervous system constantly sends signals to the brain, where they are decoded before the brain tells us what to do. This information-sharing through your nervous system and senses occurs outside your awareness so that the 'noise' you have to pay attention to doesn't overwhelm you. Imagine if you had to assess four thousand bits of information per second and pay attention to every one. You would be tired, to say the least, and some people believe that digital media are already causing information overload.

Porges (2001, 2011) speculates that this is also the system that allows us to communicate and bond with other people. When we feel safe in our environment (internal and external), we are able to have conversations, be intimate and sit still without fear, without constantly scanning for the danger around us as we might have done when we were cave people. It's not advantageous to discuss the latest colour scheme for the house and grand designs for the garden when there's a big, hungry, angry tiger on our tail. Thus, our nervous system was designed to allow us to carry out our social behaviour when the coast is clear and return to the 'safe and social' (S&S) feeling. This system also supports the brain and body in connecting with feelings of compassion and empathy. It is this important process that can be limited or wholly absent in cyberspace, which contributes to such behaviours as cyberbullying.

One of the first places we learn about communication and feelings of safety – our baseline level – is during the moments immediately after we're born, when we're held by loving parents, feeling their heartbeat and warmth as they gaze at us adoringly, smiling and cooing softly. As Siegel (2018) says in his talk entitled 'Presence, Parenting and the Planet' (online at www. drdansiegel.com/resources/video_clips/), we feel 'seen, safe, soothed and secure'. Siegel says that safety is conducive to attachment (2012). Some newborns who don't have the gentlest experiences are likely to have a baseline 'level of safety' that is lower than that of the baby who was cuddled.

When an adult holds a baby, the distance between the eyes of parent and child is approximately 30 cm, which, interestingly, is the distance nature intended babies' eyes to focus at, albeit hazily at first (Hofsten *et al.*, 2014). Have you noticed how far your smartphone, tablet or computer is from your face when you're using it? It's approximately the same distance, 30 cm! And young children tend to stand in front of a television at approximately the same distance too. What does this mean for the user of a device and what does it have to do with compassion in cyberspace and the lack of these connection-based feelings?

If 30 cm is the innate eye-gaze distance and is also associated with feelings of safety, comfort and connection, we can readily see the biological trick your nervous system plays on you when you hold a device and gaze (lovingly at times) into it and why we feel safety in cyberspace – falsely. We are held in a zone of false safety, rather as if we were in a bubble of connection through our device. Often these devices are used in safe spaces such as our own home, office or bed. Many of the cues about safety are recognized by our bodies and so we feel comfortable as we engage with/in the technology and social media spaces.

When we are not using a device and are in the real, corporeal world, we may act according to the following scenario. If, for example, I wanted to buy a coffee at a café, I'd walk towards a stranger standing behind the counter and ask for it. As I did so my body and senses would be paying attention to the sights, sounds and smells around me, I would be looking at the face of the barista as I approached and we would likely engage in some non-verbal 'safe and social' communication before either of us spoke. When the barista did speak, I would be listening for the cues of safety in the prosody (tone) of their voice. My body would be saying, 'Is this person safe to approach?' If my neuroceptive systems had not detected any danger cues and the barista had greeted me with a smile and a friendly voice, I'd engage by asking for my coffee and all would be well.

Yet, throughout the entire coffee-buying experience, my neuroceptive systems would be continually scanning the environment for danger cues. If the barista were sarcastic, angry or seemed dangerous in any way (conveyed through their body language, dilated pupils or heavier breathing), I could assess this threat and make a quick escape, should I need to – all systems fully functional for the survival of me, the human being! If something didn't feel quite right or, say, the barista suddenly swore loudly and lunged in my direction, my survival mechanisms would kick into action and my fight/flight or shutdown responses would assist me in assessing and responding to the situation. Had the barista just spilled hot water onto their skin and, therefore, instinctively jumped away from the water, my safety systems and higher-level thinking brain would quickly piece this information together to work out what had happened and why. Then, based on a brief interaction, I could have assessed that the sudden change in the barista's behaviour was not associated with me and that perhaps they had hurt themselves.

I'm likely to ask 'Are you okay?' Under these circumstances, my empathizing with the barista's pain (having scalded myself like this in the past, my mirror neurons would be reminded of my own pain) and the feeling of compassion would likely be evoked in the same moment. If, however, the barista replied by swearing at me, I might be less inclined to feel compassion and I would create a story in my mind about what kind of person they were. Would you?

Hopefully, this is making sense and you are having a virtual or imaginary scene in your mind; you may have decided that the barista is a man, wearing a beige uniform, an apron, a shirt and a nice tie. At least I think it's a nice tie.

Now, I know that, when I typed these words about the tie, I expressed the two sentences very differently, and my prosody, tone and timing all changed, along with my facial expressions. Can you work out which was the sarcastic sentence, and which the factual? You've probably considered that they can be interchangeable, and this is exactly my point. This is the type of 'test' given to artificial intelligence (AI) machines to see how human-like they actually are. This is the *how* and also *what/when/which/who* and *why* of tricky situations in cyberspace. To paraphrase Paul Gilbert, we (can/ do) have a tricky mind that can lead us into all sorts of situations and thinking patterns. When this was first discussed, it didn't relate to the digital world and cyberspace, as they were not as significant as they are today.

So, back to this digital, electronic cyberspace, where young people and adults will be spending time and regularly encountering this false safety. Young people, in particular, will be picking up their device in spaces that are, for the most part, safe enough – such as their bedrooms, or home, perhaps even school, on the bus and all manner of other places. Once they open their device to engage with an app, person, text, game or image/video, they are almost transported into the device's energy field and its bubble of false safety, where cues of danger are not always recognized by the body. We can also see this in real-world signals when young people bump into things and other people while poring over their devices! On the issue of cues and safety, I argue that using devices opens us to a number of elements, including traumas such as viewing or reading unpleasant things and misreading the intonations behind a text – as in the barista example.

Because they are viewing their device at this 30 cm distance, viewers are drawn into the transactions as though they were in the corporeal world but without the real-time neuroception feedback cues. When I speak with young people in my practice, they tell me that they react immediately and think *after*. This is where the cognitive, thinking brain and the lack of real-world signals can generate moments of non-compassion, as the reactive fight-or-flight systems can make them feel as though they're in overdrive.

Through talking to many young people in therapy, I realize that they recognize the issue but struggle with processes of 'stop, reflect respond' and take a 'fight, react or destroy' approach – they need to answer texts and posts instantly and retaliate to provocation without thinking. What is clear from what young people tell me is that they make errors of judgement around what is safe in terms of communication in cyberspace, and this makes sense when we remember that many cues are missing.

When we apply this understanding to instances of cyberbullying or retaliation online, or 'trolling', we can perceive such behaviours compassionately by seeing the incident from a place of missed cues and feeling attacked, coupled with the person's need to feel seen, soothed, safe and secure. Young people can say some very unkind things, and situations can escalate quickly in cyberspace, due to the human-based errors of digital communication and deficit of self-regulation, coupled with false safety and the desire to be seen and needed in their 'in-group', which is important for us all as social beings. But it appears as non-compassion, meanness, bullying and a high degree of disconnect through interpersonal means and also from the bodily messages and sensations that would be clear in a face-to-face conversation.

Let's say there's a group of climate-change activists online, for example, and a non-believer challenges their post or video content. It's easy to see how this can deteriorate into an attack from those of us who might otherwise be compassionate, when we are passionately defending our own posts and videos. I witness really intense debates on pages related to issues of climate change and biodiversity, or on pages run by activists, that quickly descend into unkind and non-compassionate outpourings from people who want to make changes for the good of humanity.

We can all get into tricky situations if we misread cues in the corporeal world. If we stop for a moment, then we can see that this tricky situation is magnified in a digital space, where there are so many situations that can be misinterpreted, miscommunicated and misattuned. Thus, opportunities for compassion and connection are missed. The most helpful antidotes are those based on 'early years' interventions – such as supporting parents in building powerfully-present relationships with their babies, creating a secure attachment and initiating co-created regulation. This allows young people to develop an in-built self-regulation system that gives them something to lean on to help them manage moments of miscommunication and, in turn, build their compassion towards others in cyberspace.

Tips for education staff, professionals and parents

Exploration

1. Ask young people about how they feel safe in their bodies, and have a conversation about why these signals are important. Ask them to consider how these signals are different or missing from digital communication.

2. Ask young people to explain content and context when it's written and how they can 'tell' if a text is sarcastic, passive-aggressive or unkind.

3. Ask young people to compose a brief text that can be seen as positive or negative, e.g. 'that's a nice tie' and explore how we as humans can often tell the subtle differences. Ask what they noticed or thought about themselves and others during the task.

4. Create a shared digital conversation tool that can enable young people to stop, reflect and respond and then discuss what each of these stages might look like.

5. Discuss and explore what self-regulation looks like and how this can be applied to digital communications.

6. Discuss and explore how messages about climate change can be shared without fear, while still containing the information required to evoke a desire for change; and why, when messages create fear, do people react how they do?

Actions for when a young person has reacted or retaliated online

1. When you see a young person engaging in unkind behaviour online, ask them a few 'curiously compassionate' questions about who they think the other person is, what they consider their own motivations might be, and what it is that they want to communicate to the recipient.

2. Don't berate or belittle young people who have made unkind comments, as they are likely to have been in fight/flight response online (behaving like 'keyboard warriors'). Ask them why they felt a need to respond to the person and what the underlying message was that they felt they had to respond to. These are two quite different questions and some young people may be unable to reflect on the underlying message – for example, they may think the other person was unkind about what they wrote, yet, underneath, they relate to this as a shameful comment about being useless or stupid.

3. Use compassion to reflect that you, the adult, understand and empathize with that moment of 'tricky mind' and 'fight/flight' survival reaction. Where possible, consider working together to perhaps rectify or make amends. Show kindness, care and humility in your interactions.

Section Three

Compassion for Others

Compassionate parenting: Helping to create nurturing family environments

James N. Kirby

A large and compelling body of research demonstrates the powerful impacts family environments can have on the growth and development of children. Family environments characterized by warmth, security and positive parenting can help with positive childhood growth. Conversely, family environments characterized by hostility, criticism and abuse often lead to difficulties with mental illness. This chapter focuses on how a compassionate approach can be applied to the family unit to help support and facilitate mental health and wellbeing. The chapter discusses how parenting motivations (self-image and compassion-focused goals) and fears of compassion are associated with greater reactive parenting styles (coercive, punitive), levels of parental shame, and childhood social, emotional and behavioural difficulties. It is helpful to adopt a compassionate-mind approach, and here I discuss how such approaches can be applied and, specifically, how they can be integrated with existing evidence-based parenting programmes.

Introduction

To ensure their healthy development, it is crucial for children to be raised in a family environment in which they feel cared-for, supported, secure and safe. Arguably, human offspring are the most vulnerable of any species, relying fully on their parents for at least a decade to help provide for their basic needs of shelter, food and, importantly, affiliative care (Dunbar, 2010; Hrdy, 2009; Narvaez *et al.*, 2013). Therefore, a child who has parents who are sensitive and responsive to their suffering is raised in a context that enables them to grow and flourish. In an ideal world, all children would be raised this way. However, and tragically, many millions of children around the world are nonetheless raised in family environments characterized by punishment, physical abuse and neglect (Prinz, 2015; World Health Organization, 2014; Zolotor *et al.*, 2007). It is a compassionate crisis that children throughout the world are raised in environments characterized not by care, warmth and compassion but by hostility, criticism and rejection.

A study in Brazil (Bordin *et al.*, 2006) that sought to estimate the prevalence of corporal punishment found a rate of 10.1 per cent for severe physical punishment (such as choking, shaking under-2-year-olds, kicking and beating) and 75.3 per cent for non-severe physical punishment (such as spanking with hand, spanking with object, twisting the ear). A child maltreatment study in the US found that at least 10 per cent of parents will frequently or very frequently use an object like a spoon or belt to discipline children for misbehaviour (Prinz *et al.*, 2009).

Yet, importantly, research shows smacking is ineffective at changing children's behaviour in the long term and can negatively impact parent–child attachment (D'Souza *et al.*, 2016; Klevens and Whitaker, 2007; Prinz *et al.*, 2009). This has led over forty countries (including Denmark, Germany, Israel, Sweden and Romania) to introduce legislation to ban smacking and corporal punishment and thus prevent maltreatment of children (United Nations, 2014). Moreover, the World Health Organization (WHO) (2020) has identified the three key risk factors for child maltreatment:

1. if the child is under 4 years of age
2. if the child is unwanted or fails to meet parents' expectations
3. if the child has special needs or abnormal physical features or cries persistently.

It is notable that the three key risk factors for maltreatment are childhood vulnerabilities and that, rather than protecting vulnerable children, the vulnerable are the children most punished.

While research has – importantly – focused on these obvious candidates for abuse, neglect and maltreatment, *shame* in the parent and shame and fear of inadequate parenting performance have received insufficient research attention. This is important because, even when parents are not overtly abusive or neglectful, and may even be highly motivated to be good parents, shame can induce distortions in the child–parent relationship that can cause long-term damage (Fonagy and Target, 1997; Gilbert and Andrews, 1998; Holmes and Slade, 2018; Tracy *et al.*, 2007). Furthermore, because these effects are subtle, children growing up with parents who carry a lot of shame may be unaware of the degree to which their development is being influenced by parental shame and may themselves be highly vulnerable to shame later in life (Fonagy and Target, 1997; Gilbert, 1998; Holmes and Slade, 2018; Tracy *et al.*, 2007). This chapter explores some of the core themes related to parental shame and its impact on parenting styles, and how compassion can help address and facilitate positive change so that children can be raised in nurturing family environments.

Evolutionary background

One reason why humans may be particularly sensitive to shame in their parenting role is that, in many ways, modern culture provides grossly 'abnormal' environments for child-rearing (Narvaez *et al.*, 2013). This is revealed in a brief exploration of human evolution and the hunter-gatherer lifestyle over the last 200,000 years (Dunbar, 2010).

That humans evolved to walk upright was a highly significant anatomical evolutionary change. This had the impact of narrowing the birth canal at a time when the challenges of social living were evolving larger-brained humans (Dunbar, 2010; Hrdy, 2009). The consequence was that babies were born more immature and more dependent on care (and for longer) than any other primate (Dunsworth and Eccleston, 2015; Lee, 2018). In addition, giving birth became painful and dangerous and often required help from kin (Hrdy, 2009). Post-birth learning included language, emotion regulation and social–cultural rules – all of which required lengthy and intense periods of protected learning and care (Cassidy and Shaver, 2016; Lee, 2018; Mayseless, 2016).

These and other adaptations led to an infant and child-rearing system that was more open and collective than that of other primates (Lee, 2018). Another change was also significant: early groups were typically quite small, comprising fewer than 150 individuals, which allowed for familiar and reciprocal relationships (Dunbar, 2010). Indeed, all the individuals within a group – whom every child would get to know – could take responsibility for protecting the young, looking out for them and sometimes offering comfort. This is commonly referred to as *allo*-parenting, a phenomenon in which the care of children is given by individuals other than the parents – usually, but not only, close relatives (Hrdy, 2009; Lee, 2018). Relatives and other group members were present 24/7 to aid child-rearing. Children were able to roam freely and could seek contact, comfort and play from whomever they chose; and this is still the case in hunter-gatherer groups today (Eibl-Eibesfeldt, 2017).

There are few vestiges of this style of living and child-rearing in Western industrial society. In most Western societies, only one in four grandparents is now involved in regular childcare (Australian Bureau of Statistics, 2012). That non-parental care certainly continues, but it is commonly provided by strangers for subscribed periods of time, generally from formal childcare support services such as nurseries, and schools (Australian Bureau of Statistics, 2012; Coall and Hertwig, 2010; Kirby, 2015).

Importantly, research is finding that cortisol increases over the course of the day among children who are in formal childcare, unlike those who are cared for at home by a primary caregiver (Ahnert *et al.*, 2004; Dettling *et al.*, 1999: 639–50), and the quality of the care given is an important factor in children's development and wellbeing (Lisonbee *et al.*, 2008). Schools provide contexts where children have to sit for quite long periods, separated from their family environment. In hunter-gatherer societies, co-sleeping, open breastfeeding, ease of touch and open expression of affection by kin and non-kin alike are part of everyday life (Eibl-Eibesfeldt, 2017). This is especially salient since we have known at least since Harlow's studies of monkeys in the 1950s that physical contact and touch are among the most powerful and profound regulators of affect that create a sense of safeness and comfort (Montagu, 1971). Living in a sea of strangers, as children typically do, can be highly problematic, especially when teachers are not allowed to touch or physically comfort a child in distress (Rolfe, 2005).

One consequence of modern social contexts has been a serious and significant rise in loneliness among people in Western countries such as the US, the UK and Australia, with estimates of about 10 per cent loneliness prevalent in the general population (Beutel *et al.*, 2017). Loneliness is associated with a range of mental and physical health problems (Cacioppo *et al.*, 2014) all of which are likely to impact on child-rearing. In the context of parenting, a recent survey of 2,000 mothers found that 90 per cent feel lonely since having children and 54 per cent feel friendless after giving birth. Single parents are at heightened risk of loneliness and isolation compared to parent couples (Chiu *et al.*, 2018). A recent study of 387 women who had given birth within the last 12 months found that mothers who experienced a decrease in group membership after having a baby were associated with increases in depressive symptoms compared to those who maintained their group connections (Seymour-Smith *et al.*, 2016). Moreover, a recent meta-analysis found that social isolation and loneliness are significant risk factors for early mortality, collectively increasing the risk of premature death by between 27 per cent and 30 per cent (Holt-Lunstad *et al.*, 2015). Yet, despite the increased risk of social isolation and loneliness and its known physical effects (Cacioppo *et al.*, 2014), only 15 per cent of people perceive social factors such as connectedness to others as important to mortality (Haslam *et al.*, 2018). So we are seeing a shift from supportive allo-parenting communities to more isolated, competitive and shame-vulnerable parenting.

Hrdy (2009) and Narvaez *et al.* (2013) argue that the future success of humans as a species relies on returning to cooperative breeding and allo-parenting, releasing the burden of parenting on single individuals and freeing children from entrapment when dysfunctional parents are their only source of comfort and guidance. Researchers have noted that we have steadily drifted from being a typical species that raises its young in supportive groups, to being an atypical species that isolates and disconnects from common parenting practices such as co-sleeping – consequently undermining the nurturing environments most supportive of growth (Biglan *et al.*, 2012; Gopnik, 2014; Kirby, 2016, 2017a; Narvaez *et al.*, 2013). These behaviours exemplify what has been called 'evolutionary mismatch', meaning that our brains and bodies evolved in, and to operate within, a particular ecological and social context that is now radically different (Li *et al.*, 2017).

The need to compete and the shame of failing

Part of the reason that we have created cultures that differ from those in which we evolved lies with our culture. The development of agriculture provided for rapidly increasing group sizes and the breakdown of small isolated hunter-gatherer communities, which had benefited from caring and sharing, to be replaced by increasingly powerful hierarchies often regulated by dominant males (Harrari, 2017). In these environments, competing for social place and a share of resources became more intense (Gilbert, 2018). For thousands of years, those individuals who were not able to compete were occupied and trapped in low social rank (the poor) with inadequate access to resources and often living stressful and sometimes short lives (Mann, 1986; Gilbert, 2018).

The competitive dynamic shows itself in other ways, too. For example, Western culture is placing a growing emphasis on socially comparative, competitive-driven parenting. 'How to' books provoke parental concerns about doing the 'right thing' for their child, nourish fears of being incompetent in the role and entice parents to constantly monitor themselves by standards they are supposed to be meeting, especially – but not only – in comparison with others (Gopnik, 2014). Parents can also be sensitive to their children so that their misbehaviour in public or not doing well academically is seen to reflect shame on them. Some parents are in competition with their parenting peers, leading to the rise of styles such as 'tiger parenting', where the parent invests heavily in the child to maximize success and achievement above all else (Fu and Markus, 2014). Indeed, correlational studies have found that a strong focus on goals such as status and money (compared to community feeling) is associated with being less warm and more controlling towards one's children (Kasser *et al.*, 1995).

Social competition has two aspects to it. One is focused on moving up-rank; the other is focused on avoiding moving down-rank (Gilbert *et al.*, 2007). Up-rank parents focus on wanting to excel at parenting and urging their children to do well, which they take as a reflection of themselves. Parents who wish to avoid feeling inferior and being seen as inadequate in the parenting role fear lest their child suffer in consequence, which is a down-rank focus.

Parenting styles and shame vulnerabilities

Many different motives underpin our parental styles, including those identified as: authoritarian as opposed to authoritative (Robinson *et al.*, 1995); facilitative, where parents work around the child's needs, in contrast to regulating, where they seek to enable the child to fit into their existing family routines and structures (Raphael-Leff, 1986); or responsiveness and warmth as opposed to demandingness and control (Baumrind, 1966: 887–907). The term 'parenting', as noted by Gopnik (2014), is relatively new, emerging only in the 1960s and 1970s.

Gopnik (2014) points out that 'parenting' indicates a desire or goal to turn the child into 'something', that there is some kind of outcome to be achieved, which is one-directional. Parenting is often conceptualized in terms of influencing the child; however, recent work is finding that children play an active role in influencing the parenting they receive, with their own personality factors playing a large role in determining whether they receive parental warmth or hostility (Ayob *et al.*, 2018). In contrast, the term 'being a parent' emphasizes the process of care and what one can do to nurture the child (Gopnik, 2014), and this is a bi-directional or transactional relationship between parent and child (Karraker and Coleman, 2005), where each influences the other.

Many parents report being self-critical and feeling a sense of failure, shame and guilt about their parenting efforts and perceived mistakes (Haslam *et al.*, 2015). There is an association between parental stress and dysfunctional parenting style and the child's lower levels of overall wellbeing (Abidin, 1992). A recent report on 2,200 American parents found that 90 per cent of mothers and 85 per cent of fathers felt judged by strangers and other parents, with 50 per cent saying they felt judged almost all the time (Zero to Three, 2016). Indeed, in evaluative social contexts where judgement occurs, shame is a common experience among parents (Scarnier *et al.*, 2009) and can be related to the child's 'bad' or problematic behaviour or their own perceived poor handling of such behaviour.

First-time mothers experience shame and judgement from the earliest moments of motherhood (Sutherland, 2010) and even over childbirth (Beck, 2004: 28–35) and infant feeding (Thomson *et al.*, 2015). Mothers who intended to breastfeed but are unable to do so are particularly vulnerable to shame and postnatal depression (Borra *et al.*, 2015). Thus, judgements and criticism of parenting can occur right from the moment we become parents and continue throughout parenting. In a one-year longitudinal study, Tang *et al.* (2016) surveyed 79 first-time parents and their children aged 8 months to 13 months. They found that parental self-criticism and dependency (parents' maladaptive needs to be loved and cared for and their fears of abandonment that inhibit their developing feelings of autonomy and identity) were associated with increased levels of relationship stress, which, in turn, negatively affected the child's development.

Research has found that parental concerns over child behaviour do not reflect clinical assessments of child behaviour (Sanders *et al.*, 2014), suggesting that parents are potentially more concerned over their own reputation as a good parent – depending on whether the child misbehaves – than they are over whether their child has clinical problems. More worrying is the possibility that parents are unaware of typical child behaviour, thus interpreting typical behaviour as problematic. For example, a recent report in the US of 2,200 parents found that 36 per cent of parents reported that children under the age of 2 years should have enough self-control to resist something forbidden, even though they know that this does not develop until age 3½–4 years. Moreover, 42 per cent of parents believe their children should be able to regulate their own emotions before the age of 2 (Zero to Three, 2016).

The complexities of shame

Shame is a complex, multifaceted experience that can involve emotions of anger, anxiety or disgust, various behaviours such as anger or withdrawal and a range of physiological effects that focus attention in different ways (Gilbert, 1998, 2007). 'External shame' relates to experiences in which we attend to the minds of others and believe they are in some way looking down on us; we are diminished in the minds of others. Thus, we are likely to perform acts of reparation and prevention to change their view of us.

'Internal shame' arises when our attention is focused on the self and we are preoccupied with our own negative self-evaluations. Here, acts of reparation and prevention are undergone so as to feel better in our own eyes. A third dimension is 'reflected shame', when others with whom we are associated bring shame to us (a child convicted of crimes, for instance), and we can bring shame to others too (Gilbert *et al.*, 2007). Individuals in certain cultures are less focused on individual shame but fear bringing shame and dishonour on their families and communities (Gilbert *et al.*, 2007).

All these forms of shame can texture our efforts at parenting. If shame becomes chronic, it can impact on individuals' attention-sensitivity responses to events, in that they are sensitive to social-putdown cues and have primed rapidly activated defences. This can impact negatively on their interpersonal functioning and relationships (Lewis, 1971; Tangney *et al.*, 1992; Tracy *et al.*, 2007).

In their cross-sectional survey of 198 parenting dyads, Mills *et al.* (2007) found that parents' proneness to shame was associated with psychologically controlling styles of parenting. The results linked shame with negative parental approaches towards the child as well as overprotective styles of parenting, suggesting a potential link between vulnerability and parental shame, as well as critical/rejecting and controlling parenting styles. Psychological control is a dysfunctional parenting style in which the boundary between child and parent is blurred and the parent fails to identify their child as a unique individual (Barber and Harmon, 2002: 15–52). Psychologically controlling 'tiger' parents are prone to see the child as a reflection of themselves, thus resulting in either parental pride in what the child achieves or shame about what the child fails to do well.

We have seen that external shame can trigger defensive behaviours, which may have adverse effects in a parenting context (Carona *et al.*, 2017). Scarnier *et al.* (2009) found that, in the absence of an actual observer, the mere perception of there being a critical spectator was enough to arouse parental shame. Additionally, they found that parental shame predicted mothers' preference for using corporal punishment and reduced maternal warmth, and was associated with greater efforts to distance themselves from negative child behaviour.

Matos and Pinto-Gouveia (2014) examined the impact of being shamed by a parent (compared to other figures such as teachers and peers) on depressive symptoms. In their study, they interviewed 230 adult participants from the general community and asked them to complete a shame experiences interview, which focused on that person's experiences of shame in childhood and adolescence. Results from their analyses indicated that shame memories related to the attachment figures of mother and father significantly predicted internal shame, as did shame memories related to being criticized by the caregiver. Shame memories from teachers or peers were more predictive of external shame, however. Importantly, the shame memories from attachment figures significantly predicted higher depressive symptoms than shame memories deriving from teachers or peers. The authors concluded that individuals who recall shame experiences where the self was shamed by a loved one were the ones who were generally most depressed.

Compassion and shame

While shame is derived from competitive motivation and focuses on self in arenas such as social judgement, caring motivation evolved for entirely different reasons and by very different psychological and physiological regulating processes. Shame stimulates the threat system and may close down the frontal cortex to prioritize defences (Dickerson and Kemeny, 2004). One evolutionary path of caring was the caring protection of offspring and the creation of a secure base and safe haven for them (Cassidy and Shaver, 2016). Physiologically, caring stimulates a range of systems that down-regulate threat-processing and facilitate the frontal cortex and vagus (for a review, see Seppälä *et al.*, 2017). Expressing and receiving compassion are powerful antidotes to shame, partly because of compassion's physiological effect and also because it provides an experience of being accepted, cared for and cared about (Gilbert, 2011).

However, shame may cut people off from seeking out compassionate others lest they be rejected if they get too close. It may also hinder them from being compassionate to themselves. Gilbert and colleagues found that fears of compassion are strongly linked with self-criticism, which is a form of inner shaming (2011). Consequently, there are a plethora of fears, blocks and resistances to compassion (Gilbert and Mascaro, 2017). Shame in the parenting role may inhibit some people's capacity for being open to compassion from others and to self. If this is the case, it may constitute yet a further dimension in which parents in competitive contexts can feel more isolated and more inhibited about turning to others for help or being compassionate towards themselves.

Compassion-focused parenting

It is vital that parents provide a safe and supportive environment for their children and are sensitive to the child's needs and distress, responding appropriately. The parent is typically the only source of need-fulfilment and emotion- and distress-regulation for very young children, as they are vulnerable and lack the required competencies to meet those needs themselves (Siegel and Bryson, 2011; Swain and Ho, 2016). Therefore, the numerous motives and competencies that underpin compassion are crucial to the provision of safe, predictable and secure environments for children.

Compassion can be defined as 'a sensitivity to suffering in self and others, with a commitment to alleviate and prevent it' (Gilbert, 2014: 19). Prevention of suffering is an important component of compassionate motivation. A parent who is not empathetically sensitive to the needs of their children may cause them much suffering. There can, for example, potentially be neurological damage to the developing brain of babies who are routinely left to cry alone (Bugental *et al.*, 2003; Schore, 1997); and unfed children are in danger of starving through parental neglect.

Compassion involves, first, having the sensitivity and awareness to detect a signal of suffering, and second, having a signal responsiveness to suffering and acting accordingly to alleviate and prevent it. Thus, compassion will require certain important competencies, such as the ability to *pay attention*; being emotionally moved by distress calls – that is, having *sympathy*; or having *empathy*, for example knowing that a certain type of crying might mean the baby is hungry. As children develop, compassion can mean knowing when to remove them from the source of their anxiety, and when to help them stay and cope with it (such as starting school). Thus, parents have to be able to *tolerate distress* and be *non-judgemental* – that is, non-condemning and non-critical (Gilbert, 2014; Siegel and Bryson, 2011).

Third, compassion requires action and skills. Providing parents with specific evidence-based parenting training can help them to understand and support the social, emotional and behavioural development of their children (Kirby, 2016). As we saw in Chapter 1.4, compassion moves in three directions: 1. giving compassion to others, such as friends and family members; 2. being open and responding to receiving compassion from others; and 3. self-compassion (Gilbert, 2014).

Compassion-focused parenting entails taking a CFT approach to understanding parenting motivations and behaviours. CFT, developed by Paul Gilbert over the last twenty years (see Gilbert, 2014, for review), draws on evolutionary psychology, attachment theory and applied psychology processes from neuroscience and social psychology. CFT focuses on two psychologies of compassion. The first psychology is a motivation to engage with suffering, and the second is focused on action – that is, acting specifically to help alleviate and prevent suffering. It emphasizes how the evolved brain was not developed 'perfectly' but rather has a host of complexities and trade-offs that can cause suffering (including shame, criticism, anxiety or depression). CFT emphasizes the *process* of how therapy is delivered, focusing on the fears, blocks and resistances people have to compassion, and utilizing physiological processes to help them embody change (such as body posture and vocal tone). CFT has been studied in several trials, and a systematic review conducted in 2014 included 14 evaluation studies (Leaviss and Uttley, 2015). The review concluded that CFT shows promise as an intervention for mood disorders, particularly for individuals who are very self-critical.

Importantly, compassion-focused parenting does not simply mean 'being nice' to your children; indeed, a compassion-focused parent will, for example, prevent a child from overeating or staying up too late despite the child's protests. Parenting children is seldom easy, and the parents can suffer self-doubt, stress and guilt about what to do in their role as caregivers (Haslam *et al.*, 2015; Kirby, 2017b). Thus, compassion-focused parenting requires parents to perform competencies and capacities that test their abilities, such as distress-tolerance. So it is in the interests of children that we help parents, by providing them with the skills, knowledge and confidence to adopt a style of parenting that is compassion-focused. This will help promote wellbeing in children and parents alike while preventing and alleviating suffering.

Parental investment

Fogel *et al.* (1986: 69–90) set out an influential framework for caring-nurturance and parental investment, which helps facilitate the attachment system. The framework defines five important capacities that are required: 1. *awareness* of the need to be nurturing; 2. *motivation* to nurture; 3. an *understanding* of what is needed to be nurturing; 4. the capacity to *express* nurturing feelings; and 5. having *feedback* systems. The latter capacity refers to the ability to change a behaviour depending on whether or not it has been successful (so if the new-born infant's crying is not soothed by touch or voice, the parent may need to try feeding the baby as it may be due to hunger).

This approach to caring and nurturing helps create the child's attachment system (Bowlby, 1969; Mikulincer and Shaver, 2017). Children search for attachment in three possible ways: *proximity-seeking* – the child desires to be close to the attachment figure – typically mum or dad; a *secure base* – the child needs a source of security and guidance so they can freely go out into the world, explore and develop confidence; and a *safe haven* – the child needs a source of comfort when distressed to help them regulate their emotions (Bowlby, 1969; Gilbert, 2010; Mikulincer and Shaver, 2017). The attachment system is critical to mammalian – and particularly to human – evolution, as affiliative emotions and relating to others (parents, family, friends and so on) are potentially most significant in regulating affect (Gilbert, 2014). Affiliative connection involves touch, facial expression and voice tone, among other signals (Goetz *et al.*, 2010; Porges, 2007).

Affect-regulation in compassion-focused parenting

Understanding emotional systems and affect-regulation is key to implementing compassion-focused parenting. Gilbert (2009) proposed that emotion-regulation occurs through three systems: threat (for example, self-protection or safety-seeking), drive (for example, achievement, incentive-focus and status), and soothing (for example, non-wanting, safeness and interpersonal connection) (see Figure 2.2). The aim of CFT is to enhance insight into how individuals automatically respond to threat in defensive ways, and how this can have negative and unintended consequences, such as maladaptive self-criticism (Carona *et al.*, 2017). At a deeper level, cognitive processes such as rumination, negativity bias and self-critical monitoring may reflect the human brain's evolutionary responses to threat (Matos *et al.*, 2018). By developing awareness of the tricky interplay between old-brain emotions and new-brain capacities, a context for self-compassion can be created (Gilbert, 2009). Accordingly, self-compassion has been linked to enhanced distress-tolerance, clinically significant reductions in psychopathology, reflective and flexible perspective-taking, prosocial behaviour directed towards the self and others, and better adjustment to significant life stressors, such as infertility or cancer (Mackintosh *et al.*, 2018; Macbeth and Gumley, 2012).

Compassion-focused parenting can be understood in terms of how parents increase conditions for the maturation of these three types of affective functioning, and how they can blend together and support each other (see Figure 2.2).

To date, this model of emotion-regulation has not been applied to the field of parenting (Kirby, 2016), despite the benefits that can be gained from understanding its functions. For example, children receive report cards from school indicating their level of performance compared to others in the class – which activates a competitive motive. If the child's performance is 'average' or 'slightly below average', they may feel anxious about showing the report to their parents.

Parents who are oriented towards a threat-based approach would probably respond by showing frustration and perhaps anger, in the hope that this will induce the child to study harder. This may well have the desired result: the child foregoes other activities, studies harder and achieves better grades the next term. This may give the student a short-term feeling of excitement and achievement, which is then reinforced by the parents.

However, a long-term view reveals a problem: the student realizes that, to continue receiving this reinforcement, they have to keep studying hard, lest their parents become upset with them again – thereby causing renewed threat-based anxiety. We see an interpersonal interaction between parent and child based on a cycle of threat-drive-threat, which is internalized by the child. Consequently, the child is learning to regulate their emotions through the two systems. When this is continued into adulthood, it can lead to perfectionism. As they strive for success, trapped between the threat system and the reward system, they may develop a sense of failure and become self-critical and unable to self-soothe or become their own safe space (Gilbert, 2014).

If children receive high levels of punitive parenting practices like smacking or worse maltreatment at home, they will operate from their threat-base, self-protect system, because they are scared of their parents. When their caregiver has been the activator of threat instead of soothing, children have conflicting motivation systems. This scenario has generated theories that children in families that practise punitive parenting and maltreatment develop a self-identity as the 'cause' of the problem and will self-blame because they believe they truly deserved such treatment (Gilbert, 2014). The question then becomes: 'To whom do children turn for affiliative connection and soothing when their parents hit them?' The more fortunate may be able to turn to another family member – a sibling or grandparent. Unfortunately, though, abused children are often left on their own, and such rejection reinforces their core belief that they are unworthy and unlovable. Moreover, threat can be activated from beyond the family home. Research by Horowitz *et al.* (2005) found that 50 per cent of children from inner cities in the US show symptoms of post-traumatic stress disorder due to their exposure to community-level stressors such as violence involving crime and weapons. So it is critical to determine what the environments in which children are being raised are like, as this has life-long impacts on their ability to regulate their affect and form attachments with others (Mikulincer and Shaver, 2017).

Supporting compassion-focused approaches to parenting

Importantly, evidence is emerging in parenting research that supports a compassion-focused approach. This is helpful for parents but also for the children. Both the cross-sectional survey design and experimental lab studies support this view, as do intervention evaluations of compassion-based approaches that help support parents.

Kirby *et al.* (2019) examined whether goal-orientation type predicted parenting style. Their research analysed two goal-orientations in particular: self-image goals (concerns about doing things wrong and being rejected) and compassionate goals (desires to be helpful), and whether they predicted psychologically controlling parenting (where parents control their children's thoughts and self-expression) or facilitative parenting that is warm and responsive. Their study of 151 mothers found that goal-orientation explained between 26 per cent and 40 per cent of the variance in parenting style, after factoring-in the impact of children's behavioural problems, the parents' mental health and confidence as parents. This finding is extremely important because it is – to my knowledge – the first research to indicate that shifting motivational or goal-orientation is a key pathway to modifying parenting style, whereas most parenting research takes children's behaviour to be predictive of parenting style (Sanders and Mazzuchelli, 2019).

Extending these findings, Kirby *et al.* (2019) examined the role that shame and compassion play in texturing parenting style. They predicted that parents with high levels of shame – who were rank-focused, self-image focused and feared compassion – would adopt psychologically controlling and dysfunctional parenting styles. The authors conducted an online survey of 333 parents of children aged 3–9 years. Results from hierarchical and standard linear regressions found support for their hypothesis that shame and fear of compassion explain significant variances in parenting style, with models predicting 24 per cent and 46 per cent of the variance, respectively. These findings support past research indicating that those who experience shame also find it difficult to experience compassion (Gilbert and Procter, 2006; Kirby *et al.*, 2019).

Kirby *et al.* followed with an experimental study in which 198 mothers were randomly assigned to assuming a compassion condition, a self-image condition or a control condition (Kirby *et al.*, 2019). The mothers were presented with stressful child scenarios, such as a temper-tantrum at the shops, and asked to follow either self-image instructions (*We try to get our children to do things our way because we know what is best for them*) or compassionate instructions (*We all face challenges and setbacks and disappointments. Try not to be too hard on yourself*). The authors predicted that the compassionate goals would reduce the negative emotional reactions more than the self-image goals. However, no differences were found between the conditions. The authors concluded that brief instructions are not enough to shift parental reactions when faced with difficult child behaviour scenarios but that parents need to have greater intervention and support.

In a brief intervention study conducted in 2018, Kirby and Baldwin studied the impact of a 15-minute loving-kindness meditation (LKM) in helping to improve parental reactions to difficult child behaviour. The study focused on parents of children aged 2–12 (Kirby and Baldwin, 2018). LKM entails repeating short phrases such as 'May you be safe, may you be peaceful' to oneself and others. A meta-analysis has found that LKM has a significant moderate effect on raising compassion and self-compassion levels and reducing depression (Galante *et al.*, 2014; Hoffman *et al.*, 2011).

In their 2018 study, Kirby and Baldwin randomly assigned 61 parents to watch either a 15-minute guided audio based on LKM versus a focused imagery (FI) exercise. The authors found that this brief intervention was enough to alter parents' emotional reactions: in the LKM condition, the parents felt calmer and more sympathetic towards their children, and less frustrated and angry. Moreover, LKM improved the parents' levels of self-compassion motivations compared to the FI condition. This study provided the initial evidence for the benefits of using LKM in a parenting context.

Finally, an intervention study on the feasibility and acceptability of a brief self-compassion intervention for mothers of infants was designed to support the transition to motherhood (Mitchell *et al.*, 2018). This transition can be challenging, especially when the experience does not go as expected and leaves mothers feeling guilty, ashamed or distressed. They may, for example, experience a difficult and traumatic birth (Soet *et al.*, 2003) or have difficulty with breastfeeding attachment (Hall *et al.*, 2014). Brief online resources were developed and evaluated, informed by CFT, including two videos on self-compassion meditation and a 'handy tips' sheet.

Overall, 262 mothers were recruited for the intervention, and results were examined before and after, as there was no control comparison (one of the limitations of the study). It was found that the intervention significantly increased self-compassion, reduced post-traumatic symptoms, improved the mothers' breastfeeding experience and increased the infants' satisfaction. However, the intervention had no effect on the level of shame experienced. Clearly, shame is embedded and multifaceted, and a longer intervention would probably be needed to help mothers with their shame.

Parenting to raise children's levels of compassion

An important reason to include the compassion-focused approach in evidence-based parenting programmes is to raise compassionate children. Research has documented that children with empathic parents show greater empathy themselves (Eisenberg *et al.*, 1991). In contrast, the Making Caring Common Project at Harvard University found that 80 per cent of the 10,000 adolescents they surveyed across the US said that 'achievement or happiness' is their top priority, while only 20 per cent said that their top priority was 'caring for others' (Making Caring Common, Harvard, 2014). Moreover, this study found that youths were three times more likely to agree than disagree with the statement: 'My parents are prouder if I get good grades than if I'm a caring community member'. Clearly, there is an important role for parenting interventions that encourage compassion and caring behaviour among young people, as well as a need to develop, apply and evaluate school-based educational programmes dealing with compassion.

Conclusion

The advances made towards understanding how the brain functions and the emphasis on understanding evolved caring motivational systems and affiliative emotion-processing promise the next generation of evidence-based parenting programmes an exciting future. Compassion-focused parenting has the potential to help de-stigmatize and de-shame parenting experiences and support parents in the rewarding though challenging experience of raising children. We have reason to hope that compassion-focused parenting will raise compassionate children. Summarizing, Paul Gilbert provides a poignant insight into why the area of compassion-focused parenting is so important:

> It is quite extraordinary that, given what we know about how early lives effect brain maturation and even genetic expression, we have such limited resources dedicated to the desire for 'every child to grow-up in a compassionate environment'. This failure to grasp the size and nature of the problem, of 'how children around the world are raised in appalling conditions', is probably humanity's greatest compassion failure! (Gilbert, 2014: 28)

Acknowledgement

I am grateful to Oxford University Press for permission to quote from my chapter, 'Compassion-Focused Parenting', which appeared in *The Handbook of Compassion Science* (OUP, 2017). Reproduced with permission of the Licensor through PLSclear.

Building whole-school compassionate approaches to mental health and wellbeing

Rohesia Coles

World in mental health crisis of 'monumental suffering', say experts.
(Boseley, *The Guardian*, 2018)

Abstract: This chapter examines the alarming statistics related to the mental health crisis and analyses the nature of adverse childhood experiences (ACEs), their links to mental health disorders and the impact on children and their families. It encompasses young people from 0–19 years old – the learners. From both individual and whole-school perspectives, it explores what could be done to adopt a more compassionate and trauma-informed approach to learning.

UK statistics

Let's begin with the alarming statistics. Using the International Statistical Classification of Diseases and Related Health Problems (ICD) to identify mental health disorders, the National Health Service (NHS) digitally compiled statistics from across the UK related to young people (aged 2–19) with a mental health disorder (2017). The NHS reported a significant increase in mental health issues as young people developed; by the age of 19, a staggering one in six were diagnosed as having such a disorder, most of them girls. Contributing factors that increase the likelihood of developing a mental disorder included socio-economic status, living with a parent who has poor mental health, reduced social support, small networks, and not participating in clubs, in or out of school.

In addition, nearly 60 per cent of 11–19-year-olds with a disorder had been bullied and 41.5 per cent had been cyberbullied. They were more likely to have tried tobacco, e-cigarettes and alcohol, with one in four 11–16-year-olds having self-harmed or attempted suicide. Rates of school exclusion continue along the same lines, with 6.8 per cent of excluded pupils having had a mental health disorder.

In England, even those learners who have been recognized as having special educational needs do not necessarily receive a statutory Education Health Care (EHC) Plan that would identify their educational, health and social needs and set out any additional support required. Just under half of those who have been diagnosed receive support. Even then, the data showed that the support that was received was limited, only 66.4 per cent receiving some form of professional support (from teachers or mental health workers). For the remainder, any support was informal (from family and friends). One in four reported that they had neither formal nor informal support in relation to their worries about their mental health, despite having had a diagnosis.

Although this data related to 2017 and is UK-specific, it gives a glimpse of the significant rise in diagnosed mental health disorders, showing that the support does not match the needs. This suggests a lack of resources, services, knowledge or confidence. Accordingly, we explore here some ways schools can build an ethos to support the maintenance of good mental health. Whether this is the term we use or we prefer 'emotional health' or simply 'wellbeing', just like our physical health it fluctuates in line with the circumstances affecting us at a certain time. Good mental health enhances our ability to cope with life and enables meaningful functioning and participation in play, work, school and all our activities (MentalHealth. org, 2019).

Mental health difficulties can arise from worries about starting school, friendships breaking down, being trolled on social media, losing a family member or the mental ill-health of a parent. Any deterioration might manifest itself in changes in behaviour, such as being more withdrawn, falling out with peers, missing school, becoming less engaged in learning, being seen as more disruptive, being tearful or self-harming. Whatever the cause, early identification of deterioration in the mental health of a student is crucial to addressing their needs. Sometimes the deterioration is less obvious, but there are ways to support learners to express their needs, which professionals can then address individually and at whole-school level. Recently, we have come to realize that many of the problems students present stem from their adverse childhood experiences.

Defining adverse childhood experiences

The term 'adverse childhood experiences' (ACEs), now widely employed, emanates from a study in the US that examined the causes of health problems in young adults. This survey found that encountering adversity in childhood can have a long-term negative impact on health and wellbeing and increase the risk of vulnerability (Barton *et al.*, 2015). Further international studies have shown that people who have numerous ACEs can be at greater risk of mental illness, being incarcerated, developing health-harming behaviours such as smoking and using drugs, and poor physical health. Those living in areas of deprivation risk experiencing more ACEs (Health Scotland). Health Scotland describes ACEs as 'stressful events occurring in childhood', including:

- domestic violence
- parental abandonment through separation or divorce
- a parent with a mental health condition
- being the victim of abuse (physical, sexual and/or emotional)
- being the victim of neglect (physical and emotional)
- having a member of the household in prison
- growing up in a household with adults who experience substance misuse.

The implications of ACEs

Children with a high number of ACEs are constantly on edge, their brains and bodies in a continual state of high alert, in a readied 'flight or fight' response state that is often triggered by small perceived threats (Barton *et al.*, 2016). Research has shown that children with ACEs display hypervigilance, aggression and problems with attention, decision-making and impulsivity (Brunzell *et al.*, 2015).

When children are exposed to adverse and stressful experiences, it can have a long-lasting impact on their ability to think and learn and to interact with others. The educators and professionals who understand the nature of ACEs can devise appropriate individual, community, organizational and societal responses and develop strategies for mitigating adversity and building students' resilience (de Caestecker *et al.*, 2017).

Dr Bruce Perry, American psychiatrist and senior fellow of the Child Trauma Academy, explained on *Explore Health* that the susceptibility and malleability of the brain allow external experiences to impact on it, especially if they are exceedingly traumatic. Perry believes these can be counterbalanced by connections with positive experiences and exposure to trusted adults. Further, he maintains that a degree of stress that's predictable can be good for us, as it can be an intrinsic motivator to do better. He describes how, if we recognize the negative experiences that occur throughout life, we can offset them by developing resilience to them. This is not, however, 'a predictor of the future', and we must ensure that support is offered according to each individual's needs.

If we help the learner to understand the important impact ACEs can have, we can offer a service that is both 'trauma-informed' and compassionate (de Caestecker *et al.*, 2017). Prevention and early identification constitute the crucial foundation for multi-service creativity that delivers a holistic and systemic foundation on which to build resilience. But ACEs should only help inform our support and intervention; we must not allow them to define the trajectory of a learner's life.

We must take into account positive childhood experiences, such as the presence of a trusted adult, and positive risk factors. If we can develop self-regulation in ourselves, we can support self-regulation in our learners. Self-regulation, like self-compassion, nourishes the capacity to be with the discomfort when the environment allows us to be in a safe place, so discomfort doesn't drive our behaviour. Dr Gabor Maté (ACE-Aware Scotland, 2019) points out that we will inevitably experience feelings of discomfort, pain and fear at times throughout our lives. Those experiences do not define us; but, how we regulate (or are taught to regulate) them supports resilience and the trajectory towards adulthood. We have to ensure that we don't see mental health as a single factor but look also at a person's physical health, their social and economic environment and their relationships.

ACEs exacerbate problems that can, in turn, set up a perpetual vicious cycle. What can schools do to break that cycle? Schools do have remedial functional roles but these can seem almost impossible to fulfil because of professional workload and inadequate external support. Even acts of heroic personal compassion may be ineffective because of systemic failures. We need specific, school-based strategies that help address the issue.

The systemic school approach

Many learners find school an exciting but daunting place. Teachers struggle with the demands placed on them. In the current socio-economic climate, in which healthcare and education have been undermined by economic adversity, together with huge demands to perform, staff can be so close to burnout that they are stripped of self-compassion (Fotaki, 2015).

Compassion requires emotional engagement, human connection and a sense of reward, whereas burnout degrades these qualities (Maslach, 1981; Lown, 2015). To instil a compassionate ethos, its operation requires close scrutiny. Trauma-informed approaches and interventions may be effective. They will seek not only to improve learners' experiences and staff wellbeing, reduce burnout and improve mental health and wellbeing across the school, but also aim to create the safe and secure base that models the environment we adults want learners to emulate. There is growing evidence for a trauma-responsive approach, though it is yet to be specified in the National Institute of Clinical Excellence (NICE) guidance. From research and action, however, we can see the significant difference a trauma-responsive approach makes to learners, their families and professionals.

A number of trauma-responsive strategies are known that make school approaches trauma-informed and systemic. They are based on knowledge of ACEs, with prevention as the key. Here, we suggest strategies for learners, for school staff and for caregivers.

Strategies for learners aged 0–19

We know that babies in utero experience what mothers experience. Prenatal exposure to inappropriate levels of glucocorticoids (GCs) and maternal stress can have negative consequences for infant stress-regulation (Davies *et al.*, 2011). High levels of stress and traumas pre-birth and in early childhood significantly impact on cognitive development, emotional regulation and learning. The development of emotional regulation begins at birth. Many helpful techniques are now taught, including 'self-soothing', 'skin-to-skin', 'quiet time' and 'rewards', with caregivers seeking individualized advice from midwives, health visitors, communities and family members. If a child needs more specialist support, speech and language therapists, paediatricians and occupational therapists are there to advise.

Within schools, we need to teach young people new ways of communicating (Mental Health.org, 2015). Here are some suggested approaches:

- Look at developing emotional regulation strategies that are aimed at all age groups 0–19.
- Link in with Early Years providers to discover what help is available in the community for young people outside school hours, to continue supporting positive experiences.
- Send information home so caregivers know what sort of day children have had – such as by using 'trauma bears'. A child takes a teddy home from school to signal to the adults that they have had a hard day and should ask the child about it. The bears can also be used in the school, to signify that the child holding it needs a safe place.
- Devise approaches for working with young people and their families.
- Employ positive affirmations and positive statements to improve self-esteem.
- Provide a place for learners to have a voice.
- Engineer peer-support arrangements.

- Devise alternative communication forms to let caregivers know that the child wants to talk – such as a colour card on a desk, a worry tree, or a chart for Post-it notes.
- Design 'Who am I?' passports that ask questions like: What helps me regulate? What are my triggers? What's in my self-compassion kit?
- Encourage participation in clubs both in and out of school.

Strategies for all staff (domestic workers, teachers, teaching assistants, headteachers and governors)

With recent cuts in funding, there are fewer staff within education and across health and local authority services in England. As a result, teaching staff have had to assume the roles of pastoral worker, social worker, health care professional, caregiver and so on. Teachers work long hours, and 'holiday' breaks are a myth: they continue to prepare for the following term. Staff must therefore be encouraged to look after themselves and develop their self-compassion. Research shows that focusing on self-care significantly reduces stress and increases self-efficacy (Nelsen and Gfroerer, n.d.). The many individual self-care activities include: mindfulness, sleep, eating well, physical activity, engaging in positive and enjoyable activities and talking with people one trusts.

Weare concludes that developing mindfulness for school staff has 'the capacity to improve staff occupational wellbeing and job satisfaction, improve performance, and reduce … wasted expenditure' (Weare, 2014: 18). If, as professionals, we are less emotionally overloaded, we will have more capacity to support students and respond with a compassionate mind and manner: we become the reliable, predictable, trusted adults who protect them. Every member of the school staff is an integral part of its system, from the headteacher who sets the ethos, to the lunchtime supervisors. Every experience a child has with these adults will become a memory, so training all staff in how to respond to ACEs and in self-care and compassion becomes part of a whole-school ethos, not just a specialist area.

In many cases, the behaviours that cause problems in the classroom or at home are a child's failure to communicate something important to them. Fill self-compassion boxes with such items as ear defenders, fidget toys, stress balls, wobble cushions, pop-up tents … and provide teddies or cushions to cuddle and blankets to snuggle in. Each child could have their own box, or packs could be made up and available for all. Safe spaces are needed: a zone where young people can self-regulate and feel safe until they're ready to communicate and ready for adults to intervene.

Incidents will occur during free time, breaks and lunchtimes. Yet, how often do we share the strategies with the staff in the dining room that little 'Jimmy', who hates loud noises due to living in a household of domestic violence, needs to eat his lunch with a smaller, quieter group so he can regulate? How often do we walk into environments where everyone is shouting and bells are going off ... yet, we struggle to comprehend why children are more emotionally deregulated and non-compliant, running off or throwing chairs? Think about how important having a hot meal is for the child whose caregiver at home has a terminal illness. By being more trauma-aware, we can become more compassionate. A whole-school approach that includes everyone, from the governors to the caretaker, becomes the norm and doesn't single-out one child. Look at the school's discipline policies and make them more compassionate by adopting, for instance, restorative practices.

Offering debriefs to staff after an incident or offering peer reflection when discussing situations – with outside professional help, if required – are models of shared learning and best practice. Does the school have regular access to staff counsellors or mentors? How often are these accessed? Here are a few suggested approaches:

- Hold whole-school training on mindfulness, ensuring sufficient space and time.
- Undertake whole-school training on ACEs and trauma-informed approaches.
- Have regular debriefs for all staff following incidents.
- Encourage regular reflective practice for all staff, inviting in other professionals such as educational psychologists and child and adolescent mental health staff.
- Ensure school staff counsellors are on-site at regular times and dates.
- Link up new staff with a mentor or buddy.
- Encourage self-care activities such as mindfulness.
- Look at alternative creative environments and develop safe spaces.
- Become the positive, trusted adult by being consistent and dependable.

Strategies for parents and caregivers

In the case of families that have been through numerous traumas, their relationship with educational providers may break down time after time. And we know that a child may present quite different behaviours in different environments. For example, a child who's been in numerous placements and doesn't want to be rejected by yet another adult may appear to follow the school rules, their instinct for survival overriding all else. But that same survival instinct may dictate different behaviours when they go home. A child who lives in an environment where they are exposed to high levels of verbal aggression between adults, even if it's only heard and not seen, lives in a state of deep anxiety, may struggle to concentrate or react quickly to criticism. How do we know what goes on in a learner's home so we can relate it to their ability to access learning that day? How well did they sleep? Have they had breakfast?

The current socio-economic climate in England is worsening year on year. More families require support from food banks, caregivers have numerous jobs, and parents may have poor mental health. School may be the only safe place where the students can talk about how they feel; the place where they can offload. The behaviours they exhibit, however, might not be prescriptive or what one might expect: grief may manifest itself as aggression, and abuse may cause addiction. Professionals must remain unbiased and non-judgemental, ensuring that their own assumptions of trauma and predicted responses don't influence the support they offer. If learners are in survival mode, we will see it through their behaviours. That they have a safe and stable base at school is a privilege that we, as professionals, must not take for granted. We must support the caregivers and adults in their parenting role (as they too may be experiencing, or have experienced, difficulties), and focus on the children's experiences (de Caestecker *et al.*, 2017).

Schools need to develop strategies that work with the family of each learner. There must be an identified Passport of Care that records what works for them, focusing on the positives. The Passport should identify who the learner is, things they like, what helps when they get distressed and who their trusted adult is. Traumas happen to everyone throughout their lives, so why do we wait until they arise before we put support in place? It has become the norm to be reactive. Let's strive for schools to be consistently supportive and compassionate, even when children's behaviour is challenging. Helping a learner to identify that they've had a tough morning even before they got to school will help them become reflective and to self-regulate. Such an approach can help them develop into compassionate and self-regulated adults. But first, we, the adults, must model the process. Here are a few suggested approaches:

- Encourage caregivers to meet in designated support groups at coffee mornings or after-school clubs.

- Offer caregiver training around issues like sleep hygiene, physical activity, cyber-safety and good mental health as part of a regular programme for people to access online or in person.
- Link with services such as Family Support to extinguish any stigma about social care and the perception that it's about 'taking children away'.
- Publicize parenting programmes such as Triple P, the Solihull Approach, or Non-Violence Resistance.
- Identify the needs of the community and then, if possible, resource the work in a multi-service, multi-dimensional way.
- Ensure that caregivers have access to mental health services – voluntary, self-referred, crisis services, helplines and so on
- Develop a Passport of Care: 'Who am I?'

Good practice

Worldwide, there are many examples of good practice. Here are just some that have influenced policies and helped services become more compassionate.

England

A Government green paper, *Transforming Children and Young People's Mental Health* (2017), proposed three objectives:

1. to incentivize and support all schools and colleges to identify and train a Designated Senior Lead for mental health
2. to fund new Mental Health Support Teams, to be supervised by NHS staff working in children and young people's mental health
3. to pilot a waiting time of no more than four weeks for access to specialist NHS services in mental health for children and young people.

A number of Mental Health Support Teams, jointly delivered with the DfE and NHS England, have been commissioned across England to secure faster access to mental health care. This focuses on early intervention and emotional wellbeing to provide a whole-school approach where the team acts as a link to the staff, young people and services supervised by NHS teams. The intention is to ensure that further implementation should be flexible and not add to teachers' workloads or put pressure on school funding. The ethos must remain that prevention is the key, that early identification is paramount and that all staff are trained to support learners.

In Birmingham, STICK (screening, training, intervention, consultation and knowledge) is an initiative that presents a new approach to prevention, early identification and early intervention that has been designed specifically to improve opportunities for engagement with children, young people and families in delivering mental health support. The STICK team are co-delivering and co-designing a service with Birmingham Children's Trust (Social Care) and several partners are establishing infrastructures to share skills and knowledge and improve communication and trust between key system partners to ensure cohesive delivery of quality care.

Scotland

The Scottish Government made a commitment to addressing ACEs in its Programme for Government in 2017/18 and 2018/19, building on existing commitments to progressing children's rights and the national approach to 'Getting it Right for Every Child'. The Compassionate and Connected Classroom (2019) is an excellent curricular resource published by Education Scotland.

The United States

The Compassionate Schools Project (2020) has developed a programme of lessons that 'integrate social and emotional learning, deep self-understanding, stress resiliency skills, mental fitness training, physical regulation and exercise, and nutrition education within a contemplative and compassionate framework' (see the website: www.compassionschools.org/ program). And the neurosequential model in education is available to help educators understand student behaviours and performance.

Conclusion

This chapter has attempted to outline the long-term impact of ACEs that schools need to address. It sets out a range of strategies particular to each person and group working in a school, and to caregivers. Multi-agency working is essential if schools are not to carry the burdens alone. Lastly, we must actively resist re-traumatizing learners and not punish them for behaviours that result from their adverse childhood experiences.

Section Four

Compassion for Place
(and Community)

4

4.1

Compassion in the 'second city': Made in Birmingham, England

Colin Diamond

Abstract: This chapter is about the importance of place and how professional commitment to one place – Birmingham, England – can be the driver for creativity which transforms young people's lives in the city and beyond. It tells the story of the rollercoaster journey this city's schools have been on, from the halcyon days of the 1990s when Birmingham was the inspiration for other cities, to the distressing 'Trojan Horse' episode in 2014. The story ends with the city's subsequent recovery; compassion for the city and its children runs through it. The narrative reveals how much social capital (Allan *et al.*, 2012) can be created and stored in a city's emotional bank account (Covey, 1989) when compassion is fully harnessed and aligned. Conversely, when that account was allowed to run dangerously low and raided by those pursuing their own narrow agendas, the impact on the whole community was catastrophic. Yet, this narrative ends positively. The social forces of love and compassion for the city regrouped, drawing inspiration from both long-standing and new educational initiatives.

Birmingham: Fact check

According to figures from 2018, Birmingham has a population of 1.14 million, projected to grow to 1.31 million in 2039. It is the most deprived local authority area in the West Midlands, and the sixth most-deprived in England. Forty-one per cent of the population and 50 per cent of the children live in the most deprived decile. More than one in three children live in poverty, with Ladywood constituency having the third-highest level of poverty in the UK and Sutton Coldfield the 15th-lowest (Birmingham City Council, 2018). Birmingham is super diverse: people from nearly two hundred countries have made their homes in the city. The 2011 Census revealed that 42.1 per cent of the population classify themselves as within an ethnic group other than white British, compared to 30 per cent in 2001. Over 60 per cent of the under-18 population were from a non-white

British background in 2011 compared to 44 per cent in 2001. The largest ethnic groups of young people are Asian (with British Pakistanis being the largest Asian group), white British, black and mixed-race (Birmingham City Council, 2011).

There were approximately 450 state schools and approximately fifty independent schools in the city in 2018. Precise numbers cannot be provided as the number and status of state schools frequently change within the school year, and independent schools are opening and closing frequently. In 2017, there were 205,867 pupils in schools, and 82 per cent of state schools were rated 'good' or 'outstanding' (Birmingham City Council, 2017–18).

A passionate and compassionate city: An incubator for education excellence

Birmingham has been at the forefront of educational development for many years, with several instances of intellectual and innovatory brilliance. From the days of the Lunar Society in the late eighteenth century when Birmingham was the world's equivalent of Silicon Valley, through to being recognized as the best local education authority in England at the turn of the twenty-first century, the importance of place and identity has shone through. When Forster's Elementary Education Act was passed in 1870, Birmingham was at the vanguard of establishing school boards and opened schools for children aged 5 to 13 (Stephens, 1998).

Joseph Chamberlain, who was already working to establish free primary education for children in Birmingham ahead of the 1870 Act, became a city councillor in 1869. By 1873, he had become the city's mayor and embarked on a massive programme to provide civic amenities, including more schools, libraries and parks. In 1900, the University of Birmingham became England's first civic, 'redbrick' university where students from all religions and backgrounds were accepted on an equal basis. Chamberlain was its first chancellor. Today, as the metropolis has begun its post-manufacturing regeneration symbolized by its stunning civic plaza and preparation for the high-speed railway HS2, visitors are surprised by the quality and vibrancy they find. It's come a long way from Tolkien's inspiration for Mordor – the vistas of a smoky, black hell that he saw growing up in Birmingham in the 1930s.

This is the setting in which we explore how, following a period of educational decline and trauma in the 2000s, the city has drawn on its own resources to recover educational pride and identity. Birmingham's educational social capital had been allowed to drain away and was then tarnished by the Trojan Horse affair in 2014. If allowed to drift further, this could have resulted in complete fragmentation into micro education communities with no unifying sense of place or creative collaboration. Indeed, that would have been the logical outcome of the prevailing English national education policy, which emphasizes schools' autonomy and shrinks the role of local authorities (Early and Greany, 2017).

From triumph to tragedy in 12 years: Neglect of social capital and its consequences

'We educate Birmingham children', I heard it said many times by headteachers back in 2014. It resonates still because of its unqualified generosity and inclusiveness at a time when Birmingham's education system was in crisis. Despite all that was happening, the headteachers' loyalty to, and compassion for, children across the city shone through. They wanted to find positive ways forward after the Trojan Horse affair brought national shame to the city's schools and Birmingham City Council. This damaging episode was a symptom of how the Council's custodianship of its schools had deteriorated from being recognized as outstanding under the leadership of Chief Education Officer Professor Tim Brighouse (Ofsted, 2002) to being placed in formal intervention by the DfE (DfE, 2014).

The 12 years between 2002 and 2014 had witnessed many changes in national education policy, the reduction in power of local government and the arrival of austerity in 2009 (Early and Greany, 2017). These developments seriously reduced the role and influence of all English local education authorities. For many cities, Birmingham included, the pressures of budget reductions, the national policy emphasis on school autonomy and the challenge of providing social care for poor children downgraded education, rendering it no longer a local priority. In Birmingham's case, the urgent need to improve the quality of children's social care became the number one priority when the Annual Performance Assessment judged it 'inadequate' in 2008 (CSCI and Ofsted, 2008). Yet, to judge by the accolades received, education in the city was in rude health:

> In 1998, OFSTED reported that Birmingham was a very well run LEA [local education authority]. It is now clear that it is much more than that. It is one of a very small number of LEAs which stand as an example to all others of what can be done, even in the most demanding urban environments. (Ofsted, 2002: 5)

In the last decade of the twentieth century, the collective power of schools had been galvanized by the inspirational leadership of the local education authority's senior officers. Initiatives flourished, successes were celebrated and standards rose as a result of innovative, transformational approaches that brought schools together in new 'families' with similar socio-economic characteristics (Brighouse and Woods, 2013). That era produced a generation of school leaders who had self-belief because they knew their contribution was valued by the city and celebrated nationally. This was only possible because the leaders respected and harnessed the power of place and generated social capital.

The legacy from this period can be divided into national and local influences. Nationally, the London Challenge, with Professors Tim Brighouse and David Woods as its architects, deployed school improvement strategies developed in Birmingham and adapted them for the capital with great success. Estelle Morris, Secretary of State for Education and Skills, and Member of Parliament for Yardley, had seen first-hand how schools in Birmingham had been improved, and invited Tim Brighouse to become the London Challenge's Chief Adviser. This model, in turn, was the template for other challenge areas set up by the DfE. The UFA, founded by Tim Brighouse, engaged with a wide range of adults including teachers, parents, carers and community organizations. Based on change theory, the UFA trained them to offer extra-curricular activities as a way of closing the achievement gap between young people from disadvantaged and affluent backgrounds.

But, by then, education as a priority was overtaken by the focus on children's social care, and implementation of the Children Act 2004 prevailed. Welding together an 'outstanding' education service with an 'inadequate' children's social care service in the largest urban authority in England was always going to be a challenge. The result was that, for many years, school leaders carried the torch themselves as the council no longer had the resources to shape the city's educational provision, whereas headteachers knew what best practice looked like and how to continue its traditions. Birmingham City Council was hit by austerity in 2009 and wound down its education services while ramping up investment in children's social care.

By 2014, spending on school improvement was reduced to less than £1 million per annum. The number of academies and free schools increased quickly after the implementation of the Academies Act 2010. The strongest-performing schools were allowed to convert to academy status and given considerable financial inducements to do so in the early years of the academies programme. The weaker-performing schools were either persuaded or compelled to join a multi-academy trust. The fragmentation of a formerly united civic education system was driven through in the name of neoliberal education policy with no regard whatsoever for the wider social consequences.

In response to the atrophy of local authority influence and the creation of so many semi-autonomous academies and free schools, Birmingham headteachers joined forces and formed the Birmingham Education Partnership (BEP) in 2013 with the aim of harnessing their collective strengths and supporting partnership-working. It had explicit encouragement from the City Council, which recognized its limited capacity and role in the education- and local government-policy landscapes. The BEP describes its core mission thus: 'Recognising that it takes a whole city to raise a child and that schools need to be rooted in locality, BEP champions are working with all those who support and develop Birmingham's young people' (BEP website, https://bep.education/about). With around 450 state schools in the city, the Partnership clearly had the potential to pick up where the council had left off.

The Trojan Horse

It was against this complex background that the activities subsequently known as Trojan Horse gathered momentum. Trojan Horse has been summarized as a 'co-ordinated, deliberate and sustained action ... to introduce an intolerant and aggressive Islamic ethos' into schools with a majority Muslim student population in Birmingham (Clarke, 2014: 14). The much-publicized Trojan Horse letter (purportedly sent to the council by an anonymous whistle-blower) set out a five-step plan that would allegedly ensure schools were run on Islamic principles. Analysis of the Trojan Horse affair is, still, a hotly contested narrative. It has generated more heat than light.

Some claim the letter was a hoax that precipitated a disproportionate response from the government (Holmwood and O'Toole, 2018). Ofsted inspections ordered by Michael Gove in 2014 led to the three schools within the Park View Education Trust (Park View, Nansen and Golden Hillock) being placed in special measures, along with Oldknow Primary Academy and Saltley Secondary School. The school that attracted most attention was Park View as it had previously been rated 'outstanding' (Ofsted, 2012) and feted by Chief Inspector Sir Michael Wilshaw who said, 'all schools should be like this' (*Guardian*, 2014). It had also been allowed to convert to academy status by the DfE and establish the Park View Education Trust in 2012.

The damage caused to Birmingham cannot be overstated. Its fall from educational grace in 2002 to the humiliation of being under the DfE's direction and monitored by a commissioner was demoralizing. The city that the headteachers loved and in which they had worked tirelessly to transform children's lives was a national disgrace, and the social capital so hard-won in previous years had been squandered.

Why was this allowed to happen under the noses of Birmingham City Council's officers and politicians and go on for so long? Why did the warnings made by so many headteachers go unheeded? We know that schools and the education service had been allowed to drift. Kershaw reported that, operationally, there was 'no systematic approach to filtering intelligence or data about the conduct of schools or governing bodies' (2014: 12) and numerous complaints 'about the conduct of some governing bodies [had] gone without investigation or challenge' (ibid.).

At a deeper level, a culture had developed in which, in the name of a misguided version of community cohesion and a desire not to rock the political boat, there was no challenge of the unacceptable behaviour going on in some governing bodies. The leader of the council, Sir Albert Bore, admitted in July 2014, 'We have previously shied away from tackling this problem out of a misguided fear of being accused of racism' (*Birmingham Mail*, 2014).

The Birmingham Curriculum Statement: Moving forward – the recreation of social capital

Sir Mike Tomlinson, former Chief Inspector, was appointed Education Commissioner by the Secretary of State with the remit of getting the city's education back on track. Meanwhile, the council's school improvement duties were vested with the Birmingham Education Partnership and in September 2015 Birmingham City Council's contract with the BEP began. The BEP internally strengthened its governance, appointing Baroness Estelle Morris as chair and Tim Boyes, long-standing secondary headteacher in the city, as its chief executive. This move was hugely symbolic, investing in the Birmingham headteachers' own organization and shifting the centre of gravity away from the council to an education community-owned company.

An education improvement plan was needed to secure the basic elements of the council's duties back in place. These included school improvement, safeguarding and school governance. The broken lines of communications with schools needed to be restored. By January 2015, the improvement plan was approved by the Secretary of State for Education and the journey to rebuild relationships and trust had begun.

One feature of Trojan Horse had been pressure to narrow the curriculum and remove or reduce subjects that included sex education, mixed physical education, citizenship, music and the humanities. In the revived leadership role of the council, Birmingham's Cabinet Members for Children's Services, Cllr Brigid Jones, and Inclusion and Community Safety, Cllr James McKay, signed the Birmingham Curriculum Statement in September 2015. It stated unequivocally that, 'ALL children in Birmingham will experience a broad and balanced curriculum enabling them to grow and learn in an environment without prejudice or inequality' (Birmingham City Council, 2015: 1). It was explicit about the place of the arts, physical activities, music and social, moral, spiritual and cultural education. This simple statement, underpinned by a raft of educational legislation, provided crucial affirmation of the council's moral authority in education, and it has been used extensively by headteachers and governing bodies as the touchstone for curriculum planning. It was re-issued in 2019 (Birmingham City Council, 2019) to bring it up-to-date with legislation and to ensure it remains fit for purpose and takes account of the Relationships, Health and Sex Education that is compulsory in all schools in England as of 2020. The Birmingham Curriculum Statement was subsequently recognized as an example of good practice by the DfE.

Made in Birmingham

The formal DfE intervention ended in September 2016 and the education commissioner was stood down. The improvement journey had, in reality, just begun to address some long-standing weaknesses and underinvestment in education (Birmingham City Council Education Delivery and Improvement Plan 2017/18). In 2018, a headteacher conference celebrated all that is wholesome about values-driven, compassionate, inclusive education. It was a spiritual recharging of the educational batteries that was badly needed as the counterbalance to national education policy that continued to measure only what can be measured easily – test and examination scores – while ignoring pupils' wellbeing, skills to work together and participation in performing arts and sports. A raft of home-grown Birmingham education initiatives were celebrated that reflect the contributions of the long-established UFA and the newly created BEP.

The Compassionate Education (CoED) Foundation

The CoED Foundation was launched as a charity in the House of Lords in 2013, after its establishment as a limited company the year before. It was the brainchild of Maurice Irfan Coles, who had worked successfully in Birmingham since 1982 in a range of senior capacities, including leadership of Multi-Cultural Education, Governance, School

Improvement and Secondary Schools. Its unique contribution has been to re-harness Birmingham's intellectual powerhouse to create the paradigm of compassionate education at a time when national education policy was increasingly driven by utilitarianism, market forces and reductionist approaches to teaching and learning. Compassionate education is defined as love-in-action in schools: it stands out as a call to arms to re-balance the increasingly transactional, bureaucratic model of education that has emerged in response to the DfE's obsessions with tests, exams and inspections. By 2019, CoED had celebrated the publication of two books on compassionate education, received accolades at 15 education conferences, broadened its influence across Europe via the ERASMUS graphic novel project and had many articles published across a range of journals.

UNICEF's Rights Respecting Schools Award (RRSA)

In the aftermath of Trojan Horse, new guidance was issued to all English schools in 2015 on identifying and addressing extremism and radicalization. A new Prevent Duty was introduced across all public-sector institutions including schools (DfE, 2015). There had been long-standing concerns about the Prevent strategy since its inception in 2007, and a literal interpretation in Birmingham's schools – given the social tensions following Trojan Horse – would have exacerbated tensions. So, rather than introduce a perfunctory version of Prevent that would arguably be perceived as targeting mainly Muslim communities in the city, it was decided to focus on children's rights: a critical paradigm shift from preventing unacceptable behaviours to asserting universal entitlements, mirroring the best of school behaviour policies. And the UNICEF RRSA provided the perfect vehicle for this, with its universal values and set of rights to which all children are entitled. It provided a humanist language-set that was so greatly needed, through which children from nursery age upward could identify their place in the family, their community and the outside world. Since 2015, the RRSA has been adopted by over 250 schools in the city because they know that it works in their complex communities and is free of any stigma of association with the Prevent Duty. It also provides a language-set within which to discuss Fundamental British Values as expressed by the British Government in the Prevent strategy in 2011. Its impact has been evaluated by UNICEF UK and is shown to improve attendance, attitudes and outcomes. Most critically, it has become part of the city's educational lexicon and educational moral compass which join hands among all Birmingham's children.

'No Outsiders'

Progress towards full equality for lesbian, gay, bisexual and transgender (LGBT) people in Britain was abruptly halted in 1988 when the Thatcher government introduced Section 28 of the Local Government Act banning the 'promotion' of homosexuality by local authorities and schools. This meant that teachers were prohibited from discussing even the possibility of same-sex relationships with students. Councils were forbidden from stocking libraries with literature or films that contained gay or lesbian themes. As reported in *The Independent*, 'The pernicious influence of the clause unquestionably played a huge role in legitimising hate and reinforcing playground homophobia and bullying, demonising LGBT+ children' (Sommerlad, 2018).

The clause was finally repealed in Scotland in 2001 and in the rest of the UK in 2003. It was clear that homophobia and transphobia were causing damage in British schools and beyond, and the repeal of Section 28 paved the way for detailed research into what was happening in primary settings.

Birmingham City Council commissioned Educate and Celebrate, a charity that aimed to make schools and organizations LGBT+ friendly, to work with the city's schools. Its main teaching resource was entitled 'CHIPS' (Challenging Homophobia in Primary Schools), the acronym created by Educate and Celebrate and written by local school teacher Andy Moffat. It contained a range of books with positive LGBT role models. Moffat had learnt much from how CHIPS was received in the local schools he worked in and went on to write *No Outsiders in Our Schools: Teaching the Equality Act in Primary Schools* (Moffat, 2016). He stated in the introduction to that book: 'No longer should we separate LGBT education from education about other equalities: equality is best taught in the context of British law, where all protected characteristics of the Equality Act 2010 are included in a curriculum that celebrates difference' (ibid.: 2)

The No Outsiders approach was subsequently adopted by Birmingham City Council and recommended for use in its schools. Moffat has hosted over 60 No Outsiders training sessions at Parkfield Community School and trained at least another 30 Birmingham primary schools. In 2019, the teaching of No Outsiders was the subject of protests organized by parents, despite having been taught at Parkfield and other schools in Birmingham without issue for several years. The catalyst for the protests was the forthcoming introduction of mandatory Health, Relationships and Sex Education in all English schools in 2020 which has generated concerns within conservative religious groups. Uniquely in Birmingham, there have been protracted protests and demands that Parkfield's school leaders quit, echoing 'Trojan Horse' unacceptable behaviours pre-2014 (Diamond, 2019a, 2019b). The organizations best placed to deal with scenarios such as this, in which headteachers are exposed and isolated, are found within the communities that schools serve. Birmingham City Council and its headteachers are rising to this challenge and producing teaching materials rooted in an understanding of place.

The Birmingham Standing Advisory Committee for Religious Education (SACRE)

The Birmingham SACRE was one of the few local organizations to emerge with credit from Ian Kershaw's report:

> It is our view that Birmingham SACRE has undertaken its responsibilities in advising on a locally agreed syllabus with due diligence and sensitive care in meeting the needs of a variety of young people from a wide range of world religions. (Kershaw, 2014: 15)

It is mentioned here because the role of RE teaching, given all that happened during the Trojan Horse furore and the wider growth of extremist and intolerant views in English society, has become more important than ever. *The Birmingham Agreed Syllabus for Religious Education* (Birmingham City Council, 2007), based on 24 dispositions that students are encouraged to cultivate, is well-regarded nationally (Birmingham City Council, n.d.). Locally, it binds together all state schools as it must be used by any school that does not have a religious character, and that includes all academies and free schools. In an era of fragmented school structures that can introduce artificial boundaries and divisions, the Birmingham SACRE remains a city-wide force that unifies schools within a multi-faith community.

Birmingham Music Service

This service weighed anchor from Birmingham City Council in 2013 and moved into a new community-interest company. It has since thrived, working with over 90 per cent of schools in the city, during a decade in which music has been downgraded in schools – because it wasn't included in the philistine English Baccalaureate that contains no performing arts subjects – and there has been an overall impoverishment in schools as education spending has been reduced by 14 per cent in real terms since 2010 nationally (Institute for Fiscal Studies, 2018). The directors of Services for Education are value-driven and have put affordable instrument tuition, free loans and ensembles at the core of the Music Service's delivery model in the city. It would have been easy to run with a market-driven model that catered mainly for families in the affluent areas that can afford instruments and tuition. Exactly the opposite happens. The Music Service analyses the city's youth population through the lenses of free school meal entitlement and special educational needs. This enables them to track and target schools with the highest social–economic needs and steer the music tutors into these areas. Building on that approach are the initiatives aimed at the 27 special schools located in areas with the highest levels of deprivation. Additionally, the service works with the Virtual School for children who are in the care of the city. Year 4 children in care are receiving one-to-one 30-minute instrument lessons weekly and there are plans to extend that up the age range.

It takes a city to raise a child

Children growing up will form attachments that start at home, widen out as they start playgroups and nursery and embed within their local communities (Winnicott, 1964). Many young people born in Birmingham will rarely, if ever, leave their postcode area and venture further afield into the city centre. Social mobility is determined principally by socio-economic status. Birmingham is a cash-poor city with nearly half of its adult population in the bottom decile of deprivation and many families therefore simply don't have the resources to enable their children to take advantage of what happens in the city centre. So it is vital that social capital is developed among the young to help them form attachments and belonging beyond their immediate neighbourhoods. That can only happen when they feel secure in their local community and the city's leaders celebrate what happens there first.

For me, as Director of Education, this provided compelling reasons to spend time in schools learning about how they did things, how they celebrated their achievements, but also, critically, how they related to their local community. In Marsh Hill, for example, the primary school children walk around the whole neighbourhood in a fancy dress procession once a year, building and reinforcing those links. In Washwood Heath, the local academy trust runs an annual Grand Iftari with the widest possible range of guests from the community. And, in Longbridge, a fish-and-chip supper is organized at school on a Friday night to bring the parents in to an event where they feel fully at home. Opportunities to join in city-wide events are less common but the children and young people do come together for extraordinary sports and music gatherings.

The DfE states that it will develop world-class education that builds, *inter alia*, 'character, resilience and well-being' (DfE, 2019). It is hard to find evidence of this aim in operation as education policy remains fixated on harvesting data from the narrowest set of outcomes possible. The more sophisticated data that is less easy to measure – on wellbeing, community contribution and engagement – and participation in creative arts and sports remain ignored. Ofsted reports on a narrow slice of school life derived from desk-top analysis and a superficial visit. The examples illustrated in this chapter are all home-grown in Birmingham as the antidote to a neoliberal national education policy. They are about local agency and power rather than a compliance culture. And they demonstrate that the power of social capital can transcend government policies that are released onto communities with no reference to local realities.

Section Five

Compassion for Planet

Education for survival: Compassion for planet

Maurice Irfan Coles

Abstract: This chapter formed the bedrock of Coles' TEDx talk in Doncaster (2019). It outlines the terrifying and undeniable imperatives for tackling the climate emergency, the greatest existential threat in the history of the planet. It examines some of the political and economic responses to the crisis and argues that religion and science now speak with one voice. It introduces the concept of 'spiritual ecology', which combines, in compassionate just cause, the two great streams of secular science and ancient spiritual/religious/indigenous traditions. It aims to offer a series of practical, educational and compassionate solutions that demonstrate that the health and wellbeing of both the individual and the collective depend on the health and wellbeing of the planet and all its species.

The terrifying and undeniable imperatives for change

As I began writing this in my conservatory in the spring of 2019, I looked out on lush grass, beautiful flowering azaleas and rhododendrons, early vegetables – all accompanied by a chorus of singing birds and sustained by a large variety of bees. I found it almost impossible to contemplate that, unless politicians and big businesses urgently take remedial action, our five 3-year-old grandchildren will see the end of the grandeur of this world. The scope and scale of what is now a 'climate crisis' rather than climate change, and global heating rather than 'warming', are such that it almost defies individual human comprehension. To deny that it is happening, as vested interests continue to do, is nothing short of evil. The 'denying' politicians and big businessmen can only be described as 'ecopaths', a condition that deifies greed, selfishness and power at the expense of planetary survival. As David Wallace-Wells expresses so forcefully in *The Uninhabitable Earth*:

> It is worse, much worse, than you think. The slowness of climate change is a fairy tale, perhaps as pernicious as the one that says it isn't happening at all, and comes to us bundled with several others in an anthology of comforting delusions … (Wallace-Wells, 2019: 3)

He outlines clearly the devastating facts behind our 'Anthropocene Age', the geologic era in which we live, which is defined by human intervention in the life of the planet – an intervention that, unless reversed, could well drive us to the edge of extinction. Since Wallace-Wells's book, we have been overwhelmed by evidence of the terrifying impact on climate and species survival. Two extensively researched reports by over 2,500 scientists from 130 countries have been produced by the UN intergovernmental platforms. In addition, in January 2019, the *UN Environment Foresight Brief* published evidence of the catastrophic decline of insects, which provided another clear and stark warning to humanity about the impact of its present behaviours (UN Environment, 2019).

In 2018, the Intergovernmental Panel on Climate Change (IPCC) published its *Special Report on Global Warming of 1.5 °C,* which warns that **we have only a dozen years for global warming to be kept to a maximum of 1.5°C**. This major report outlines the dramatic differences that simply restricting warming to 1.5°C above pre-industrial levels would have on the global environment. The consequences of exceeding 1.5°C are almost too horrifying to contemplate.

A second report, published in May 2019 by the Intergovernmental Science-Policy Platform on Biodiversity and Ecosystem Services (IPBES-Science and Policy for People and Nature), examines the impact of global warming by assessing the state of biodiversity and the ecosystem. Based on the most comprehensive study of nature ever conducted, it argues that the environment is in steep decline and that one million plants, insects and other creatures are in danger of extinction, many within decades from now. For some time, scientists have been maintaining that we are on the verge of the sixth mass species extinction – the only one for which humankind is directly responsible!

To compound the bad news, the UN Environment organization charted the research concerning the decline of the insect populations, which make up about half of all known living organisms. Without insects, humans would struggle to survive, but the continued use of insecticides, the fragmentation of habitats and the changing climate are placing multiple threats on the insects, and their populations are in steep decline. The analysis found that:

Across the world, more than 40 per cent of insect species are declining and a third are endangered. The rate of extinction is eight times faster than that of mammals, birds and reptiles. The total mass of insects is falling by a precipitous 2.5 per cent a year, according to the best data available, suggesting they could vanish within a century ... The world's insects are hurtling down the path to extinction, threatening a catastrophic collapse of nature's ecosystems. (UN Environment Programme, 2019).

Equally alarming are the same patterns evident in our oceans, which are fast becoming deoxygenated and filled with plastic and micro-plastic. Add what we now also know about the even more devastating effects of the majority of the world's estimated 7.7 billion people eating meat, and we have a perfect storm. As wildlife biologist Liz Bonnin, presenter of the BBC's 'Meat: A Threat to Our Planet?', says:

Unless we do things very differently ... the impact the meat industry has on our environment is only going to get worse. As demand increases, so do greenhouse gas emissions, so does pollution, so does the destruction of biodiversity. Which leads to one very obvious question: should we just stop eating meat? (BBC One, 2019)

In short, therefore, *every* piece of evidence we have points to the catastrophic damage humans are inflicting on the planet, and thus on ourselves. Intuitive and indigenous wisdom has always understood the interdependent relationship between all living things, and now science has, at long last, caught up. Discoveries from the previously secret worlds of trees, fish, birds and bees and other insects confirm that all living things have what we humans would call 'feelings' and are far more organized and intelligent than we ever imagined. Even plants emit remotely detectable ultrasounds that can reveal their stress (Khait *et al.*, 2019). Peter Wohlleben's wonderful book, *The Hidden Life of Trees: What they feel, how they communicate* (2015) demonstrates how the forest is a social network in which trees share a symbiotic relationship with everything around them. Wohlleben uses science to describe how trees are like human families with parents supporting children, sharing nutrients and communicating often through scent, through chemical compounds and electrical impulses. He likens the forest to a 'wood-wide web', a term borrowed from Dr Suzanne Simard's work on how trees communicate (A Future of OUR Choosing, n.d.).

Similarly, Jennifer Ackerman's *The Genius of Birds* (2016) throws new light onto our old perception of 'bird-brain', of our avian friends having 'limited intelligence'. 'A flood of new research has overturned the old views, and people are starting to accept that birds are far more intelligent than we ever imagined – in some ways closer to primate relatives than to their reptilian ones' (ibid.: 2).

Cognitive intelligence has more to do with the number of neurons and neural pathways than brain size, and birds exhibit densities and connections remarkably like ours. Although avian brains are organized in a very different way, 'they share similar genes and neural circuits and are capable of feats of quite extraordinary mental power' (ibid.: 5).

Even fish have their own secret and complex lives (see PETA's *The Hidden Lives of Fish*, n.d.). As Dr Theresa Burt de Perera of Oxford University writes: 'We're now finding that [fish] are very capable of learning and remembering, and possess a range of cognitive skills that would surprise many people' (ibid.). Dr Culum Brown, a Macquarie University biologist studying the evolution of cognition in fish, similarly argues that 'Fish are more intelligent than they appear. In many areas, such as memory, their cognitive powers match or exceed those of "higher" vertebrates including non-human primates' (ibid.).

So, science has spoken again and again. The question is: how should we respond and what can we do? Doing nothing is a death sentence. The gradualism adopted by many governments is almost as bad. The polar ice caps won't wait while politicians fiddle; a million species will die and it will simply be too late to avert global disaster. Rather, what is required is a concerted, unified scientific and spiritual response by governments, by communities and by individuals. Similarly, the carbon and other industries, economists and those who work across education must take up the challenge. Given the fractured nature of our world and the well-funded sociopathic, ecopathic deniers, it seems an impossibly tall order.

But there is hope. To use a phrase coined by Joanna Macy, environmental activist and author, for some time there has been a 'Great Turning', a move away from the industrialized carbon-fuelled paradigm towards one that is more integrated and infinitely more balanced. This 'turning' has been given a strong impetus by the young, by some bankers and lawyers, by religious and spiritual leaders, by an increasing number of politicians and, unsurprisingly, by thousands of scientists.

Despite the rise of populist movements that sustain anachronistic shibboleths like 'national sovereignty' and spout hollow promises to restore former glories while dismissing all evidence and rational thought, there are moments in human history when, 'Once in a lifetime, the longed-for tide of justice can arise and hope and history rhyme' (Heaney, 1991). Perhaps, just perhaps, this is one such moment; a moment when we can 'hope for a great sea-change'. Such optimism might appear unwarranted, but what has happened recently is an incredible outpouring of compassion for the planet. Birthed by science, spirituality and technology and midwifed by social and mainstream media, compassion for the planet for the first time in human history brings together and galvanizes representatives drawn from all five existing generations, ranging from Attenborough – in his 90s – at one end to Thunberg – in her teens – at the other. This intergenerational tour de force has the ground-breaking UN work as its intellectual driver, and spiritual and religious leaders including the Dalai Lama, Thích Nhất Hạnh and Pope Francis as its champions. Furthermore, business leaders and bankers are increasingly realizing that responding effectively to the damage caused by global warming is in our enlightened self-interest.

Scientific and technological responses

Scientists and technologists have been arguing for some time that we have the technology we need to solve the carbon-fuelled crisis. This could cost a very significant sum but that's nothing compared to the costs that will be incurred if we don't act NOW. We have old 'technologies' like planting trees and new technology centred on carbon capture and promoting renewables. The problem is not the technology: it is the greed, lust for power and defence of the selfish vested interests of the few, at the planetary expense of the many. It follows, therefore, that these issues have to be addressed on all levels, from the individual to the community, to the political, to the national and international.

All experts agree, however, that, although individual initiatives will be helpful, it is the politicians and the business people who will make or break attempts to save the planet. Many believe that these secular scientific and technological responses are sufficient to meet these growing crises. Others believe they aren't. In an interview, Gus Speth, environmental activist, lawyer and adviser to the UN and several US presidents, for example, encapsulated the problem thus:

> I used to think that top environmental problems were biodiversity loss, ecosystem collapse and climate change. I thought that thirty years of good science could address these problems. I was wrong. The top environmental problems are selfishness, greed and apathy, and to deal with these we need a cultural and spiritual transformation. (Speth, 2014)

His words echo those of religious, indigenous and spiritual leaders who argue that ecocide is not only a threat to our physical survival but also to our spiritual and emotional wellbeing. As Father Thomas Berry

(1914–2009), an eco-theologian in the tradition of Pierre Teilhard de Chardin, eloquently put it:

> There is now a single issue before us: survival. Not merely physical survival but survival in a world of fulfillment, survival in a living world, where the violets bloom in the springtime, where the stars shine down in all their mystery, survival in a world of meaning. (Teilhard de Chardin, cited in Vaughan-Lee, 2016: 17)

In short, we are talking here about survival of the human spirit itself. So how do the ecological and the spiritual combine as one?

Spiritual responses

Spiritual development is a fundamental plank of many education jurisdictions throughout the world, but 'spiritual' is a tricky word. Sandra Ingerman's definition, however, is beautifully succinct: 'spirit is who we are beyond our skin' (Vaughan-Lee, 2016: 211). Brother Wayne Teasdale refers to 'an individual's solitary search for and discovery of the absolute or the divine' (Teasdale, 2010: 10). Although primarily personal, spirituality is played out dynamically in the collective and has moral, social and cultural dimensions. It exists both inside us and between the people and elements of nature with whom we interact. It is, in short, *relational*. Deborah Eden Tull explores this in depth in her 2018 book, *A Relational Mindfulness*, in which she explores meditation as an attitude of mind and way of life. For her, meditation 'is the key to both personal healing and global sustainability' (Tull, 2018: x) because it helps end the myth of our separation from each other and the Earth. 'Compassion through Spiritual Development' (Coles, 2015: 41–57) offers a detailed synthesis and typology of spirituality. How, then, does the spiritual merge with the ecological?

The word 'ecology' was originally coined in 1886 by German scientist Ernst Haeckel. Grounded in the natural-history output of philosophers including Hippocrates and Aristotle, it derives from the Greek *oikos* meaning 'house' or 'environment' plus *logia*, 'the study of'. It has been defined variously as 'the study of the interrelationships of organisms with their environment and each other', as 'the economy of nature', and as 'the biology of ecosystems'.

The contemporary bringing-together of aspects of spiritual and of ecology is comparatively recent, however. What are its fundamental principles? How did it arise and why is it so important? Satish Kumar explains briefly online (Kumar, 2014), and the Audiopedia cartoon 'What is spiritual ecology?' (2017) renders it graphically in six minutes.

The CoED Foundation argues that spiritual ecology combines, in common compassionate just cause, the two great streams of secular science and ancient spiritual/religious/indigenous traditions. It aims to rescue us and our beautiful shared Earth by stressing the scientific and intuitive wisdom that we are all interconnected and that the health and wellbeing of both the individual and of the collective depends on the health and wellbeing of the planet and its entire species. It demands that humanity take seriously and urgently its role as guardian of the planet. Fortified with its bedrock of love, spirit and connectivity, spiritual ecology is an existential clarion call, a cry to all to become sacred activists.

Its recent origins are largely to be found in the works of Catholic Thomas Berry, Evangelical Matthew Fox, Sufi Llewellyn Vaughan-Lee, Jain Satish Kumar and Buddhist Joanna Macy. For Macy, there are two main drivers: deep ecology (also known as biocentrism) and the living systems theory. Deep ecology is based on the work of Norwegian philosopher Arne Naess, who coined the term in the 1970s. It is essentially an ethical position that stresses human interdependence with the planet, removes humans as the ultimate measure and arbiter of value, and argues that, for the planet to survive, we must liberate ourselves from our species' arrogance, which is driving us all down a road to disaster. As the late Judi Bari, who survived an assassination attempt in her campaign to save the American Redwoods, put it:

> Deep ecology or biocentrism is a law of nature that exists independently of whether humans recognize it or not ... And the failure of modern society to acknowledge this — as we attempt to subordinate all of nature to human use — has led us to the brink of collapse of the Earth's life support systems ... Biocentrism is ancient native wisdom ... but in the context of today's industrial society, biocentrism is profoundly revolutionary, challenging the system to its core. (Bari, cited in Macy and Young Brown, 2014: 43)

The living systems theory evolved because scientists altered their focus from studying separate entities to understanding the relationships between them. Like Wohlleben's trees and Ackerman's birds, they demonstrate that nature is self-organizing and based on a coherence and constancy that permits the variety of life forms to arise from interactions. As Macy and Young Brown argue:

> The system self-generates from adaptive co-operation between its parts for mutual benefit. Order and differentiating go hand in hand; components diversify as they coordinate and invent new responses. (ibid.: 41)

In other words, the Earth can be seen as an intelligent, self-organizing living system. Margulis and Lovelock developed a hypothesis that saw the entire biosphere behaving in this way. This became known as the *Gaia Theory*, named after the early Greek goddess of the Earth. Again, the science resonated with spiritual and religious traditions that argued that the Earth is a living being endowed with a soul and intelligence – what was called the *anima mundi*, the soul of the world. In his *Working with Oneness* (2002), Llewellyn Vaughan-Lee expands on this, cogently arguing that we are all interconnected and that we have forgotten that the world belongs to God and that the Earth is our mother. Many practising Hindus start their day with the prayer: 'I offer my salutations to the consort of Vishnu, Mother Earth, asking her to forgive me for stepping on her, whose body is clothed with oceans and mountain ranges' (Srinivasan, 2011: 337).

The concept of Mother Earth, expressed slightly differently according to context and time, exists in the Neoplatonic great chain of being and in aspects of Taoist, Hindu and Buddhist thinking. Perhaps, however, it is the indigenous people of Australia and North America who felt it most and expressed it best. The wonderful composite response that Chief Sealth (Seattle) made in c. 1854 to his Duwamish tribal assembly in reply to President Franklin Pierce captures the biocentric world view:

> The President in Washington sends word that he wishes to buy our land. But how can you buy or sell the sky; the land? The idea is strange to us. If we do not own the freshness of the air and the sparkle of the water, how can you buy them ...? Every part of the Earth is sacred to my people. We are part of the Earth and it is part of us. ... The rivers are our brothers ... they feed our children. So you must give the rivers the kindness that you would give any brother ... Will you teach your children what we have taught our children? That the Earth is our mother? What befalls the Earth befalls all the sons of the Earth ... This we know: the Earth does not belong to man, man belongs to the Earth. All things are connected like the blood that unites us all. Man did not weave the web of life; he is merely a strand in it. Whatever he does to the web, he does to himself. (Seattle, 1854. Many versions of this speech survive – see Wikipedia)

A similar image exists in Buddhist and in Hindu cosmology. Known as Indra's web (net or jewels), it is central to Buddhist thinking concerning universal interconnectivity. The net is a metaphor for what Thích Nhất Hạnh, founder of 'engaged Buddhism', has termed 'interbeing': that is, the integration of the universal and the particular. Hạnh maintains that each of us is a particular being, and each particular being is also the entire phenomenal universe.

For many secularists, this worldview will be a step too far. What is undeniable, however, is that we are all connected and that this connection brings with it a huge moral responsibility – a responsibility to act not just for ourselves but as guardians of the whole planet and its entire species. This concept of humans as 'caretakers' has a long and distinguished history. It is embodied in Buddhism in the 'bodhisattva', a soul that has chosen to return to Earth to help end suffering, as personal salvation is now inseparable from that of the collective.

Islam places responsibility on humans as God's vice-regents, as Allah's earthly *khalifas*. Both Western and Orthodox Christian traditions speak of 'stewardship', where humans are accountable for maintaining the Earth. Pope Francis (2013–) adopted his papal name in inspirational honour of the patron saint of the animals and the poor, St. Francis of Assisi (1181/2–1226). The Pope published a passionate, lengthy reflection, *Laudato Si': On Care for Our Common Home* (Pope Francis, 2015). Using the language of St. Francis, he compared the Earth to a beautiful sister and mother whom we have harmed because of our greed. He points to the disproportionate impact climate change has on the poor and argues that we must bring the whole human family together to seek a long-term sustainable future.

Sacred activism

What is common to most religious and spiritual traditions is the concept of sacred activism, love-in-action that unites spiritual wisdom with practical deeds to create a powerful divine force capable of transforming us and saving our planet and its myriad species. As Neil Douglas Klotz puts it, sacred activism means 'working to create a loving, just, sacred and sustainable world through means that are loving, just, sacred and sustainable' (Vaughan-Lee, 2019: iv). Andrew Harvey, in his *The Hope* outlines 'the five forms of service' required to support this vision: service to the divine, to yourself as an instrument of the divine, to all sentient beings in your life, to the local and global community (Harvey, 2009: 119–29). Fox *et al.*, in *Order of the Sacred Earth* (2018), go a step further when they describe a new order similar to the old holy orders. They argue that the order will become:

… a community and movement of people from varied backgrounds of belief systems who share a sacred vow to preserve Mother Earth and to become the best lovers … they can be on behalf of Mother Earth. (ibid.: 4)

The beauty is that any individual, any school can join this order – it is totally inclusive, but they have to commit to action. The pledge is simply: 'To defend Mother Earth, to work and live as generously as we can on behalf of Mother Earth and her creatures so that future generations might live and thrive and take in her beauty and her health '.

Even simpler for schools to read and adapt is Llewellyn Vaughan-Lee and Hilary Hart's *Spiritual Ecology: 10 Practices to Reawaken the Sacred in Everyday Life* (2017). Their book outlines how an individual's ecological practice can be absorbed into the everyday fabric of their lives. Vaughan-Lee provides the commentary and Hart the practices. Spiritual ecology and sacred activism have a simple spiritual truth at their heart: that it is no longer about the individual's path to 'salvation' (however one chooses to define it) but, rather, it is about the collective. The individual's spiritual journey becomes meaningful when it interacts and connects with the spiritual journey of others, when we move from the 'me' to the 'we'. Sustainability of our entire planetary system is at the heart of sacred activism. It is, of course, also at the heart of secular approaches, in the fields of both education and politics (mainstream and street).

Political responses

There's a word that describes the political responses of many governments: pusillanimous – small-minded and mean-spirited. Everything is reduced to a crude political calculation that focuses on gaining or retaining power, often underpinned by a lack of political compassionate courage among politicians to spell out certain truths to the electorate in case their message and their party are rejected. Well-meaning leaders who proudly articulate their ecological aims often back away from forcing through the policies required. The most mean-spirited reject the science and continue with 'business as usual'. These politicians are almost invariably supported by big donations from the fossil fuel lobbyists, and their own wealth is often tied into the most harmful polluters. It will take great political courage to stand up on behalf of the planet because our whole economic system has been based on the burning of 'cheap' fossil fuels.

Although almost a century has elapsed since H.G. Wells famously warned that 'human history becomes more and more a race between education and catastrophe', it has never been so relevant. Wells went on to urge, 'Let us learn the truth and spread it far and wide as our circumstances allow. For the truth is the greatest weapon we have'. This ought to apply in rational democratic societies. So when Ban Ki-moon, UN Secretary-General, launched the historic IPCC report with the words, 'Science has spoken. There is no ambiguity in the message' (Ban, 2014), one could be forgiven for thinking that that was the end of any debate.

The problem is, however, that we live in a 'post-truth political age', an age when emotion undermines reason and mendacious politicians and the press can appeal, at one and the same time, to base instincts and loftier sentiments. US President Trump is the master of such tactics. His environmental policies, according to 'Environmental policy of the Donald Trump administration' (Wikipedia, 2019), comprise a systematic rejection of the green policies of the Obama administration and provide a frightening litany of reversal, the most dramatic of which is US withdrawal from the 2016 Paris Accord wherein 195 states agreed to devise and implement their own policies to ensure that greenhouse gas emissions were limited so that global warming did not increase beyond 1.5 °C. Trump's stance is perhaps unsurprising in that his big financial backers, and those of the Republican Party, are energy and fossil fuel-burning companies. He has also surrounded himself with courtiers from the world of climate denial.

Sadly, Trump is not the only world leader who puts profit above planet. Scott Morrison in Australia – who can now barely see above Sydney's smoke – and Brazil's Bolsonaro are fervent deniers, supported by media outlets like Murdoch's Fox News. Bolsonaro has declared his intention to end protection for the land rights of indigenous tribes, eliminated departments with responsibility for climate change and deforestation, and appointed Ernesto Araújo Minister of Foreign Affairs. Araújo has called global warming a plot by 'cultural Marxists' – which is reminiscent of Trump previously blaming the Chinese. And what *about* the Chinese?

Economic responses

In his report of June 2019, Professor Philip Alston, the UN Special Rapporteur on extreme poverty and human rights, argues that:

> Climate change will have devastating consequences for people in poverty. Even under the best-case scenario, hundreds of millions will face food insecurity, forced migration, disease, and death. Climate change threatens the future of human rights and risks

undoing the last fifty years of progress in development, global health, and poverty reduction. (Alston, 2019)

Although the richer world will hardly be immune from its effects, the poor (who contribute least to global warming) will be in the front line and will not have the financial means or infrastructure to mitigate the effects. It will further exacerbate the yawning gap between rich and poor, both in poor and richer nations, while poverty spreads alarmingly in European and North American countries (Wilson and Pickett, 2010; Resolution Foundation, 2019; Coles, 2015).

The problems are all interrelated but it's the impact of climate change and species extinction, *ecocide*, that hastens the worsening crises. It's horrifying that the carbon industries have known about the hugely damaging effects of their products for over 70 years and yet have chosen not merely to suppress the information but to actively propagate an alternate vision in which they have invested billions (Alston, 2019). Many of the big oil companies are facing legal challenges which, if they were to lose, will bring little solace and less respite as the wheels of justice grind so slowly that by the time the process is completed, it may well be too late to avert catastrophe.

2019 marked a terrifying watershed in our knowledge and understanding of climate Armageddon and of the perilous power wielded by the vested interests determined to persuade us that the overwhelming scientific proof is nothing more than fake news, an elaborate hoax! The *Guardian*, quoting research conducted by Richard Heede of the Climate Accountability Institute, revealed the top 20 firms behind a third of all climate emissions. It transpires that they are all private or state-owned gas, coal or oil companies. The article cites climate scientist Michael Mann, who is unequivocal:

> The great tragedy of the climate crisis is that seven and a half billion people must pay the price – in the form of a degraded planet – so that a couple of dozen polluting interests can continue to make record profits. It is a great moral failing of our political system that we have allowed this to happen. (Taylor and Watts, 2019)

Disillusioned with many career politicians, young people across the globe are taking to direct action in their demands for climate protection and justice. Direct action – when groups of disempowered people have taken to the streets to protest against the policies and actions of their rulers – has a long history. The massive international demonstrations against US involvement in Vietnam, civil rights marches and the Arab Spring are recent examples. Many of those involved were young people/student-led, often with intergenerational support. Thanks to the internet, they quickly become international. The Occupy Movement, which started in the US in 2011 as an 'occupy Wall Street' campaign against economic injustice, grew exponentially.

Similarly, in response to the frightening rise of gun violence and the killing of so many school and college students by lone gunmen in the US, groups like 'Never Again MSD' led to a 'lie-in' outside the White House and an '#Enough! National School Walkout' in which an estimated 3,000 schools and nearly one million students took part. Across the world, for a range of causes, young people are taking to the streets, often in concerted action and in extraordinary numbers. Cue the international phenomenon that is Greta Thunberg, the young Swedish school student whose lone school strike (beginning August 2018) against her government's lack of action over climate change has led to a worldwide school strike movement.

The international phenomenon of Greta Thunberg

Bullies always try to find and exploit what they consider to be a weakness in their victims. Thus, in the absence of argument against Greta's unequivocal message, the right-wing press and commentators attack her age, her lack of experience, even her Asperger's syndrome. She is being paid, manipulated and used, they claim. Even the trillion-dollar OPEC argues that young activists like her are now a threat to them. Its Secretary-General, Mohammad Barkindo, was reported in the *Guardian* as saying that there was a growing mass mobilization against oil, which was 'beginning to … dictate policies and corporate decisions, including investment'. Even OPEC officials' own families and children were 'asking about their future because … they see their peers on the street campaigning against this industry'. Greta tweeted in response, 'Thank you! Our biggest compliment yet!' (Watts, 2019).

Greta appears unfazed by all this vilification: in fact, it adds to her resolve to support school strikes throughout the globe. Her message resonates with millions of young people, across all generations, and with the powerful. Her widely reported short speeches to the UN, Davos, UK and European parliaments are perfect examples of speaking truth to power. It is perhaps because her message is simple, heartfelt and based on scientific facts that her profile and influence are international in scope. Her short book, *No One is Too Small to Make a Difference* (Thunberg, 2019), provides a brilliant, affordable and accessible resource for all primary, secondary and tertiary institutions.

The political and educational responses to the climate strikes inspired by Greta have varied. Some see her work as a splendid example of active global citizenship at work, a rallying cause around which all young people can unite. Others believe it to be totally wrong, that young people should remain in school and 'learn', and argue that there are a range of alternative actions that should be taken to involve young people.

The international phenomenon of Extinction Rebellion

In the same year as Greta Thunberg began her protest, three people – Gail Bradbrook, Roger Hallam and Simon Bramwell – working from the small English town of Stroud in Gloucestershire sparked a non-violent civil disobedience movement, Extinction Rebellion (XR). They were protesting against climate breakdown, ecological collapse and species extinction. XR, too, has become an international movement purposefully causing mass disruption in over 25 countries. The authors of the handbook *This is Not a Drill* (Extinction Rebellion, 2019) cogently make the case for a Declaration of Rebellion, arguing that the bonds of the social contract are null and void because 'the government has rendered them invalid by its continued failure to act appropriately'(ibid.: 2). XR demands citizenship assemblies and the declaration of Climate Emergencies.

Mainstream responses to the existential threat and declaration of climate emergencies

There is no agreed definition of a climate emergency, and each government, local authority area, school, company and individual sets their own priorities. Indeed, every person should declare a 'climate emergency of the heart' because each of us must address this existential issue in our own lives. The overarching aim is for all parties involved to produce action plans to help reduce their carbon footprint and combat species extinction. Many British local councils and American states have declared their intention and are in the process of action-planning. The issue for most governments is not intent but outcome – an outcome hindered if, like the UK, you continue to indirectly subsidize the fossil fuel industry and persist with plans to build new runways at major airports. And hindered if, like Canada, you approve the expansion of an oil pipeline at almost the same time as declaring a climate emergency project.

Much of the political pressure has been applied by groups like the Greens, who enjoyed enormous success in the European Elections of 2019 and support a Global Green New Deal (GGND), an updated economic plan to move away from carbon-based fuels and towards zero emissions by 2030, coupled with social and economic reforms designed to address ever-growing inequalities. Its authors consciously evoked the spirit of President Franklin D. Roosevelt's New Deal programme of public works and economic reforms, which reversed the impact of the Great Depression.

Naomi Klein, in *On Fire* (2019), outlines the why, what and how of progressing a green new deal. Similarly, Ann Pettifor in *The Case for the Green New Deal* (2019), proposes a radical new understanding of the international monetary system and offers a global road map to wrestle the wealth back from the privileged 1 per cent.

The European Union, with its new European Green Deal, is committed to reducing carbon emissions to zero by 2050. Speaking ahead of her European Parliament debate in December 2019, Ursula von der Leyen, President of the European Commission, announced:

> This is a very special day. This morning, the College of Commissioners agreed on the European Green Deal … [which] is, on the one hand, our vision for a climate neutral continent in 2050, and it is on the other hand a very dedicated roadmap to this goal. It is fifty actions for 2050. Our goal is to reconcile the economy with our planet, to reconcile the way we produce and the way we consume … (European Commission, 2019)

The major obstacles to such changes are not merely rich individuals and intransigent leaders: they go deeper because they're ideologically systemic. Resistance to radical action, however greatly it's needed, goes to the heart of the neoliberal discourse that has dominated our political and economic landscape since the Thatcher–Reagan era and has a vice-like hold on many of our institutions. Against all economic evidence, neoliberals continue to argue that individual wealth-creation is paramount and that state intervention and regulation are, by definition, a bad thing because they limit private enterprise. Small government trumps big government; and private enterprise is more productive than public ownership. At its foundation is a Darwinian worldview that humans are innately competitive and this spirit should therefore be nurtured and encouraged. This worldview has become the norm in many education systems.

Educational responses

In his excellent book, *Educating for Hope in Troubled Times* (2014), Professor David Hicks asks: 'What is education for?' Drawing on the work of Harvey (2005), Gray (2009) and Hayward (2012), he contrasts neoliberal perspectives with what is sometimes known, at least in the UK, as the 'welfare state ideology'. This ideology, like compassionate education, stresses cooperation as opposed to competition, service as opposed to selfishness, and argues that it is the role of the state and the school to promote equality and justice for all. As such, schools should be about the survival of the kindest, not the survival of the fittest. Both systems share a desire for the individual to achieve and prosper and thus benefit all of society. The processes, perspectives and means of achieving these aims are, however, radically different. A government's worldview influences its pedagogy because pedagogy cannot be meaningfully separated from content, delivery, assessment and context. In the final analysis, education is about power: about how the 'powerful' define the purposes of education and how they translate their perceptions into curriculum vision, design, delivery, monitoring and assessment.

Teaching compassionately in a system that unintentionally discourages it can be difficult, but teachers have always led the way. This is particularly true in areas related to the environment. Whether it be the old 'nature studies', 'outdoor' or 'environmental education', 'conservation' or 'education for sustainability', teachers have been at the forefront of developing curriculum content and processes that aim to prepare young people for collaboration with each other and the natural world. Many young children, particularly in urban areas, first learn about growing plants, caring for pets and animals, about trees and birds, at school.

It is not that we are short of resources to support these endeavours. In fact, the opposite is true. There are now so many resources available that it can be overwhelming. The foundation for many of these has been the UN's Sustainable Development Goals.

Education for Sustainable Development

Education for Sustainable Development (ESD) is a UN programme that encourages changes in knowledge, skills, values and attitudes in education to facilitate a more sustainable and just society globally. It aims to empower and equip current and future generations to meet their needs by using a balanced, integrated approach to the economic, social and environmental dimensions of sustainable development. The concept of sustainable development, the overarching paradigm of the UN, was described in the 1987 Brundtland Commission Report as 'development that meets the needs of the present without compromising the ability of future generations to meet their own needs' (United Nations, 1987: 41). Although it has been argued that 'sustainability' is still predominantly anthropocentric – viewing the planet intrinsically as a resource for humans to exploit – it has nonetheless proved to be a major initiative for helping the young understand and assume responsibility for our shared Earth. The ESD programme has led to the production of some excellent materials.

In 2012, for example, UNESCO published its first-rate open-access *Education for Sustainable Development Sourcebook*, a key theoretical and practical tool (UNESCO, 2012). It is a complete package replete with suggestions for integrating the key messages into existing curricula, teaching pedagogy tips, practical activities and assessment tools. The U.S. Partnership for Education for Sustainable Development also offers a range of practical resources from kindergarten to grade 12 and higher education.

One of the most detailed and useful examples of whole-systems thinking, however, can be found in the *Scottish Curriculum for Excellence: Learning for Sustainability* (LfS). It is part of the Scottish pupil entitlement and professional standards for teachers. LfS is:

> ... an approach to life and learning which enables learners, educators, schools and their wider communities to build a socially-just, sustainable and equitable society. An effective whole school and community approach to LfS weaves together global citizenship, sustainable development education and outdoor learning to create coherent, rewarding and transformative learning experiences. (Education Scotland, n.d.)

One key concept that has been popularized since the introduction of ESD is that of 'eco-warrior'. Originally coined in the 1990s, the term related to activists like Greenpeace and others who were prepared to engage in direct action against those destroying the environment. Some education systems have adopted the concept. Northern Ireland Curriculum, for example, has published an eco-warriors' booklet, available online, which encompasses a wide range of suggested learning intentions and activities suitable for 9–11-year-olds but which has wider application. It contains lesson activities for a range of curriculum areas (Northern Ireland Curriculum, n.d.).

The most comprehensive and detailed package, however, which can culminate in an internationally recognized award, is 'Eco-Schools'. This is an international programme of the Foundation for Environmental Education (FEE) that aims to empower students to be the change our sustainable world needs by engaging them in fun, action-orientated and socially responsible learning. Presently, the Eco-Schools programme extends from nursery level to universities and is implemented in 67 countries, involving 51,000 schools and institutions and over 19 million students. It is the largest international network of teachers and students in the world. At the school level, it offers a number of age-appropriate, well-thought-out and well-constructed packages that are free to download and use and can be accompanied by paid teacher training. At college and university level, the programme is known as EcoCampus.

The programme's aims are expressed through its three structural elements – The Seven Step Framework, the Eco-Schools Topics and assessment for the international Green Flag award. To succeed, the programme requires support from school leaders and active involvement from staff, who, as well as being committed, must be willing to involve students in decision-making. The Eco-Schools Seven Steps methodology comprises a series of carefully engineered measures to help schools maximize the success of their Eco-School ambitions. While the Seven Steps are the most important aspect of the Eco-Schools programme, schools also work on important topics that lend the programme even more structure: pollution, marine issues, biodiversity, litter, global citizenship, healthy living, school grounds, transport, energy, waste and water.

Though these many initiatives are excellent in themselves, the fields of spiritual ecology and sacred activism are largely missing from the school curriculum. Similarly, schools have yet to address issues of what psychologists are calling 'eco-anxiety' – that is, deepening worry about the planet and feeling powerless to do anything about it. The medical term for this condition is 'solastalgia'.

The disciplines of eco-psychology, eco-therapy and eco-literacy are expanding, however. Eco-psychology is about the 'greening' of psychology, developing a human identity with, and compassion for, the natural world (Roszak *et al.*, 1995: 16), along with recognizing that human psychological stress is bound up with the ecocide we have inflicted on Mother Earth. If eco-psychology concentrates on the psyche, eco-therapy focuses on the mind–body–spirit relationship.

Many educators know intuitively that time spent in nature is imperative for health and wellbeing, especially for urban children. Some people outside Japan have taken up 'forest bathing' (*shinrin-yoku*) – that is, spending mindful time in the woods. Similarly, Daniel Goleman (the author of *Emotional Intelligence*) has, with Senoia Barlow and Lisa Bennett from the Center for Ecoliteracy, produced a practical book that guides teachers in supporting emotionally engaged eco-literate students (Goleman *et al.*, 2012). This follows on from Goleman's *Ecological Intelligence*, published in 2009.

In times of crisis, there are always those who see further and more clearly than their contemporaries. At the time of his death in 1997, Paulo Freire was writing a book about ecology that was published posthumously by his widow, Ana Maria Freire, in 2000. In it, he argues:

> It is urgent that we assume the duty to fight for the ethical principles of respect of life of human beings, life of other animals, the life of birds, the life of the rivers and the life of the forest. I do not believe in the love between human beings if we cannot become capable of loving the world ... Ecology has to be present in every radical practice ... [in order that we end] the practices of polluting the oceans, the waters, the fields, the devastation of the forest, and those which threaten the animals and birds. (Freire, 2000: 66–7)

True to his principles, Freire was one of the founders of eco-pedagogy, which is taught in Paulo Freire Institutes throughout the world. Key to his thinking is praxis, which has been played out in institutions that not only teach people the critical thinking of ecopedagogy but also engage them in learning through action. For example, a study conducted with 10-year-old children in West Scotland concluded that interactive dramatic education was successful in engaging students in the ecological, social and political dimensions of global problems such as solid waste and deforestation (McNaughton, 2010).

Over twenty years ago, Joanna Macy and Molly Young Brown published *The Guide to the Work That Reconnects*, which was updated in 2014 under the title *Coming Back to Life*. It is a practical book of hope, which acknowledges and builds on the denial and despair many feel in the face of ever-deepening global crises. It is aimed at parents and teachers and those who have to help young people navigate these turbulent waters. Chapter 11, 'The Work that Reconnects with Children and Teens', provides an ideal starting point for teachers. Unsurprisingly, compassion is at the heart of this work: it is the antidote to desperate times.

Compassionate responses

In the preface to his seminal book, *A Spirituality Named Compassion*, Matthew Fox writes:

> Compassion is everywhere. Compassion is the world's richest energy source. Now that the world is a global village we need

compassion more than ever – not for altruism's sake, not for philosophy's sake or theology's sake, but for survival's sake. (Fox, 1999: xi)

The CoED Foundation's typology of compassion echoes the work of Fox and Freire (see Figure 1.3 in Chapter 1.1). Compassion for planet, at the apex of this typology, must become education's dynamic response to the climate emergency. It aims to equip all young people with the knowledge, skills and attitudes they need to become eco-warriors and for them to realize that they have a major part to play in countering the greed and avarice that has led to this crisis. Young people must hold politicians and big business to account and must be encouraged to devise new creative ways and solutions to restore natural balance. Compassion for planet is a perspective, a way of seeing and acting in the world that must now become *the* driver in school and college curricula.

As well as the skills, knowledge and attitudes that are transmitted through the discrete subject areas connected to ecology – like aspects of science, maths, RE and geography as well as through cross-curricular approaches – children also need to understand what interdependent nature does for them, and how their future depends on it. It is already abundantly clear that the old order – our species' arrogance, greed and perpetual growth – will not die easily. Powerful vested interests conspire to maintain the status quo, heedless of the impact on us all. Learners therefore need yet greater concentration on the attitudes and skills that underpin virtues like campaigning, courage, resilience and truth – especially talking truth to power! Elements of spiritual ecology and sacred activism will need to provide optimism and stave off the potential for grief and despair.

Very young children understand concepts like recycling, reusing and reducing; and, as they grow, they understand refusing and even rebelling against what is happening – the 'Five Rs' (Figure 5.1).

Even the higher-order skills can be rendered very simply. It is about changing our collective mindset from one that puts the individual first, to one that considers the whole. For us as educators, it is about encouraging all young people to fall in love with the cosmos, to move from the 'me' to the 'we', and for them to realize that the 'we' is the whole planet. A simple slogan helps to capture it all: *FROM 'ME' TO 'WE': CHANGE THE PRONOUN, CHANGE THE WORLD.*

Figure 5.1: The five Rs

Source: The CoED Foundation

Compassion's ecological roadmap: Our 'starter for 10'

Ecocide is so life-threatening that what is now required is concerted and coordinated action planning at every level of our school and college systems. How educational institutions are funded, organized, inspected and controlled varies from country to country, and each jurisdiction must chart its own course. To assist in this journey we offer a simple roadmap, from government to learner level:

1. Central/Federal governments must offer clear, resourced direction that assists schools and colleges to review and revise their curriculum through the prism of compassion for the planet. This will require specialist educational personnel to orchestrate and prioritize existing curriculum and training resources, as well as developing new materials and courses. Such direction must be reflected in policies generally, and in inspection/review regimes in particular.

2. Local and state governments and academy trusts must provide on-the-ground support and development. All school services for which they have responsibility must prioritize the climate emergency, be they responsible for curriculum development, policies and support, resource

development, or teacher, management and governor training, or school meal provision.

3. All institutions responsible for initial teacher training and continuing professional development – be they a school, college or university – must review their current provision and incorporate compassion for the planet in appropriate course content and pedagogy.

4. All schools, academies, trusts and colleges must audit their present curriculum provision. In particular, they should examine their spiritual, moral, social and cultural offer in the light of climate emergency, spiritual ecology and sacred activism.

5. All schools and colleges – in collaboration with career guidance officers, local businesses and entrepreneurs – must help learners develop the 'green' skills required to bring about a carbon-neutral world.

6. All secular and religious schools should encourage service to the planet, and place the concept of guardianship and stewardship of the Earth at the centre of their pedagogy. Schools can justify this by reference to their own religious and ethical traditions.

7. All schools and colleges should become eco-schools or eco-colleges, and all learners should be encouraged to become eco-warriors.

8. All schools and colleges should declare their own climate emergency and collaboratively develop their own policies for safeguarding the planet, proactively involving the students, parents and local communities.

9. All governors/managers and school leaders should ensure that climate emergency becomes a central plank in their policies, reviews, school improvement plans and staff appraisal.

10. Schools and colleges must capitalize on the inspiration provided by 'young elders' like Greta Thunberg and Malala Yousafzai. This will help students voice their concerns and propose actions and solutions at home, in the community and in schools via such mechanisms as eco-committees, pupil voice and Young People Parliaments.

Some tips for schools and colleges and their staff

What can schools and colleges do in practical terms? We identify possible avenues to explore for all those involved with young people:

1. Begin by considering your own thoughts and feelings about this existential issue of our age.

2. Be open and honest with your learners but stress the hopeful aspects too.

3. Audit your 'spiritual' provision. Where, for example, do young people experience the joy, awe, wonder and benefits of nature?

4. Encourage your institution to become an eco-school and to appoint a named teacher and named governor/manager as lead officers.
5. Devise a 'safeguarding our planet' policy.
6. Explore the resources available to support sustainable education. David Hicks' aforementioned book, for instance, is an excellent practical resource. Each chapter deals with a particular issue and ends with 'ideas for teaching', and 'five things a school can do'.
7. Develop your own networks.
8. Devise strategies for dealing with the grief and worry that children of all ages and adults might experience because of the climate crisis.
9. Encourage pupil agency so that young people feel that they can play an active part in the wonder of oneness and in reversing the decline.
10. Use assemblies and creative arts to help the young express their concerns and celebrate what nature does for us.

Section Six

Bringing It All Together

Education's blueprint for survival

Maurice Irfan Coles, Philip Barlow, Gilroy Brown, Louise Darby and Manjit Shellis

Abstract: This chapter argues that any blueprint for survival needs to start with the individual who declares a climate emergency in their heart. As well as individuals, schools and education services can adopt various approaches. Using the future-mapping process, we offer seven detailed criteria against which schools can measure themselves. In addition, we provide blueprints for compassionate learning walks and a compassionate guarantee that all schools can adopt. Finally, we use our typology of compassion and our Pedagogy of Compassion (populated) model to bring it all together.

Introduction

This final chapter argues simply that adoption of the compassionate perspective, of the all-pervading principle of love-in-action, is the first existential step from which everything else follows. As the Tao put it, 'A journey of a thousand miles begins with a single step'. For most people working in education, that single step has already been taken.

Compassion is the bedrock of this profession. Compassionate education starts with each individual: the learner, the teacher, the leader, the governor, the politician. If each of us scrutinizes our areas of expertise through the lens of compassion for planet, collectively we can co-construct a blueprint for survival. If each stakeholder in a school declared their 'own climate emergency of the heart', they could begin to generate compassionate responses, which, taken together, will have a huge impact.

The authors of this chapter all live and work in Birmingham. At various times, most of them have been employed in the city's education service and thus bring immense knowledge and expertise about what worked best for the city, before its social education service was eviscerated. Some of these practices – such as supported self-evaluation and a forerunner of learning walks – predated the Tim Brighouse years. Others, like the Partnership Model of Working, and Birmingham Guarantees, were very much his inspiration. Wragg and colleagues examined some of the success of this work in *Improving Literacy in the Primary School* (1988).

Later, as we have seen, the Labour Government asked Tim Brighouse and David Woods, who had been Birmingham's Chief Adviser under Tim, to transfer the Birmingham experience to London. Together, they constructed the acclaimed 'London Challenge', which they based on a system of collaboration. They provide an elegant account of their work in *The Story of the London Challenge* (2014). The Challenge supported the rise in teaching standards by peer-to-peer review; headteachers helped one another to turn good schools into outstanding ones; and the Challenge offered a 'pupil pledge', providing young Londoners with access to sport, the arts and university life. The results, as in Birmingham, were impressive. By the time the Tory Government put an end to the Challenge, children on free school meals in London fared 50 per cent better at GCSEs than their peers elsewhere. Arguably, the successes of Birmingham and London were the forerunners of a local compassionate education system.

Such a system is not, in itself, radical because, as a principle, it begins where schools are at, working with them collaboratively and supportively in using their existing planning mechanisms to build compassionately. For example, schools are now well accustomed to the tried-and-tested iterative action planning format and its seven-step cycle:

1. Establish the criteria.
2. Audit existing practice.
3. Devise an action plan and prioritize according to the audit findings.
4. Determine allocation of responsibilities, financial implications and training requirements.
5. Devise a realistic time frame.
6. Monitor and evaluate the results, building on identified strengths and addressing highlighted weaknesses.
7. Amend the criteria in the light of developing knowledge and changing circumstances, and then begin the next action-planning cycle.

We have argued in this book that, in many educational jurisdictions, even those that claim to be 'school-led', it is the state that determines the major policies, itemizes the required knowledge, skills, attitudes and often the content that it expects to be transmitted. In some, it also instructs teachers on how they should teach. It is against *its* criteria that the state inspects to ensure that schools are complying. Their schools build their own policies within this wider external framework. Imagine the change if the government simply added 'compassion for planet' to its list of aims and values, for that in itself could spark national debate. Or what if the government decided to include compassion as one of the areas its inspection regime covers? But if it doesn't, there's nothing to stop schools adding the promotion of compassion to their own value statements and declaring themselves compassionate institutions.

Consistent with the future mapping process, here we offer lists of descriptive criteria that highlight, for example, the characteristics of a compassionate school or a compassionate teacher. Behind the seven areas we detail are a series of assumptions – the rationale for which is the essence of this book. The lists provide both a baseline and a direction of travel for the schools that undertake their own compassionate journey towards the pedagogy of compassion. Because pedagogy is about politics, however, we start with our elected representatives, and end with the nature of a compassionate child: for that, in the final analysis, is our yardstick.

1. Compassionate local, national and international politicians are those who …

- position compassion as a fundamental human value at the heart of all policies and practices
- care deeply about all those they represent
- work tirelessly towards equality and equity
- uphold all the support services that disadvantaged people need to thrive
- co-construct, with all stakeholders, policies and pedagogies that support the development of compassionate schools and compassionate communities
- engage in constructive and on-going dialogue with all those involved in the educative process
- devise supportive and constructive review processes (involving all stakeholders as partners) that are done *with* rather than done *to*
- actively listen to the expertise of professionals in the fields of education and related disciplines
- are committed to acting on best practice and research so it can be translated into policy and action
- are passionate advocates for the pedagogy of compassion and education for survival.

2. A compassionate teacher is one who …

- listens more than they talk
- uses positive and hopeful language
- demonstrates kindness and open body language

- treats every child first and foremost as a human being
- actively develops positive relationships with, and between, the students
- notices both positive and negative changes in their students
- uses restorative practice to help mend and heal, including adopting a 'clean slate' approach every lesson
- teaches with passion, care and humour
- connects the classroom to the real world and the planetary issues of our age
- aligns their teaching to the way the human brain learns.

3. A compassionate classroom is one where ...

- students think and work as 'we' and not just 'me'
- students are encouraged to lead and to support the learning needs of others
- the resources of the local communities are brought into the classroom
- cooperative group work is employed
- dialogue, not just debate, is encouraged and space made for it
- positive talk is encouraged on the part of both teachers and students
- compassionate knowledge, skills and attitudes are nurtured
- relevant, real-world issues are incorporated
- difference is valued and multiple perspectives are constantly sought
- coaching for personal development is valued as much as developing subject knowledge.

4. A compassionate school is one that ...

- welcomes everybody and has the golden thread of love-in-action at its heart
- treats learners, teachers and staff as human beings, encouraging their wellbeing and sense of belonging
- encourages compassionate relationships: between all staff, between learners, between staff and learners, and between staff, parents and the community
- uses restorative practice to manage behaviour
- collaborates rather than competes with other schools
- recruits teachers for their capacity to engage young people, not just their subject knowledge
- continually examines its practice in relation to the emotional and spiritual, as well as academic impact on young people
- uses the community and its wider resources to help educate the child

- listens to, and encourages, input from young people and all staff in developing policies and practices
- encourages the students to 'improve' themselves not just 'prove' themselves, thereby building a learning culture rather than a performance-orientated one
- co-constructs a compassionate curriculum that is meaningful to the students and builds compassionate skills and qualities as well as knowledge
- places compassion for the planet at the heart of its ethos.

5. Compassionate school leaders are those who ...

- recognize that compassion must be caught, taught and cultivated
- build a compassionate ethos and understand the knowledge, skills and attitudes that compassion requires
- strive to create a no-blame culture
- ensure that all learners, teachers and staff feel safe, supported and connected
- seek to understand before they act, always assume good intentions and self-check their initial response
- act as role models by manifesting the qualities of compassion in all that they do
- see failure as an integral component of learning for both teachers and young people
- build the leadership capacity of all students so that they can meaningfully contribute to the improvement of the school
- strive to 'see and hear' people by building trust at all levels across the school
- encourage people to challenge them so that they, themselves, continue to grow and learn
- ensure that there are safe mechanisms for the school community to voice dissent
- are not afraid of showing their vulnerabilities to other staff and to students
- use their leadership for the service of others, striving to improve others' lives
- inspire others through encouragement and empowerment
- are humble and understand that leadership requires learning from others around them
- accept accountability and uphold their ethics to a high standard

- seek influence rather than authority, encourage rather than demand, and lead with hope
- are deeply concerned about how their team members feel and their degree of job satisfaction
- see 'excellence' as a group effort in which every individual is valued and their efforts celebrated.

6. Compassionate school managers and governors are those who ...

- understand the attitudes outlined in 'acts for love' (see Figure 1.6 in Chapter 1.2) and practise them
- know the school well
- are generous with their time and have a high profile and supportive presence in the school
- are genuine and humble critical friends, who are there to serve the school and community
- have a sound knowledge of their policies and the confidence and competence to hold the school to account
- have the courage to challenge government education policies and robustly interrogate any external reviews imposed
- understand and monitor the implementation of policies that safeguard students and safeguard the planet
- are advocates for a compassionate school and exemplify the ideal of selfless service.

7. A compassionate child is one who ...

- sees kindness as a strength
- accepts the complexity and messiness of learning
- sees things from multiple perspectives and is non-judgemental
- listens with empathy and is sensitive to the changing moods of those around them
- feels connected to others: adults, other young people and the planet
- feels connected to nature, seeing its beauty with awe and a sense of wonder
- practises self-compassion and is prepared to fail and make mistakes
- is hopeful about the future and is a powerful advocate for climate justice
- has an awareness of their own emotional, spiritual and physical health
- is an active planetary citizen who engages in volunteering or social action to make a positive difference to all living things.

In addition to these criteria, CoED has devised three major audit proformas on Compassionate Knowledge, Compassionate Skills and Compassionate Attitudes. These can be downloaded from its website free of charge and printed as A3 hand-outs to be used for training purposes. Each seeks evidence of where these KSAs are taught, caught or cultivated.

Training on the pedagogy of compassion is an integral part of the blueprint. At present, it rarely happens and, yet, with each passing day, more scientific and other insights become available in support of its implementation. The required training encompasses everything from whole-school to governors, subject-specific and age phases. There are, however, an increasing range of online courses available. The Greater Good Science Center and the Charter for Compassion Education Institute offer some excellent modules. To date, however, there appears to be little on compassionate assessment, monitoring and evaluation at classroom, whole-school or system level.

How do you know your school has become compassionate?

A compassionate assessment system is predicated on the following premises:

- It is done 'with' rather than 'to'.
- It involves as many stakeholders as possible, including pupils and parents.
- It is open, honest and reflective and seeks critical comments.
- It operates on a no-blame/no-shame culture.
- It does not make league tables of compassionate schools, from best to worst.
- It is formative in that it seeks to offer next-step advice on areas of improvement.
- It accredits prior external validation like Rights Respecting, ECO and Healthy Schools awards.

Essentially, it's your own intuitive wisdom of the heart that can become your guide. For parents, asking and answering the simple question: 'Would I want my child to be educated here?' is an excellent starting point. Your initial impressions count, and they are almost invariably right. It is on reflection that these insights can be translated into cognitive judgements.

For those involved in school, a more refined methodology is to undertake compassionate learning walks. Learning walks are straightforward mechanisms through which, in a non-threatening manner, participants can gain knowledge and insights about aspects of provision. They have been used in most areas of school life and have involved all stakeholders, including students and parents. Our blueprint with six 'footprints' is one model (see Figure 6.1).

THE COMPASSIONATE LEARNING WALK

FOOTPRINT ONE: AGREEING THE FOCUS

Start with a key question: "What should we look at on the walk"? Are we, for example going to focus in turn on the compassionate skills, knowledge and attitudes of the pupils? Are we going to examine pupil agency? If we are looking at compassion for planet, what key elements do we propose to focus on?

FOOTPRINT TWO: ESTABLISH THE TEAM

Some simple questions: How big should the team be? What should be the criteria for team selection? Will we involve young people in the walk?

FOOTPRINT THREE: PREPARING THE WALK

The sorts of questions might be:

1. What training and briefing will we offer before the walk begins?
2. What information will we be providing to those we are planning to observe and interact with?
3. What are we going to see?
4. What are we going to ask?
5. Who are we going to talk to?
6. What are we hoping to hear?
7. How will we collect our evidence?

FOOTPRINT FOUR: THE ROOM VISITS

Some issues for discussion:

1. How long should we spend in a room?
2. What will we do when we get there?
3. How can we minimise our disruptive influence?
4. How and when shall we record our evidence?
5. What questions might we ask the pupils and the teaching staff?

FOOTPRINT FIVE: THE LEARNING ENVIRONMENT

This footprint is designed to help walkers come to conclusions about the learning environment both within rooms and about other areas like corridors, external areas, and dining rooms. Some basic questions might be:

1. How does the compassionate environment support learning?
2. What are the criteria for a good learning environment?
3. How is the environment organised and what does it tell us?
4. Do we see evidence of the golden thread of compassion?

FOOTPRINT SIX: DEBRIEF AND FEEDBACK TO COLLEAGUES AND PUPILS

The Basic question is "How should we debrief colleagues/young people and what feedback systems should we put into place?"

Figure 6.1: The compassionate learning walk

Source: The CoED Foundation

One successful aspect of the school improvement process in both Birmingham and London was the school guarantee, or pledge, that listed a number of key values, actions and aspirations the school pledged that students would receive during their years there. The CoED Foundation and the Birmingham Governor Network devised the following compassionate guarantee. Ideally, this would have been built-on with a student guarantee, where the students, in turn, promised to operate in certain compassionate ways.

The Compassionate Guarantee: 'The magnificent 12'

The school, its governors/managers, parents and carers guarantee that:

1. We adhere to the Golden Rule and try to treat everybody and the planet as we would wish to be treated.
2. We will do our best to ensure that this Golden Thread of love-in-action runs through everything we do in school and beyond.
3. We will teach about compassion and teach compassionately.
4. We will do our best to model compassionate behaviour at all times with everybody, and ensure that there is always one adult in whom you can confide.
5. We will do our best to teach you to become emotionally and spiritually literate and to become self-compassionate.
6. We will promote a rights-respecting ethos and one that is eco-friendly.
7. We will practise restorative justice principles and help you to do the same.
8. We will make sure that we help you achieve your highest possible potential in all areas of school life.
9. We will offer you the widest possible curriculum that affirms and celebrates a range of cultural and faith backgrounds.
10. We will do our best to help you play an active role in both school and community.
11. We will do all in our power to safeguard you from harm, wherever it may lurk.
12. We will provide you with the moral compass to practise love-in-action and become good citizens of the UK, the world and the planet.

Conclusion

In his TEDx talk in Doncaster in 2019, 'Education for Survival: Compassion for Planet', Maurice Irfan Coles envisages a world which has successfully addressed many of our climate problems by 2030, and highlights how this has been achieved. Similarly, Bruce Gill, in his brilliant CoED Foundation

Think Piece (2017), writes an imaginary Ofsted report from 2027 in which he describes a successful compassionate school. Both are based on the pedagogy of compassion in which schools address the issues of the day systematically, using the Golden Rule and Golden Thread as their guides. This book aimed to help schools navigate turbulent waters so that they, too, can become places of compassion. Let us end, therefore, by returning to the Pedagogy of Compassion model (Figure 1.4), but this time populating the five key areas with our compassionate insights (Figure 6.2).

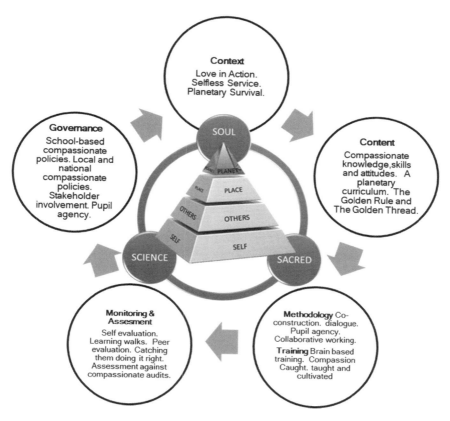

Figure 6.2: The pedagogy of compassion (populated version)

Source: The CoED Foundation

We can sum up the whole book in the simple phrase we saw earlier:

FROM 'ME' TO 'WE': CHANGE THE PRONOUN, CHANGE THE WORLD.

Afterword

Maurice Irfan Coles

The aim of this volume has been to provide the rationale for making a paradigm shift from a pedagogy of individualism and competition to a pedagogy of compassion. It charts the rationale for a change from selfishness to service, from planetary business-as-usual to one that places compassion for planet – and hence for ourselves, for others and for communities – at the heart of all we do. It offers a range of practical strategies to assist schools in undertaking their own compassionate journeys.

The 23 authors involved in *Education for Survival* struggled to contain in one book their enthusiasm and passion for the tasks in hand. So we hoped to make it two. Bill Gent and I had to take some difficult decisions as to where the excellent work of these authors would be placed – in the present volume, in printed form, or in a proposed Volume 2, which would be in electronic form only. Each volume would be self-contained so each chapter could be read as a stand-alone. The CoED Foundation is still committed to producing such an electronic book, and information about our progress will be kept up-to-date on our website.

References

Abidin, R.R. (1992) 'The determinants of parenting behavior'. *Journal of Clinical Child Psychology*, 21 (4), 407–12.

ABS (Australian Bureau of Statistics) (2012) *Childhood Education and Care, Australia, June 2011* (Catalogue No. 4402.0). Canberra: Australian Bureau of Statistics.

ACE-Aware Scotland (2019) *Keynote ACES to Assets 2019 – Dr Gabor Maté – Trauma as Disconnection from the Self* [video]. Online. www.youtube.com/watch?v=tef5_HK5Zlc (accessed 30 March 2020).

Ackerman, J. (2016) *The Genius of Birds*. London: Corsair.

Adams, R. (2014) 'Ofsted inspectors make U-turn on "Trojan Horse" school, leak shows'. *The Guardian*, 30 May. Online. https://tinyurl.com/ofqc3oa (accessed 16 March 2020).

A Future of OUR Choosing (2012) *Do Trees Communicate?* [video]. Online. www.youtube.com/watch?v=iSGPNm3bFmQ (accessed 13 May 2019).

Ahnert, L., Gunnar, M.R., Lamb, M.E. and Barthel, M. (2004) 'Transition to child care: Associations with infant–mother attachment, infant negative emotion, and cortisol elevations'. *Child Development*, 75 (3), 639–50.

Alexander, R. (ed.) (2010) *Children, Their World, Their Education: Final report and recommendations of the Cambridge Primary Review*. London: Routledge.

Allan, J. and Catts, R. (eds) (2012) *Social Capital, Children and Young People: Implications for practice, policy and research*. Bristol: Policy Press.

Alston, P. (2019) *Visit to the United Kingdom of Great Britain and Northern Ireland: Report of the Special Rapporteur on extreme poverty and human rights*. New York: United Nations General Assembly. Online. https://undocs.org/A/HRC/41/39/Add.1 (accessed 29 March 2020).

Altenfelder Santos Bordin, I., Silvestre Paula, C., Do Nascimento, R. and Seixas Duarte, C. (2006) 'Severe physical punishment and mental health problems in an economically disadvantaged population of children and adolescents'. *Revista Brasileira de Psiquiatria*, 28 (4), 290–6.

Anderson, C., Hildreth, J.A.D. and Howland, L. (2015) 'Is the desire for status a fundamental human motive? A review of the empirical literature'. *Psychological Bulletin*, 141 (3), 574–601.

Ayoub, M., Briley, D.A., Grotzinger, A., Patterson, M.W., Engelhardt, L.E., Tackett, J.L., Harden, K.P. and Tucker-Drob, E.M. (2019) 'Genetic and environmental associations between child personality and parenting'. *Social Psychological and Personality Science*, 10 (6), 711–21.

Bakan, J. (2012) *The Corporation: The pathological pursuit of profit and power*. Rev. ed. London: Constable.

Bakshi, R. (2012) *Civilizational Ghandi* (Gateway House Research Paper 6). Online: https://www.gatewayhouse.in/wp-content/uploads/2015/12/Civilizational-Gandhi-Online.pdf (accessed 20 June 2020).

Balch, O. (2013) 'The relevance of Gandhi in the capitalism debate'. *The Guardian*, 28 January. Online. https://tinyurl.com/vx5hdfd (accessed 15 March 2020).

Ban, K. (2014) 'Opening remarks at launch of Intergovernmental Panel on Climate Change Synthesis Report'. Online. https://tinyurl.com/rlcktpo (accessed 29 March 2020).

Bandes, S.A. (2017) 'Compassion and the rule of law'. *International Journal of Law in Context*, 13 (2), 184–96.

Bangham, G. and Leslie, J. (2019) 'Who owns all the pie? The size and distribution of Britain's £14.6 trillion of wealth'. Online. https://tinyurl.com/sc7jpw3 (accessed 28 March 2020).

Barber, B.K. and Lovelady Harmon, E. (2002) 'Violating the self: Parental psychological control of children and adolescents'. In Barber, B.K. (ed.) *Intrusive Parenting: How psychological control affects children and adolescents*. Washington, DC: American Psychological Association, 15–52.

Bargh, J. (2017) *Before You Know It: The unconscious reasons we do what we do*. New York: Touchstone.

Baring, A. (1993) *The Birds Who Flew beyond Time*. Bath: Barefoot Books.

Barkow, J.H. (1989) *Darwin, Sex and Status: Biological approaches to mind and culture*. Toronto: University of Toronto Press.

Barton, E.R, Newbury, A. and Roberts, J. (2018) *An Evaluation of the Adverse Childhood Experience (ACE)-Informed Whole School Approach*. Cardiff: Public Health Wales. Online. https://tinyurl.com/rr5goed (accessed 29 March 2020).

Basran, J., Pires, C., Matos, M., McEwan, K. and Gilbert, P. (2019) 'Styles of leadership, fears of compassion, and competing to avoid inferiority'. *Frontiers in Psychology*, 9, Article 2460, 1–14. Online. https://tinyurl.com/rq57vux (accessed 15 March 2020).

Bass, R.V. and Good, J.W. (2004) 'Educare and educere: Is a balance possible in the educational system?'. *Educational Forum*, 68 (2), 161–8.

Baumsteiger, R. (2019) 'What the world needs now: An intervention for promoting prosocial behavior'. *Basic and Applied Social Psychology*, 41 (4), 215–29.

BBC One (2019) *Meat: A Threat to Our Planet?* Online. www.bbc.co.uk/programmes/m000bqsh (accessed 30 March 2020).

Beck, C.T. (2004) 'Birth trauma: In the eye of the beholder'. *Nursing Research*, 53 (1), 28–35.

Belfield, C., Farquharson, C. and Sibieta, L. (2018) *2018 Annual Report on Education Spending in England*. London: Institute for Fiscal Studies.

Bentham, J. (1791) *Panopticon; or The Inspection House, Volume 1*. London: T. Payne.

BEP (Birmingham Education Partnership) (n.d.) 'Our mission'. Online. https://bep.education/about/ (accessed 22 June 2020).

Bergland, C. (2013) 'The neuroscience of empathy'. *Psychology Today*, 10 October. Online. https://tinyurl.com/mjn4nbu (accessed 15 March 2020).

Bergold, S. and Steinmayr, R. (2016) 'The relation over time between achievement motivation and intelligence in young elementary school children: A latent cross-lagged analysis'. *Contemporary Educational Psychology*, 46, 228–40.

Beutel, M.E., Klein, E.M., Brähler, E., Reiner, I., Jünger, C., Michal, M., Wiltink, J., Wild, P.S., Münzel, T., Lackner, K.J. and Tibubos, A.N. (2017) 'Loneliness in the general population: Prevalence, determinants and relations to mental health'. *BMC Psychiatry*, 17, Article 97, 1–7. Online. https://tinyurl.com/wlodync (accessed 15 March 2020).

Biglan, A., Flay, B.R., Embry, D.D. and Sandler, I.N. (2012) 'The critical role of nurturing environments for promoting human well-being'. *American Psychologist*, 67 (4), 257–71.

Birmingham City Council (n.d.) 'Faith Makes a Difference: RE in Birmingham'. Online. https://www.faithmakesadifference.co.uk/content/24-dispositions (accessed 22 June 2020).

Birmingham City Council (2007) *Birmingham Agreed Syllabus for Religious Education*. Online. https://www.faithmakesadifference.co.uk/content/agreed-syllabus (accessed 20 June 2020).

Birmingham City Council (2011). 'Census 2011'. Online. https://www.birmingham.gov.uk/directory/35/population_and_census/category/447 (accessed 30 June 2020).

Birmingham City Council (2015) *Birmingham Curriculum Statement*. Online. https://www.birmingham.gov.uk/downloads/file/1491/birmingham_curriculum_statement (accessed 20 June 2020).

Birmingham City Council (2017) *Education Delivery and Improvement Plan 2017/18*. Online. https://www.birmingham.gov.uk/download/downloads/id/4340/education_services_delivery_and_improvement_plan_2017_to_2018.pdf (accessed 22 June 2020).

Birmingham City Council (2018). 'Infograph'. Online. No longer available.

Bloom, P. (2017) 'Empathy and its discontents'. *Trends in Cognitive Sciences*, 21 (1), 24–31.

Blunt Bugental, D., Martorell, G.A. and Barraza, V. (2003) 'The hormonal costs of subtle forms of infant maltreatment'. *Hormones and Behavior*, 43 (1), 237–44.

Böckler, A., Tusche, A. and Singer, T. (2016) 'The structure of human prosociality: Differentiating altruistically motivated, norm motivated, strategically motivated, and self-reported prosocial behavior'. *Social Psychological and Personality Science*, 7 (6), 530–41.

Borra, C., Iacovou, M. and Sevilla, A. (2015) 'New evidence on breastfeeding and postpartum depression: The importance of understanding women's intentions'. *Maternal and Child Health Journal*, 19, 897–907.

Boseley, S. (2018) 'World in mental health crisis of "monumental suffering", say experts'. *The Guardian*, 9 October. Online. https://tinyurl.com/vzv23ds (accessed 16 March 2020).

Bowlby, J. (1969) *Attachment and Loss, Volume 1: Attachment*. London: Hogarth Press.

Breit, S., Kupferberg, A., Rogler, G. and Hasler, G. (2018) 'Vagus nerve as modulator of the brain–gut axis in psychiatric and inflammatory disorders'. *Frontiers in Psychiatry*, 9, Article 44, 1–15. Online. https://tinyurl.com/u6pjb4v (accessed 15 March 2020).

Brighouse, T. (2019) *The Priestley Lecture*. Birmingham: University of Birmingham. Online: www.birmingham.ac.uk/schools/education/events/2019/06/priestley-lecture.aspx (accessed 22 June 2020).

References

Brighouse, T. and Woods, D. (2013) *The A–Z of School Improvement: Principles and practice*. London: Bloomsbury.

Brown, G. and Coles, M.I. (2015) 'Compassion through cultural development'. In Coles, M.I. (ed.) *Towards the Compassionate School: From golden rule to golden thread*. London: Trentham Books, 76–94.

Brown, S.L. and Brown, R.M. (2015) 'Connecting prosocial behavior to improved physical health: Contributions from the neurobiology of parenting'. *Neuroscience and Biobehavioral Reviews*, 55, 1–17.

Brunzell, T., Waters, L. and Stokes, H. (2015) 'Teaching with strengths in trauma-affected students: A new approach to healing and growth in the classroom'. *American Journal of Orthopsychiatry*, 85 (1), 3–9.

Buber, M. (1923) *Ich und Du* [Trans. Smith, R.G. *I and Thou*]. Leipzig: Insel Verlag.

Bulman, M. (2019) 'UN tears into Tory-led austerity as "ideological project causing pain and misery" in devastating report on UK poverty crisis'. *The Independent*, 22 May. Online. https://tinyurl.com/uzvxqba (accessed 15 March 2020).

Buss, D.M. (2016) *Evolutionary Psychology: The new science of the mind*. 5th ed. London: Routledge.

Byrne, J. (2015) 'See this illustration of Kristin Neff's three steps for self-compassion'. Online. https://www.lionsroar.com/three-steps-for-self-compassion-illustrated/ (accessed 25 June 2020).

Cacioppo, S., Capitanio, J.P. and Cacioppo, J.T. (2014) 'Towards a neurology of loneliness'. *Psychological Bulletin*, 140 (6), 1464–504.

Carona, C., Rijo, D., Salvador, C., Castilho, P. and Gilbert, P. (2017) 'Compassion-focused therapy with children and adolescents'. *British Journal of Psychiatry Advances*, 23 (4), 240–52.

Carter, C.S., Ben-Ami Bartal, I. and Porges, E.C. (2017) 'The roots of compassion: An evolutionary and neurobiological perspective'. In Seppälä, E.M., Simon-Thomas, E., Brown, S.L., Worline, M.C., Cameron, C.D. and Doty, J.R. (eds) *The Oxford Handbook of Compassion Science*. New York: Oxford University Press, 173–88.

CASEL (Collaborative for Academic, Social, and Emotional Learning) (2019) 'What is SEL?'. Online. https://casel.org/what-is-sel/ (accessed 18 September 2019).

Cassidy, J. and Shaver, P.R. (eds) (2016) *Handbook of Attachment: Theory, research, and clinical applications*. 3rd ed. New York: Guilford Press.

Chance, M.R.A. (ed.) (1988) *Social Fabrics of the Mind*. Hove: Lawrence Erlbaum Associates.

Charter for Compassion Education Institute (2019) 'The Science of Compassion Course'. Online. https://charterforcompassion.org/the-science-of-compassion-course (accessed 20 June 2020).

Charter for Compassion (2020) 'Charter for Compassion Education Institute'. Online. https://charterforcompassion.org/cei-home (accessed 16 March 2020).

Chiao, J.Y. (2017) 'Cultural neuroscience of compassion and empathy'. In Seppälä, E.M., Simon-Thomas, E., Brown, S.L., Worline, M.C., Cameron, C.D. and Doty, J.R. (eds) *The Oxford Handbook of Compassion Science*. New York: Oxford University Press, 147–58.

Chiu, M., Rahman, F., Vigod, S., Lau, C., Cairney, J. and Kurdyak, P. (2018) 'Mortality in single fathers compared with single mothers and partnered parents: A population-based cohort study'. *Lancet Public Health*, 3 (3), e115–23.

Clarke, K. (2016) *Kind of Blue: A political memoir*. London: Macmillan.

Clarke, P. (2014) *Report into Allegations Concerning Birmingham Schools Arising from the 'Trojan Horse' Letter*. London: Department for Education.

Coall, D.A. and Hertwig, R. (2010) 'Grandparental investment: Past, present, and future'. *Behavioral and Brain Sciences*, 33 (1), 1–59.

Coles, M.I. (ed.) (2015) *Towards the Compassionate School: From golden rule to golden thread*. London: Trentham Books.

Colonnello, V., Petrocchi, N. and Heinrichs, M. (2017) 'The psychobiological foundation of prosocial relationships: The role of oxytocin in daily social exchanges'. In Gilbert, P. (ed.) *Compassion: Concepts, research and applications*. London: Routledge, 105–19.

Commission for Social Care Inspection and Ofsted (2008) *2008 Annual Performance Assessment of Services for Children and Young People in Birmingham City Council*. Online. https://files.api.beta.ofsted.gov.uk/v1/file/50003639 (accessed 20 June 2020).

Commissioner for Wales (2015) 'Well-being of Future Generations (Wales) Act 2015. Online. https://futuregenerations.wales/about-us/future-generations-act/ (accessed 20 June 2020).

Compassionate Schools Project (n.d.) 'Compassionate Schools Project program'. Online. www.compassionschools.org/program/ (accessed 16 March 2020).

Conroy, D.E., Willow, J.P. and Metzler, J.N. (2002) 'Multidimensional fear of failure measurement: The performance failure appraisal inventory'. *Journal of Applied Sport Psychology*, 14 (2), 76–90.

Conway, C.C. and Slavich, G.M. (2017) 'Behavior genetics of prosocial behavior'. In Gilbert, P. (ed.) *Compassion: Concepts, research and applications*. London: Routledge, 151–70.

Corrigan, J.G. (2019) *Red Brain Blue Brain: Living, loving and leading without fear*. Kindle edition. Sydney: Castleflag Pty Ltd.

Covey, S.R. (1989) *The Seven Habits of Highly Effective People*. New York: Free Press.

Cowan, C.S.M., Callaghan, B.L., Kan, J.M. and Richardson, R. (2016) 'The lasting impact of early-life adversity on individuals and their descendants: Potential mechanisms and hope for intervention'. *Genes, Brain and Behavior*, 15 (1), 155–68.

Crocker, J. and Canevello, A. (2008) 'Creating and undermining social support in communal relationships: The role of compassionate and self-image goals'. *Journal of Personality and Social Psychology*, 95 (3), 555–75.

Crocker, J. and Canevello, A. (2012) 'Egosystem and ecosystem: Motivational perspectives on caregiving'. In Brown, S.L., Brown, R.M. and Penner, L.A. (eds) *Moving beyond Self-Interest: Perspectives from evolutionary biology, neuroscience, and the social sciences*. New York: Oxford University Press, 211–23.

Crocker, J. and Park, L.E. (2004) 'The costly pursuit of self-esteem'. *Psychological Bulletin*, 130 (3), 392–414.

Curran, T. and Hill, A.P. (2019) 'Perfectionism is increasing over time: A meta-analysis of birth cohort differences from 1989 to 2016'. *Psychological Bulletin*, 145 (4), 410–29.

Darwin, C. (1871) *The Descent of Man*. New York: D. Appleton and Company.

Decety, J. and Cowell, J.M. (2014) 'Friends or foes: Is empathy necessary for moral behavior?'. *Perspectives on Psychological Science*, 9 (5), 525–37.

Decety, J. and Ickes, W. (eds) (2011) *The Social Neuroscience of Empathy*. Cambridge, MA: MIT Press.

de Caestecker, L. *et al.* (2017) *Tackling the Attainment Gap by Preventing and Responding to Adverse Childhood Experiences (ACEs)*. Edinburgh: NHS Health Scotland. Online. https://tinyurl.com/vsdolhg (accessed 30 June 2020).

Deming, W.E. (1994) *The New Economics for Industry, Government, Education*. 2nd ed. Cambridge, MA: MIT Press.

Dettling, A.C., Gunnar, M.R. and Donzella, B. (1999) 'Cortisol levels of young children in full-day childcare centers: Relations with age and temperament'. *Psychoneuroendocrinology*, 24 (5), 519–36.

DfE (Department for Education) (n.d.) 'Department for Education'. Online. https://tinyurl.com/z687yr4 (accessed 16 March 2020).

DfE (Department for Education) (2014a) *Equality Objectives*. London: Department for Education. Online. https://tinyurl.com/skvh54l (accessed 16 March 2020).

DfE (Department for Education) (2014b) 'Education commissioner for Birmingham announced'. Press release, 25 September. Online. https://tinyurl.com/pwmdb6d (accessed 16 March 2020).

DfE (Department for Education) (2015) 'Protecting children from radicalisation: The prevent duty'. Online. https://www.gov.uk/government/publications/protecting-children-from-radicalisation-the-prevent-duty (accessed 22 June 2020).

DfE (Department for Education) (2019) *Relationships Education, Relationships and Sex Education (RSE) and Health Education: Draft statutory guidance for governing bodies, proprietors, head teachers, principals, senior leadership teams, teachers*. London: Department for Education.

DHSC (Department of Health and Social Care) and DfE (Department for Education) (2017) 'Transforming children and young people's mental health provision: A green paper'. Online. https://tinyurl.com/y3kox3pe (accessed 25 March 2020).

Diamond, C. (2019a) 'Parkfield School and No Outsiders: We must learn from Trojan Horse history in Birmingham'. *Schools Week*, 20 March. Online. https://tinyurl.com/syzwxkr (accessed 16 March 2020).

Diamond, C. (2019b) 'There is a way out of the schools LGBT protest mess – but ministers need to get behind it'. *The Guardian*, 6 August. Online. https://tinyurl.com/u4wtlvb (accessed 16 March 2020).

Dickerson, S.S. and Kemeny, M.E. (2004) 'Acute stressors and cortisol responses: A theoretical integration and synthesis of laboratory research'. *Psychological Bulletin*, 130 (3), 335–91.

Dobson, A. (2003) *Citizenship and the Environment*. Oxford: Oxford University Press.

Dobson, A. (2016) *Environmental Politics: A very short introduction.* Oxford: Oxford University Press.

Dorling, D. (2018) *Peak Inequality: Britain's ticking time bomb.* Bristol: Policy Press.

D'Souza, A.J., Russell, M., Wood, B., Signal, L. and Elder, D. (2016) 'Attitudes to physical punishment of children are changing'. *Archives of Disease in Childhood*, 101 (8), 690–3.

Duffell, N. (2014) *Wounded Leaders: British elitism and the entitlement illusion: A psychohistory.* London: Lone Arrow Press.

Dunbar, R.I.M. (2010) 'The social role of touch in humans and primates: Behavioural function and neurobiological mechanisms'. *Neuroscience and Biobehavioral Reviews*, 34 (2), 260–8.

Dunbar, R. (2014) *Human Evolution: A Pelican introduction.* London: Pelican.

Dunsworth, H. and Eccleston, L. (2015) 'The evolution of difficult childbirth and helpless hominin infants'. *Annual Review of Anthropology*, 44, 55–69.

Durante, F. and Fiske, S.T. (2017) 'How social-class stereotypes maintain inequality'. *Current Opinion in Psychology*, 18, 43–8.

Earley, P. and Greany, T. (eds) (2017) *School Leadership and Education System Reform.* London: Bloomsbury Academic.

Edge, D. and Lemetyinen, H. (2019) 'Psychology across cultures: Challenges and opportunities'. *Psychology and Psychotherapy: Theory, research and practice*, 92 (2), 261–76.

Education Scotland (n.d.) 'What is learning for sustainability?' Online. https://education.gov.scot/improvement/learning-resources/a-summary-of-learning-for-sustainability-resources (accessed 30 June 2020).

Eibl-Eibesfeldt, I. (2017) *Human Ethology.* London: Routledge.

Einstein, A. (1946) Letter to *New York Times* (quoted in Stavrianos, L.S., 2004, *Lifelines from Our Past.* London: Routledge).

Eisenberg, N., Fabes, R.A., Schaller, M., Carlo, G. and Miller, P.A. (1991) 'The relations of parental characteristics and practices to children's vicarious emotional responding'. *Child Development*, 62 (6), 1393–408.

Elkes, N. (2014) '"We're sorry": Council leader admits staff ignored Trojan Horse issue for "fear of being accused of racism"'. *Birmingham Mail*, 18 July. Online. https://tinyurl.com/ujwana2 (accessed 15 March 2020).

ESP (Education Support Partnership) (2018) *Teacher Wellbeing Index 2018.* London: Education Support Partnership. Online. https://tinyurl.com/rm2nmvv (accessed 16 March 2020).

European Commission (2019) 'Press remarks by President von der Leyen on the occasion of the adoption of the European Green Deal Communication'. Online. https://ec.europa.eu/commission/presscorner/detail/en/speech_19_6749 (accessed 9 June 2020).

Etcoff, N. (1999) *Survival of the Prettiest: The science of beauty.* New York: Doubleday.

Extinction Rebellion (2019) *This is Not a Drill: An Extinction Rebellion handbook.* London: Penguin.

Fogel, A., Melson, G.F. and Mistry, J. (1986) 'Conceptualizing the determinants of nurturance: A reassessment of sex differences'. In Fogel, A. and Melson, G.F. (eds) *Origins of Nurturance: Developmental, biological and cultural perspectives on caregiving.* Hillsdale, NJ: Lawrence Erlbaum Associates, 53–90.

Fonagy, P. and Target, M. (1997) 'Attachment and reflective function: Their role in self-organization'. *Development and Psychopathology,* 9 (4), 679–700.

Fotaki, M. (2015) 'Why and how is compassion necessary to provide good quality healthcare?'. *International Journal of Health Policy and Management,* 4 (4), 199–201.

Foucault, M. (1979) *Discipline and Punish: The birth of the prison.* Trans. Sheridan, A. Harmondsworth: Penguin.

Fox, M. (1999) *A Spirituality Named Compassion: Uniting mystical awareness with social justice.* Rochester, VT: Inner Traditions International.

Fox, M., Wilson, S. and Listug, J.B. (2018) *Order of the Sacred Earth: An intergenerational vision of love and action.* Rhinebeck, NY: Monkfish Book Publishing Company.

Freire, P. (1970) *Pedagogy of the Oppressed.* Trans. Ramos, M. New York: Herder and Herder.

Freire, P. (2000) Cited by Carlos Alberto Torres in (2014) *First Freire: Early writings in social justice education.* New York: Teachers College Press.

Fromm, E. (1956) *The Art of Loving.* New York, NY: Harper and Row.

Fu, A.S. and Markus, H.R. (2014) 'My mother and me: Why tiger mothers motivate Asian Americans but not European Americans'. *Personality and Social Psychology Bulletin,* 40 (6), 739–49.

Galante, J., Galante, I., Bekkers, M.-J. and Gallacher, J. (2014) 'Effect of kindness-based meditation on health and well-being: A systematic review and meta-analysis'. *Journal of Consulting and Clinical Psychology,* 82 (6), 1101–14.

Garner, R. (2013). 'Michael Gove creating "neo Victorian" curriculum for primary schools, says professor who led massive review into sector'. *The Independent,* 24 September. Online. https://tinyurl.com/yc8z27nq (accessed 20 June 2020).

Gardner, H. (1983) *Frames of Mind: The theory of multiple intelligences.* London: Heinemann.

Germer, C.K. (2009) *The Mindful Path to Self-Compassion.* New York: Guilford Press.

Germer, C.K. and Siegel, R.D. (eds) (2012) *Wisdom and Compassion in Psychotherapy: Deepening mindfulness in clinical practice.* New York: Guilford Press.

Gilbert, P. (1989) *Human Nature and Suffering.* Hove: Lawrence Erlbaum Associates.

Gilbert, P. (1997) 'The evolution of social attractiveness and its role in shame, humiliation, guilt and therapy'. *British Journal of Medical Psychology,* 70 (2), 113–47.

Gilbert, P. (1998) 'What is shame? Some core issues and controversies'. In Gilbert, P. and Andrews, B. (eds) *Shame: Interpersonal behavior, psychopathology, and culture.* New York: Oxford University Press, 3–38.

Gilbert, P. (2000) 'Social mentalities: Internal "social" conflict and the role of inner warmth and compassion in cognitive therapy'. In Gilbert, P. and Bailey, K.G. (eds) *Genes on the Couch: Explorations in evolutionary psychotherapy*. Hove: Brunner-Routledge, 118–50.

Gilbert, P. (2007) 'The evolution of shame as a marker for relationship security: A biopsychosocial approach'. In Tracy, J.L., Robins, R.W. and Price Tangney, J. (eds) *The Self-Conscious Emotions: Theory and research*. New York: Guilford Press, 283–309.

Gilbert, P. (2009) *The Compassionate Mind: A new approach to life's challenges*. London: Constable and Robinson.

Gilbert, P. (2010) *Compassion Focused Therapy: Distinctive features*. London: Routledge.

Gilbert, P. (2011) 'Shame in psychotherapy and the role of compassion focused therapy'. In Dearing, R.L. and Price Tangney, J. (eds) *Shame in the Therapy Hour*. Washington, DC: American Psychological Society, 325–54.

Gilbert, P. (2014) 'The origins and nature of compassion focused therapy'. *British Journal of Clinical Psychology*, 53 (1), 6–41.

Gilbert. P. (ed.) (2017a) *Compassion: Concepts, research and applications*. London: Routledge.

Gilbert, P. (2017b) 'Compassion as a social mentality: An evolutionary approach'. In Gilbert, P. (ed.) *Compassion: Concepts, research and applications*. London: Routledge, 31–68.

Gilbert, P. (2018) *Living like Crazy*. 2nd ed. York: Annwyn House.

Gilbert, P. (2019a) 'Explorations into the nature and function of compassion'. *Current Opinion in Psychology*, 28, 108–14.

Gilbert, P. (2019b) 'Psychotherapy for the 21st century: An integrative, evolutionary, contextual, biopsychosocial approach'. *Psychology and Psychotherapy: Theory, Research and Practice*, 92 (2), 164–89.

Gilbert, P., Bhundia, R., Mitra, R., McEwan, K., Irons, C. and Sanghera, J. (2007) 'Cultural differences in shame-focused attitudes towards mental health problems in Asian and non-Asian student women'. *Mental Health, Religion and Culture*, 10 (2), 127–41.

Gilbert, P., Broomhead, C., Irons, C., McEwan, K., Bellew, R., Mills, A., Gale, C. and Knibb, R. (2007) 'Development of a striving to avoid inferiority scale'. *British Journal of Social Psychology*, 46 (3), 633–48.

Gilbert, P. and Choden (2013) *Mindful Compassion*. London: Constable and Robinson.

Gilbert, P., Clarke, M., Hempel, S., Miles, J.N.V. and Irons, C. (2004) 'Criticizing and reassuring oneself: An exploration of forms, styles and reasons in female students'. *British Journal of Clinical Psychology*, 43 (1), 31–50.

Gilbert, P. and Mascaro, J. (2017) 'Compassion fears, blocks and resistances: An evolutionary investigation'. In Seppälä, E.M., Simon-Thomas, E., Brown, S.L., Worline, M.C., Cameron, C.D. and Doty, J.R. (eds) *The Oxford Handbook of Compassion Science*. New York: Oxford University Press, 399–418.

Gilbert, P., Price, J. and Allan, S. (1995) 'Social comparison, social attractiveness and evolution: How might they be related?'. *New Ideas in Psychology*, 13 (2), 149–65.

References

Gilbert, P. and Procter, S. (2006) 'Compassionate mind training for people with high shame and self-criticism: Overview and pilot study of a group therapy approach'. *Clinical Psychology and Psychotherapy*, 13, 353–79.

Gilbert, T. (2015) 'Using the Psychological Concept of Compassion to Inform Pedagogic Strategies for Higher Education Seminars'. PhD thesis, University of Hertfordshire.

Gill, B. (2017) *Compassion-Based Educational Transformation* (Think Piece No. 5). Birmingham: CoED Foundation. Online. https://tinyurl.com/uxjzxk7 (accessed 16 March 2020).

Ginott, H.G. (1972) *Teacher and Child: A book for parents and teachers*. New York: Macmillan.

Goetz, J.L., Keltner, D. and Simon-Thomas, E. (2010) 'Compassion: An evolutionary analysis and empirical review'. *Psychological Bulletin*, 136 (3), 351–74.

Goleman, D. (1995) *Emotional Intelligence*. New York: Bantam Books.

Goleman, D. (2009) *Ecological Intelligence: The coming age of radical transparency*. New York: Penguin.

Goleman, D., Bennett, L. and Barlow, Z. (2012) *Ecoliterate: How educators are cultivating emotional, social, and ecological intelligence*. San Francisco: Jossey-Bass.

Goleman, D. and Davidson, R.J. (2017) *Altered Traits: Science reveals how meditation changes your mind, brain, and body*. London: Penguin.

Goodall, J. (1991) *Through a Window: Thirty years with the chimpanzees of Gombe*. London: Penguin.

Gopnik, A. (2016) *The Gardener and the Carpenter: What the new science of child development tells us about the relationship between parents and children*. London: Vintage.

Gray, J., O'Regan, J.P. and Wallace, C. (2018) 'Education and the discourse of global neoliberalism'. *Language and Intercultural Communication*, 18 (5), 471–7.

Hall, H., McLelland, G., Gilmour, C. and Cant, R. (2014) '"It's those first few weeks": Women's views about breastfeeding support in an Australian outer metropolitan region'. *Women and Birth*, 27 (4), 259–65.

Harari, Y.N. (2015) *Sapiens: A brief history of humankind*. London: Vintage.

Hargreaves, A. (2019) 'Leadership ethics, inequality and identity'. *Principal Connections*, 23 (1), 14–17. Online. https://tinyurl.com/wyyyq4t (accessed 25 March 2020).

Harvey, A. (2009) *The Hope: A guide to sacred activism*. London: Hay House.

Harvey, D. (2005) *A Brief History of Neoliberalism*. Oxford: Oxford University Press.

Haslam, D.M., Patrick, P. and Kirby, J.N. (2015) 'Giving voice to working mothers: A consumer informed study to program design for working mothers'. *Journal of Child and Family Studies*, 24, 2463–73.

Haslam, S.A., McMahon, C., Cruwys, T., Haslam, C., Jetten, J. and Steffens, N.K. (2018) 'Social cure, what social cure? The propensity to underestimate the importance of social factors for health'. *Social Science and Medicine*, 198, 14–21.

Hawkes, N. and Hawkes, J. (2018) *The Inner Curriculum: How to nourish wellbeing, resilience and self-leadership.* Woodbridge: John Catt Educational.

Hayward, B. (2012) *Children, Citizenship and Environment: Nurturing a democratic imagination in a changing world.* London: Routledge.

Heaney, S. (1991) *The Cure at Troy: A version of Sophocles' Philoctetes.* New York: Noonday Press.

Heroic Imagination Project (n.d.) Resource library on heroism. Online. https://www.heroicimagination.org/library (accessed 29 June 2020).

Hicks, D. (2014) *Educating for Hope in Troubled Times: Climate change and the transition to a post-carbon future.* London: Trentham Books.

Ho, A.K., Sidanius, J., Pratto, F., Levin, S., Thomsen, L., Kteily, N. and Sheehy-Skeffington, J. (2012) 'Social dominance orientation: Revisiting the structure and function of a variable predicting social and political attitudes'. *Personality and Social Psychology Bulletin*, 38 (5), 583–606.

Hobfoll, S.E. (2018) *Tribalism: The evolutionary origins of fear politics.* Cham: Palgrave Macmillan.

Hofmann, S.G., Grossman, P. and Hinton, D.E. (2011) 'Loving-kindness and compassion meditation: Potential for psychological intervention'. *Clinical Psychology Review*, 31 (7), 1126–32.

Holmes, J. and Slade, A. (2018) *Attachment in Therapeutic Practice.* London: SAGE Publications.

Holmwood, J. and O'Toole, T. (2018) *Countering Extremism in British Schools? The truth about the Birmingham Trojan Horse affair.* Bristol: Policy Press.

Holt, J. (1964) *How Children Fail.* London: Pitman.

Holt-Lunstad, J., Smith, T.B., Baker, M., Harris, T. and Stephenson, D. (2015) 'Loneliness and social isolation as risk factors for mortality: A meta-analytic review'. *Perspectives on Psychological Science*, 10 (2), 227–37.

Horowitz, K., McKay, M. and Marshall, R. (2005) 'Community violence and urban families: Experiences, effects, and directions for intervention'. *American Journal of Orthopsychiatry*, 75 (3), 356–68.

Howe, S. (2019) 'Our obsession with exams is failing to equip young people with the right skills for the future, says Future Generations Commissioner for Wales'. Press release, 21 October. Online. https://tinyurl.com/rcro8ws (accessed 25 March 2020).

Hrdy, S.B. (2009) *Mothers and Others: The evolutionary origins of mutual understanding.* Cambridge, MA: Harvard University Press.

Huang, J.Y. and Bargh, J.A. (2014) 'The selfish goal: Autonomously operating motivational structures as the proximate cause of human judgement and behavior'. *Behavioral and Brain Sciences*, 37 (2), 121–35.

IPCC (2018) *Global Warming of 1.5°C: An IPCC Special Report on the impacts of global warming of 1.5°C above pre-industrial levels and related global greenhouse gas emission pathways, in the context of strengthening the global response to the threat of climate change, sustainable development, and efforts to eradicate poverty.* Geneva: IPCC.

Ikeda, D. (2005) 'The university of the twenty-first century – cradle of world citizens'. Online. https://tinyurl.com/rgcvhad (accessed 28 March 2020).

Janoff-Bulman, R. (2009) 'To provide or protect: Motivational bases of political liberalism and conservatism'. *Psychological Inquiry*, 20 (2–3), 120–8.

References

Jennings, P.A. (ed.) (2019) *The Mindful School: Transforming school culture through mindfulness and compassion*. New York: Guilford Press.

Johnson, A.P. (2007) *The Inner Curriculum*. Unionville, NY: Royal Fireworks Press.

Karraker, K.H. and Coleman, P.K. (2005) 'The effects of child characteristics on parenting'. In Luster, T. and Okagaki, L. (eds) *Parenting: An ecological perspective*. 2nd ed. Mahwah, NJ: Lawrence Erlbaum Associates, 147–76.

Kasser, T., Ryan, R.M., Zax, M. and Sameroff, A.J. (1995) 'The relations of maternal and social environments to late adolescents' materialistic and prosocial values'. *Developmental Psychology*, 31 (6), 907–14.

Keltner, D., Gruenfeld, D.H. and Anderson, C. (2003) 'Power, approach, and inhibition'. *Psychological Review*, 110 (2), 265–84.

Kershaw, I. (2014) *Investigation Report: Trojan Horse letter*. London: Eversheds LLP.

Khait, I., Lewin-Epstein, O., Sharon, R., Saban, K., Perelman, R., Boonman, A., Yovel, Y. and Hadany, L. (2019) 'Plants emit informative airborne sounds under stress'. Online. www.biorxiv.org/content/10.1101/507590v4 (accessed 15 March 2020).

Kirby, J.N. (2015) 'The potential benefits of parenting programs for grandparents: Recommendations and clinical implications'. *Journal of Child and Family Studies*, 24, 3200–12.

Kirby, J.N. (2016) 'The role of mindfulness and compassion in enhancing nurturing family environments'. *Clinical Psychology: Science and Practice*, 23 (2), 142–57.

Kirby, J.N. (2017a) 'Compassion interventions: The programmes, the evidence, and implications for research and practice'. *Psychology and Psychotherapy: Theory, Research and Practice*, 90 (3), 432–55.

Kirby, J.N. (2017b) 'Compassion-Focused Parenting'. In Seppälä, E.M., Simon-Thomas, E., Brown, S.L., Worline, M.C., Cameron, C.D. and Doty, J.R. (eds) *The Oxford Handbook of Compassion Science*. New York: Oxford University Press, 92–106.

Kirby, J.N. and Baldwin, S. (2018) 'A randomized micro-trial of a loving-kindness meditation to help parents respond to difficult child behavior vignettes'. *Journal of Child and Family Studies*, 27, 1614–28.

Kirby, J.N. and Gilbert, P. (2017) 'The emergence of the compassion focused therapies'. In Gilbert, P. (ed.) *Compassion: Concepts, research and applications*. London: Routledge, 258–85.

Kirby, J.N., Grzazek, O. and Gilbert, P. (2019) 'The role of compassionate and self-image goals in predicting psychological controlling and facilitative parenting styles'. *Frontiers in Psychology*, 10, Article 1041, 1–14. Online. https://tinyurl.com/vjh7m5p (accessed 25 March 2020).

Kirby, J.N., Sampson, H., Day, J., Hayes, A. and Gilbert, P. (2019) 'Human evolution and culture in relationship to shame in the parenting role: Implications for psychology and psychotherapy'. *Psychology and Psychotherapy: Theory, Research and Practice*, 92 (2), 238–60.

Klein, N. (2019) *On Fire: The burning case for a Green New Deal*. London: Allen Lane.

Klevens, J. and Whitaker, D.J. (2007) 'Primary prevention of child physical abuse and neglect: Gaps and promising directions'. *Child Maltreatment*, 12 (4), 364–77.

Koopmann-Holm, B. and Tsai, J.L. (2017) 'The cultural shaping of compassion'. In Seppälä, E.M., Simon-Thomas, E., Brown, S.L., Worline, M.C., Cameron, C.D. and Doty, J.R. (eds) *The Oxford Handbook of Compassion Science*. New York: Oxford University Press, 273–86.

Kukk, C.L. (2017) *The Compassionate Achiever: How helping others fuels success*. New York: HarperOne.

Kumar, S. (2014) 'Love can save the world'. Video presentation at the Future NOW Spiritual Ecology Conference. Online: www.youtube.com/watch?v=5F_ZdepTA0A (accessed 9 June 2020).

Kuyken, W., Weare, K., Ukoumunne, O.C., Vicary, R., Motton, N., Burnett, R., Cullen, C., Hennelly, S. and Huppert, F. (2013) 'Effectiveness of the Mindfulness in Schools Programme: Non-randomised controlled feasibility study'. *British Journal of Psychiatry*, 203 (2), 126–31.

Lavelle, B.D. (2017) 'Compassion in schools'. In Seppälä, E.M., Simon-Thomas, E., Brown, S.L., Worline, M.C., Cameron, C.D. and Doty, J.R. (eds) *The Oxford Handbook of Compassion Science*. New York: Oxford University Press.

Leach, J. and Moon, B. (2008) *The Power of Pedagogy*. London: SAGE Publications.

Leaviss, J. and Uttley, L. (2015) 'Psychotherapeutic benefits of compassion-focused therapy: An early systematic review'. *Psychological Medicine*, 45 (5), 927–45.

Lee, R.B. (2018) 'Hunter-gatherers and human evolution: New light on old debates'. *Annual Review of Anthropology*, 47, 513–31.

Lewis, H.B. (1971) *Shame and Guilt in Neurosis*. New York: International Universities Press.

Li, N.P., Van Vugt, M. and Colarelli, S.M. (2018) 'The evolutionary mismatch hypothesis: Implications for psychological science'. *Current Directions in Psychological Science*, 27 (1), 38–44.

Lin, I.M., Tai, L.Y. and Fan, S.Y. (2014) 'Breathing at a rate of 5.5 breaths per minute with equal inhalation-to-exhalation ratio increases heart rate variability'. *International Journal of Psychophysiology*, 91 (3), 206–11.

Lisonbee, J.A., Mize, J., Lapp Payne, A. and Granger, D.A. (2008) 'Children's cortisol and the quality of the teacher–child relationships in child care'. *Child Development*, 79 (6), 1818–32.

Loewenstein, G. and Small, D.A. (2007) 'The scarecrow and the tin man: The vicissitudes of human sympathy and caring'. *Review of General Psychology*, 11 (2), 112–26.

Lowes, T.D. (2016) 'To What Extent Do Ofsted Inspectors' Values Influence the Inspection Process (2005–2012)? An examination of Ofsted inspectors' perceptions'. EdD thesis, University of Hull.

Lown, B.A. (2015) 'Compassion is a necessity and an individual and collective responsibility: Comment on "Why and how is compassion necessary to provide good quality healthcare?"'. *International Journal of Health Policy and Management*, 4 (9), 613–14.

MacBeth, A. and Gumley, A. (2012) 'Exploring compassion: A meta-analysis of the association between self-compassion and psychopathology'. *Clinical Psychology Review*, 32 (6), 545–52.

Mackintosh, K., Power, K., Schwannauer, M. and Chan, S.W.Y. (2018) 'The relationships between self-compassion, attachment and interpersonal problems in clinical patients with mixed anxiety and depression and emotional distress'. *Mindfulness*, 9 (3), 961–71.

Macy, J. and Young Brown, M. (2014) *Coming Back to Life: The updated guide to the work that reconnects*. Gabriola Island, BC: New Society Publishers.

Making Caring Common Project (2014) 'The children we mean to raise: The real messages adults are sending about values'. Online. https://mcc.gse.harvard.edu/reports/children-mean-raise (accessed 25 March 2020).

Mann, M. (1986) *The Sources of Social Power*. Cambridge: Cambridge University Press.

Maratos, F.A., Gilbert, P. and Gilbert, T. (2019) 'Improving well-being in higher education: Adopting a compassionate approach'. In Gibbs, P., Jameson, J. and Elwick, A. (eds) *Values of the University in a Time of Uncertainty*. Cham: Springer, 261–78.

Maratos, F.A., Mogg, K., Bradley, B.P., Rippon, G. and Senior, C. (2009) 'Coarse threat images reveal theta oscillations in the amygdala: A magnetoencephalography study'. *Cognitive, Affective, and Behavioral Neuroscience*, 9 (2), 133–43.

Maratos, F.A., Montague, J., Ashra, H., Welford, M., Wood, W., Barnes, C., Sheffield, D. and Gilbert, P. (2019) 'Evaluation of a compassionate mind training intervention with school teachers and support staff'. *Mindfulness*, 10, 2245–58.

Maratos, F.A. and Pessoa, L. (2019) 'What drives prioritized visual processing? A motivational relevance account'. *Progress in Brain Research*, 247, 111–48.

Maratos, F.A., Sheffield, D., Wood, W., McEwan, K., Matos, M. and Gilbert, P. (in preparation) 'The physiological effects of a compassionate mind training course with school teachers and support staff'.

Marsh, A.A. (2019) 'The caring continuum: Evolved hormonal and proximal mechanisms explain prosocial and antisocial extremes'. *Annual Review of Psychology*, 70, 347–71.

Maslach, C. and Jackson, S.E. (1981) 'The measurement of experienced burnout'. *Journal of Organizational Behavior*, 2 (2), 99–113.

Maternal and Child Nutrition Study Group (2013) 'Maternal and child nutrition: Building momentum for impact'. *The Lancet*, 382 (9890), 372–5.

Matos, M., Duarte, C., Duarte, J., Pinto-Gouveia, J., Petrocchi, N., Basran, J. and Gilbert, P. (2017) 'Psychological and physiological effects of compassionate mind training: A pilot randomised controlled study'. *Mindfulness*, 8 (6), 1699–712.

Matos, M., Duarte, J., Duarte, C., Gilbert, P. and Pinto-Gouveia, J. (2018) 'How one experiences and embodies compassionate mind training influences its effectiveness'. *Mindfulness*, 9 (4), 1224–35.

Matos, M. and Pinto-Gouveia, J. (2014) 'Shamed by a parent or by others: The role of attachment in shame memories relation to depression'. *International Journal of Psychology and Psychological Therapy*, 14 (2), 217–44.

Mayseless, O. (2016) *The Caring Motivation: An integrated theory*. New York: Oxford University Press.

McAdam, E. and Lang, P. (2009) *Appreciative Work in Schools: Generating future communities*. Chichester: Kingsham Press.

McEwan, K. and Gilbert, P. (2016) 'A pilot feasibility study exploring the practising of compassionate imagery exercises in a nonclinical population'. *Psychology and Psychotherapy: Theory, Research and Practice*, 89 (2), 239–43.

McGhee, P.E. (1979) *Humor: Its origins and development*. San Francisco: W.H. Freeman.

McNaughton, M.J. (2010) 'Educational drama in education for sustainable development: Ecopedagogy in action'. *Pedagogy, Culture and Society*, 18 (3), 289–308.

Mental Health Foundation (2020) 'What is mental health?'. Online. https://tinyurl.com/syfqkco (accessed 30 March 2020).

Mikulincer, M. and Shaver, P.R. (2017) 'An attachment perspective on compassion and altruism'. In Gilbert, P. (ed.) *Compassion: Concepts, research and applications*. London: Routledge, 187–202.

Mills, R.S.L., Freeman, W.S., Clara, I.P., Elgar, F.J., Walling, B.R. and Mak, L. (2007) 'Parent proneness to shame and the use of psychological control'. *Journal of Child and Family Studies*, 16 (3), 359–74.

Mitchell, A.E., Whittingham, K., Steindl, S. and Kirby, J. (2018) 'Feasibility and acceptability of a brief online self-compassion intervention for mothers of infants'. *Archives of Women's Mental Health*, 21 (5), 553–61.

Moffat, A. (2017) *No Outsiders in Our School: Teaching the Equality Act in primary schools*. London: Routledge.

Monbiot, G. (2020) 'Lab-grown food will soon destroy farming – and save the planet'. *The Guardian*, 8 January. Online. https://tinyurl.com/tmzqsw3 (accessed 30 March 2020).

Montagu, A. (1971) *Touching: The human significance of the skin*. New York: Columbia University Press.

Mourshed, M., Chijioke, C. and Barber, M. (2010) *How the World's Most Improved School Systems Keep Getting Better*. London: McKinsey and Company. Online. https://tinyurl.com/y7pbouz8 (accessed 30 March 2020).

Munby, S. (2019) *Imperfect Leadership: A book for leaders who know they don't know it all*. Bancyfelin: Crown House Publishing.

Narvaez, D. (2017) 'Evolution, child raising, and compassionate morality'. In Gilbert, P. (ed.) *Compassion: Concepts, research and applications*. London: Routledge, 173–86.

Narvaez, D., Panksepp, J., Schore, A.N. and Gleason, T.R. (eds) (2013) *Evolution, Early Experience and Human Development: From research to practice and policy*. New York: Oxford University Press.

Neel, R., Kenrick, D.T., White, A.E. and Neuberg, S.L. (2016) 'Individual differences in fundamental social motives'. *Journal of Personality and Social Psychology*, 110 (6), 887–907.

Neff, K. (2011) *Self-Compassion: Stop beating yourself up and leave insecurity behind*. London: Hodder and Stoughton.

References

Nelsen, J. and Gfroerer, K. (n.d.) 'Self care for teachers'. Online. www.positivediscipline.com/articles/self-care-teachers (accessed 30 March 2020).

Newmark, B. (2019) 'Why teach?'. Online. https://bennewmark.wordpress.com/2019/02/10/why-teach/ (accessed 30 March 2020).

NHS Digital (2018) 'Mental health of children and young people in England, 2017 [PAS]'. Online. https://tinyurl.com/ybvhfa9u (accessed 30 March 2020).

NHS Health Scotland (2019) *Adverse Childhood Experiences in Context.* Edinburgh: NHS Health Scotland. Online. https://tinyurl.com/tu5oh7e (accessed 16 March 2020).

Northern Ireland Curriculum (n.d.) *Eco-Warriors: Key Stage 2 Years 6 and 7 (Ideas for Connecting Learning).* Belfast: Council for the Curriculum, Examinations and Assessment. Online. https://tinyurl.com/sd6rdta (accessed 16 March 2020).

OECD (Organisation for Economic Co-operation and Development) (2016) *What Makes a School a Learning Organisation? A guide for policy makers, school leaders and teachers.* Paris: Organisation for Economic Co-operation and Development. Online. https://tinyurl.com/t2y3npb (accessed 30 March 2020).

Ofsted (2012) *Inspection Report: Park View Business and Enterprise School, 11–12 January 2012.* Manchester: Ofsted.

Ofsted (2019) 'Amanda Spielman at the Muslim Teachers' Association'. Online. https://tinyurl.com/tktmafy (accessed 28 March 2020).

Ofsted and Audit Commission (2002) *Inspection of Birmingham Local Education Authority.* Online. www.educationengland.org.uk/documents/pdfs/2002-ofsted-birmingham.pdf (accessed 23 June 2020).

Pani, L. (2000) 'Is there an evolutionary mismatch between the normal physiology of the human dopaminergic system and current environmental conditions in industrialized countries?'. *Molecular Psychiatry*, 5 (5), 467–75.

Paton, G. (2013) 'Leading academic criticises "Victorian"-style curriculum'. *The Telegraph*, 24 September. Online. www.telegraph.co.uk/education/educationnews/10330917/Leading-academic-criticises-Victorian-style-curriculum.html (accessed 30 March 2020).

Penner, L.A., Dovidio, J.F., Piliavin, J.A. and Schroeder, D.A. (2005) 'Prosocial behavior: Multilevel perspectives'. *Annual Review of Psychology*, 56, 365–92.

Perryman, J. (2006) 'Panoptic performativity and school inspection regimes: Disciplinary mechanisms and life under special measures'. *Journal of Education Policy*, 21 (2), 147–61.

PETA (People for the Ethical Treatment of Animals) (n.d.) 'The hidden lives of fish'. Online. https://tinyurl.com/t3to58s (accessed 28 March 2020).

Peterson, A. (2017) *Compassion and Education: Cultivating compassionate children, schools and communities.* London: Palgrave Macmillan.

Petrocchi, N. and Cheli, S. (2019) 'The social brain and heart rate variability: Implications for psychotherapy'. *Psychology and Psychotherapy: Theory, Research and Practice*, 92 (2), 208–23.

Pettifor, A. (2019) *The Case for the Green New Deal.* London: Verso Books.

Piff, P.K. and Moskowitz, J.P. (2017) 'The class–compassion gap: How socioeconomic factors influence compassion'. In Seppälä, E.M., Simon-Thomas, E., Brown, S.L., Worline, M.C., Cameron, C.D. and Doty, J.R. (eds) *The Oxford Handbook of Compassion Science*. New York: Oxford University Press, 317–30.

Plowright, D. (2008) 'Using self-evaluation for inspection: How well prepared are primary school headteachers?'. *School Leadership and Management*, 28 (2), 101–26.

Poggi Davis, E., Glynn, L.M., Waffarn, F. and Sandman, C.A. (2011) 'Prenatal maternal stress programs infant stress regulation'. *Journal of Child Psychology and Psychiatry*, 52 (2), 119–29.

Pope Francis (2015) *Laudato Si' – Encyclical on Climate Change and Inequality: On care for our common home*. New York: Melville House Publishing.

Porges, S.W. (2001) 'The polyvagal theory: The phylogenetic substrates of a social nervous system'. *International Journal of Psychophysiology*, 42 (2), 123–46.

Porges, S.W. (2007) 'The polyvagal perspective'. *Biological Psychology*, 74 (2), 116–43.

Porges, S.W. (2011) *The Polyvagal Theory: Neurophysiological foundations of emotions, attachment, communication, and self-regulation*. New York: W.W. Norton and Company.

Porges, S.W. (2017) 'Vagal pathways: Portals to compassion'. In Seppälä, E.M., Simon-Thomas, E., Brown, S.L., Worline, M.C., Cameron, C.D. and Doty, J.R. (eds) *The Oxford Handbook of Compassion Science*. New York: Oxford University Press, 189–202.

Price Tangney, J., Wagner, P., Fletcher, C. and Gramzow, R. (1992) 'Shamed into anger? The relation of shame and guilt to anger and self-reported aggression'. *Journal of Personality and Social Psychology*, 62 (4), 669–75.

Prinz, R. (2015) 'Public health approach to parenting and family support: A blended prevention strategy to reduce child abuse and neglect'. In Bentovim, A. and Gray, J. (eds) *Eradicating Child Maltreatment: Evidence-based approaches to prevention and intervention across services*. London: Jessica Kingsley Publishers, 106–21.

Prinz, R.J., Sanders, M.R., Shapiro, C.J., Whitaker, D.J. and Lutzker, J.R. (2009) 'Population-based prevention of child maltreatment: The US Triple P System Population Trial'. *Prevention Science*, 10 (1), 1–12.

Raghanti, M.A., Edler, M.K., Stephenson, A.R., Munger, E.L., Jacobs, B., Hof, P.R., Sherwood, C.C., Holloway, R.L. and Lovejoy, C.O. (2018) 'A neurochemical hypothesis for the origin of hominids'. *Proceedings of the National Academy of Sciences of the United States of America*, 115 (6), E1108–16.

Raphael-Leff, J. (1986) 'Facilitators and regulators: Conscious and unconscious processes in pregnancy and early motherhood'. *British Journal of Medical Psychology*, 59 (1), 43–55.

Ravitch, D. (2010) *The Death and Life of the Great American School System: How testing and choice are undermining education*. New York: Basic Books.

Raworth, K. (2017) *Doughnut Economics: Seven ways to think like a 21st century economist*. White River Junction, VT: Chelsea Green Publishing.

Ricard, M. (2015) *Altruism: The power of compassion to change yourself and the world*. London: Atlantic Books.

References

Robinson, C.C., Mandleco, B., Frost Olsen, S. and Hart, C.H. (1995) 'Authoritative, authoritarian, and permissive parenting practices: Development of a new measure'. *Psychological Reports*, 77 (3), 819–30.

Rodway, C., Tham, S.-G., Ibrahim, S., Turnbull, P., Windfuhr, K., Shaw, J., Kapur, N. and Appleby, L. (2016) 'Suicide in children and young people in England: A consecutive case series'. *Lancet Psychiatry*, 3 (8), 751–9.

Roeser, R.W., Colaianne, B.A. and Greenberg, M.A. (2018) 'Compassion and human development: Current approaches and future directions'. *Research in Human Development*, 15 (3–4), 238–51.

Rolfe, H. (2005) *Men in Childcare* (Working Paper 35). Manchester: Equal Opportunities Commission.

Roszak, T., Gomes, M.E. and Kanner, A.D. (eds) (1995) *Ecopsychology: Restoring the earth, healing the mind*. San Francisco: Sierra Club Books.

Sachs, J. (2011) *The Price of Civilization: Economics and ethics after the fall*. London: Bodley Head.

Sanders, M.R., Kirby, J.N., Tellegen, C.L. and Day, J.J. (2014) 'The Triple P-Positive Parenting Program: A systematic review and meta-analysis of a multi-level system of parenting support'. *Clinical Psychology Review*, 34 (4), 337–57.

Sanders, M.R. and Mazzucchelli, T.G. (2018) 'How parenting influences the lives of children'. In Sanders, M.R. and Mazzucchelli, T.G. (eds) *The Power of Positive Parenting: Transforming the lives of children, parents, and communities using the Triple P System*. New York: Oxford University Press, 5–31.

Santor, D.A. and Walker, J. (1999) 'Garnering the interest of others: Mediating the effects among physical attractiveness, self-worth and dominance'. *British Journal of Social Psychology*, 38 (4), 461–77.

Sapolsky, R.M. (2005) 'The influence of social hierarchy on primate health'. *Science*, 308 (5722), 648–52.

Sapolsky, R.M. (2017) *Behave: The biology of humans at our best and worst*. London: Bodley Head.

Scarnier, M., Schmader, T. and Lickel, B. (2009) 'Parental shame and guilt: Distinguishing emotional responses to a child's wrongdoings'. *Personal Relationships*, 16 (2), 205–20.

Schopenhauer, A. (1839) *Über die Grundlage der Moral* (On the Basis of Morality). Royal Danish Society.

Schore, A.N. (1997) 'Early organization of the nonlinear right brain and development of a predisposition to psychiatric disorders'. *Development and Psychopathology*, 9 (4), 595–631.

Scott, C.L. (2015a) *The Futures of Learning 1: Why must learning content and methods change in the 21st century?* (Education Research and Foresight Working Paper 13). Paris: United Nations Educational, Scientific and Cultural Organization. Online. https://unesdoc.unesco.org/ark:/48223/pf0000234807 (accessed 25 March 2020).

Scott, C.L. (2015b) *The Futures of Learning 2: What kind of learning for the 21st century?* (Education Research and Foresight Working Paper 14). Paris: United Nations Educational, Scientific and Cultural Organization. Online. https://unesdoc.unesco.org/ark:/48223/pf0000242996 (accessed 25 March 2020).

Scott, C.L. (2015c) *The Futures of Learning 3: What kind of pedagogies for the 21st century?* (Education Research and Foresight Working Paper 15). Paris: United Nations Educational, Scientific and Cultural Organization. Online. https://unesdoc.unesco.org/ark:/48223/pf0000243126 (accessed 25 March 2020).

Scottish Government (n.d.) 'Getting it right for every child (GIRFEC)'. Online. www.gov.scot/policies/girfec/ (accessed 16 March 2020).

Seattle (1854) 'Letter to all'. Online. www.csun.edu/~vcpsy00h/seattle.htm (accessed 7 July 2020).

Seppälä, E.M., Simon-Thomas, E., Brown, S.L., Worline, M.C., Cameron, C.D. and Doty, J.R. (eds) (2017) *The Oxford Handbook of Compassion Science.* New York: Oxford University Press.

Seymour-Smith, M., Cruwys, T., Haslam, S.A. and Brodribb, W. (2017) 'Loss of group memberships predicts depression in postpartum mothers'. *Social Psychiatry and Psychiatric Epidemiology,* 52 (2), 201–10.

Sidanius, J., Kteily, N., Sheehy-Skeffington, J., Ho, A.K., Sibley, C. and Duriez, B. (2013) 'You're inferior and not worth our concern: The interface between empathy and social dominance orientation'. *Journal of Personality,* 81 (3), 313–23.

Siegel, D.J. (2012) *The Developing Mind: How relationships and the brain interact to shape who we are.* New York: Guilford Press.

Siegel, D.J. (2017) *Mind: A journey to the heart of being human.* New York: W.W. Norton and Company.

Siegel, D.J. (2019) 'The mind in psychotherapy: An interpersonal neurobiology framework for understanding and cultivating mental health'. *Psychology and Psychotherapy: Theory, Research and Practice,* 92 (2), 224–37.

Siegel, D.J. and Payne Bryson, T. (2011) *The Whole-Brain Child.* New York: Delacorte Press.

Singer, T. and Bolz, M. (eds) (2013) *Compassion: Bridging practice and science.* Munich: Max Planck Society. Online. www.compassion-training.org/?page=download&lang=en (accessed 3 December 2019).

Singer, T. and Klimecki, O.M. (2014) 'Empathy and compassion'. *Current Biology,* 24 (18), R875–8.

Smith, P.K. and Brain, P. (2000) 'Bullying in schools: Lessons from two decades of research'. *Aggressive Behavior,* 26 (1), 1–9.

Soet, J.E., Brack, G.A. and DiIorio, C. (2003) 'Prevalence and predictors of women's experience of psychological trauma during childbirth'. *Birth,* 30 (1), 36–46.

Sommerland, J. (2018) 'Section 28: What was Margaret Thatcher's controversial law and how did it affect the lives of LGBT+ people?' *The Independent,* 24 May. Online. www.independent.co.uk/news/uk/politics/section-28-explained-lgbt-education-schools-homosexuality-gay-queer-margaret-thatcher-a8366741.html (accessed 8 June 2020).

Sommers-Spijkerman, M.P.J., Trompetter, H.R., Schreurs, K.M.G. and Bohlmeijer, E.T. (2018) 'Compassion-focused therapy as guided self-help for enhancing public mental health: A randomized controlled trial'. *Journal of Consulting and Clinical Psychology,* 86 (2), 101–15.

References

Speth, G. (2014) In Crockett, D. 'Connection will be the next big human trend'. *Huffington Post*. Online. https://www.huffingtonpost.co.uk/daniel-crockett/nature-connection-will-be-the-next-big-human-trend_b_5698267.html (accessed 29 June 2020).

Spikins, P. (2017) 'Prehistoric origins: The compassion of far distant strangers'. In Gilbert, P. (ed.) *Compassion: Concepts, research and applications*. London: Routledge, 16–30.

Srinivasan, A.V. (2011) *Hinduism for Dummies*. Hoboken, NJ: Wiley.

Stephens, W.B. (1998) *Education in Britain, 1750–1914*. New York: St Martin's Press.

Suddendorf, T. (2018) 'Inside our heads: Two key features created the human mind'. *Scientific American*, September, 42–7.

Suler, J. (2004) 'The online disinhibition effect'. *CyberPsychology and Behavior*, 7 (3), 321–6.

Sutherland, J.-A. (2010) 'Mothering, guilt and shame'. *Sociology Compass*, 4 (5), 310–21.

Swain, J.E. and Ho, S.S. (2017) 'Parental brain: The crucible of compassion'. In Seppälä, E.M., Simon-Thomas, E., Brown, S.L., Worline, M.C., Cameron, C.D. and Doty, J.R. (eds) *The Oxford Handbook of Compassion Science*. New York: Oxford University Press, 65–78.

Sznycer, D., Tooby, J., Cosmides, L., Porat, R., Shalvi, S. and Halperin, E. (2016) 'Shame closely tracks the threat of devaluation by others, even across cultures'. *Proceedings of the National Academy of Sciences of the United States of America*, 113 (10), 2625–30.

Talks at Google (2019) *Presence, Parenting, and the Planet – Dan Siegel – Talks at Google* [video]. Online. www.youtube.com/watch?v=Ouzb_Urt7LQ (accessed 30 March 2020).

Tang, E., Luyten, P., Casalin, S. and Vliegen, N. (2016) 'Parental personality, relationship stress, and child development: A stress generation perspective'. *Infant and Child Development*, 25 (2), 179–97.

Taylor, M. and Watts, J. (2019) 'Revealed: The 20 firms behind a third of all carbon emissions'. *The Guardian*, 9 October. Online. https://tinyurl.com/vyw8p2r (accessed 28 March 2020).

Teasdale, W. (2001) *The Mystic Heart: Discovering a universal spirituality in the world's religions*. Novato, CA: New World Library.

TEDx Talk (2019) *Compassion for Planet* [video]. Online. https://www.ted.com/talks/maurice_irfan_coles_education_for_survival_compassion_for_planet (accessed 23 June 2020).

The Audiopedia (2017) *What is Spiritual Ecology? What Does Spiritual Ecology Mean? Spiritual Ecology Meaning* [video]. Online. www.youtube.com/watch?v=Ccuha_IGO9M (accessed 30 March 2020).

Thomson, G., Ebisch-Burton, K. and Flacking, R. (2015) 'Shame if you do – shame if you don't: Women's experiences of infant feeding'. *Maternal and Child Nutrition*, 11 (1), 33–46.

Thunberg, G. (2019) *No One is Too Small to Make a Difference*. London: Penguin.

Tost, H., Kolachana, B., Hakimi, S., Lemaitre, H., Verchinski, B.A., Mattay, V.S., Weinberger, D.R. and Meyer-Lindenberg, A. (2010) 'A common allele in the oxytocin receptor gene (OXTR) impacts prosocial temperament and human hypothalamic-limbic structure and function'. *Proceedings of the National Academy of Sciences of the United States of America*, 107 (31), 13936–41.

Tracy, J.L., Robins, R.W. and Price Tangney, J. (eds) (2007) *The Self-Conscious Emotions: Theory and research*. New York: Guilford Press.

Tull, D.E. (2018) *Relational Mindfulness: A handbook for deepening our connection with ourselves, each other, and the planet*. Somerville, MA: Wisdom Publications.

Twenge, J.M. (2013) 'The evidence for generation me and against generation we'. *Emerging Adulthood*, 1 (1), 11–16.

Tyler, G. (2020) *Food Banks in the UK* (House of Commons Briefing Paper No. 8585). Online. https://tinyurl.com/re9yayw (accessed 23 June 2020).

UK Government (n.d.) 'Find and compare schools in England'. Online. www.gov.uk/school-performance-tables (accessed 16 March 2020).

United Nations (1987) *Report of the World Commission on Environment and Development: Our common future*. Online. https://sustainabledevelopment. un.org/content/documents/5987our-common-future.pdf (accessed 9 June 2020).

United Nations Environment Programme (2009) *Global Green New Deal: Policy brief 2009*. Online. https://www.unenvironment.org/resources/report/global-green-new-deal-policy-brief-march-2009 (accessed 24 June 2020).

United Nations Environment Programme (2019) 'Insect declines are a stark warning to humanity'. Online. www.unenvironment.org/pt-br/node/24654 (accessed 28 March 2020).

UNESCO (United Nations Educational, Scientific and Cultural Organization) (2012) *Education for Sustainable Development: Sourcebook*. Paris: United Nations Educational, Scientific and Cultural Organization. Online. https://unesdoc.unesco.org/ark:/48223/pf0000216383 (accessed 28 March 2020).

United Nations (2019) 'Sustainable development Goal 4'. Online. https://sustainabledevelopment.un.org/sdg4 (accessed 20 June 2020).

United Nations Sustainable Development Solutions Network (2020) *World Happiness Report 2020*. Online. https://worldhappiness.report/ (accessed 20 June 2020).

UN Tribune (2014) 'The 42 countries that have banned corporal punishment'. *UN Tribune*, 20 November. Online. https://tinyurl.com/y9934w77 (accessed 28 March 2020).

Van Kleef, G.A., Oveis, C., Van der Löwe, I., LuoKogan, A., Goetz, J. and Keltner, D. (2008) 'Power, distress, and compassion: Turning a blind eye to the suffering of others'. *Psychological Science,* 19 (12), 1315–22.

Vaughan-Lee, L. (2002) *Working with Oneness*. Inverness, CA: Golden Sufi Center.

Vaughan-Lee, L. (2016) *Spiritual Ecology: The cry of the earth*. 2nd ed. Point Reyes, CA: Golden Sufi Center.

Vaughan-Lee, L. (2019) *Including the Earth in Our Prayers: A global dimension to spiritual practice*. Point Reyes, CA: Golden Sufi Center.

References

Vaughan-Lee, L. and Hart, H. (2017) *Spiritual Ecology: 10 practices to reawaken the sacred in everyday life*. Point Reyes, CA: Golden Sufi Center.

Von Hofsten, O., Von Hofsten, C., Sulutvedt, U., Laeng, B., Brennen, T. and Magnussen, S. (2014) 'Simulating newborn face perception'. *Journal of Vision*, 14 (13), Article 16, 1–9. Online. https://tinyurl.com/uxh47qa (accessed 28 March 2020).

Wallace-Wells, D. (2019) *The Uninhabitable Earth: A story of the future*. London: Allen Lane.

Wang, Z., Jetten, J. and Steffens, N.K. (2020) 'The more you have, the more you want? Higher social class predicts a greater desire for wealth and status'. *European Journal of Social Psychology*, 50 (2), 360–75.

Watts, J. (2019) '"Biggest compliment yet": Greta Thunberg welcomes oil chief's "greatest threat" label'. *The Guardian*, 5 July. Online. https://tinyurl.com/utht4wh (accessed 16 March 2020).

Weare, K. (2013) 'Developing mindfulness with children and young people: A review of the evidence and policy context'. *Journal of Children's Services*, 8 (2), 141–53.

Weare, K. (2014) *Evidence for Mindfulness: Impacts on the wellbeing and performance of school staff*. Tonbridge: Mindfulness in Schools Project. Online. https://tinyurl.com/gvm43op (accessed 28 March 2020).

Welford, M. and Langmead, K. (2015) 'Compassion-based initiatives in educational settings'. *Educational and Child Psychology*, 32 (1), 71–80.

Well, T. (2017) 'Compassion is better than empathy: Neuroscience explains why'. *Psychology Today*, 4 March. Online. https://tinyurl.com/va4q2to (accessed 28 March 2020).

Weng, H.Y., Lapate, R.C., Stodola, D.E., Rogers, G.M. and Davidson, R.J. (2018) 'Visual attention to suffering after compassion training is associated with decreased amygdala responses'. *Frontiers in Psychology*, 9, Article 771, 1–12. Online. https://tinyurl.com/vhznej4 (accessed 28 March 2020).

Wetherall, K., Robb, K.A. and O'Connor, R.C. (2019) 'Social rank theory of depression: A systematic review of self-perceptions of social rank and their relationship with depressive symptoms and suicide risk'. *Journal of Affective Disorders*, 246, 300–19.

WHO (World Health Organization) (2020) *Child Maltreatment* (Fact Sheet). Online. https://www.who.int/news-room/fact-sheets/detail/child-maltreatment (accessed 23 June 2020).

Wigglesworth, C. (2012) *SQ21: The twenty-one skills of spiritual intelligence*. New York: SelectBooks.

Wikipedia (2020a) 'Environmental policy of the Donald Trump administration'. Online. https://tinyurl.com/y9ukac9l (accessed 30 March 2020).

Wikipedia (2020b) 'Neoliberalism'. Online. https://en.wikipedia.org/wiki/Neoliberalism (accessed 24 June 2020).

Wilkinson, R. (2001) *Mind the Gap: Hierarchies, health and human evolution*. New Haven: Yale University Press.

Wilkinson, R. and Pickett, K. (2010) *The Spirit Level: Why equality is better for everyone*. London: Penguin.

Williams, K.D., Forgas, J.P. and Von Hippel, W. (2013) *The Social Outcast: Ostracism, social exclusion, rejection, and bullying*. New York: Psychology Press.

Wine and Water Watch (2016) '"We scientists don't know how to do that"… What a commentary!'. Online. https://tinyurl.com/y6emc555 (accessed 30 March 2020).

Winnicott, D.W. (1964) *The Child, the Family and the Outside World*. Harmondsworth: Penguin.

Wohlleben, P. (2016) *The Hidden Life of Trees: What they feel, how they communicate: Discoveries from a secret world*. Vancouver: Greystone Books.

Wolfe, R.N., Lennox, R.D. and Cutler, B.L. (1986) 'Getting along and getting ahead: Empirical support for a theory of protective and acquisitive self-presentation'. *Journal of Personality and Social Psychology*, 50 (2), 356–61.

Woods, D. and Brighouse, T. (eds) (2014) *The Story of London Challenge*. London: London Leadership Strategy.

Wragg, E.C., Wragg, C.M., Haynes, G.S. and Chamberlin, R.P. (1998) *Improving Literacy in the Primary School*. London: Routledge.

Yeager, D.S., Dahl, R.E. and Dweck, C.S. (2018) 'Why interventions to influence adolescent behavior often fail but could succeed'. *Perspectives on Psychological Science*, 13 (1), 101–22.

Zero to Three (2016) *National Parent Survey Report*. Online. https://tinyurl.com/jmed7m6 (accessed 20 August 2020).

Zohar, D. and Marshall, I. (2001) *SQ: Spiritual intelligence: The ultimate intelligence*. London: Bloomsbury.

Zolotor, A.J., Theodore, A.D., Coyne-Beasley, T. and Runyan, D.K. (2007) 'Intimate partner violence and child maltreatment: Overlapping risk'. *Brief Treatment and Crisis Intervention*, 7 (4), 305–21.

Index